W9-CFI-917

Guide to the Offshore Wildlife of the Northern Atlantic

GUIDE TO THE

 University of Texas Press, Austin

Number Forty-seven
The Corrie Herring Hooks Series

OFFSHORE WILDLIFE

of the Northern Atlantic

Michael H. Tove

Copyright © 2000 by Michael H. Tove
All rights reserved
Printed in Hong Kong

First edition, 2000

Requests for permission to reproduce material from this work
should be sent to Permissions, University of Texas Press, Box 7819,
Austin, TX 78713-7819.

⊚ The paper used in this book meets the minimum requirements
of ANSI/NISO Z39.48-1992 (R 1997) (Permanence of Paper).

Library of Congress Cataloging-in-Publication Data

Tove, Michael H. (Michael Henry), 1953–
    Guide to the offshore wildlife of the northern Atlantic /
Michael H. Tove.—   1st ed.
        p.   cm. — (The Corrie Herring Hooks series ; no. 47)
    Includes bibliographical references and index.
    ISBN 0-292-78171-7 (pbk. : alk. paper)
    1. Marine animals—North Atlantic Ocean—Identification.
I. Title.   II. Series.
QL128.T68   2000
591.77'31—dc21   99-050862

This book is dedicated to my father, Samuel B Tove, who introduced me to the sea and instilled in me a love of wildlife. He had the vision to see this work as a possibility even before I did, and in fact urged me to write a field guide years before I thought it was ever possible. I also dedicate it to my loving wife, Miraflor C. Tove, who has supported and encouraged me to press on when the tedium seemed overwhelming. Finally, I remember with fondness my first years as a bird-watcher with Duncan Hollar and Bruce Pikaard, who started me in the hobby, and those early days chasing around the wilds of Greensboro, North Carolina.

CONTENTS

PREFACE

The first time I went to sea, I was eight years old. My father took me on a deep-sea fishing trip. I watched him catch a couple of King Mackerel and, with his help, caught a Spanish Mackerel. That experience was the start of my fascination with the sea and its wildlife. Like most boys, I was particularly enamored with the large and spectacular sea creatures, especially sharks and whales. When I was about fourteen, my family and I were taking our annual week-long vacation at the beach. There were a lot of small sharks being caught in the surf and one fisherman I was chatting with said to me, "If you think that's something, you ought to see the shark they caught off the pier last night. It took eight hours to land and it weighed 1,300 pounds." Naturally, I was interested and persuaded my parents to drive me to the pier. Expecting something ten feet long lying on the pier, I was disappointed that no shark was in evidence. Finally, I looked over the side and saw it suspended on block and tackle by its tail. It was nearly as long as the pier was high and three times the girth of the man cutting it down. Although I cannot be sure, I've always felt it was a Great White.

I started bird-watching in college—in fact, on a marine biology field excursion to the Tampa Bay area where I was introduced to the concept of using a field identification guide. I found it fascinating that one could identify a bird by matching what one saw through binoculars with a series of stylized paintings in a book. My interest grew rapidly from there. A few years later, I took my first pelagic trip into the Gulf of Maine where I saw shearwaters, petrels, and jaegers for the first time. I also saw my first whales. Over the next twelve years, I did a lot of traveling in search of birds. In the early 1980s, I attended graduate school in Utah. Landlocked, I found myself increasingly drawn to the ocean. I made several trips to Monterey Bay, California, where a "back-burner" interest in whales began to flourish.

In 1986 I returned home to North Carolina and soon started to organize pelagic bird-watching trips out of the Cape Hatteras area. At first, these trips were organized solely to give me and my birding friends an opportunity to get offshore, but it soon grew into much more. From the early days of those efforts, two dates stand out in my mind as pivotal. The first was May 25, 1991. It was a flat calm day with a magical early-morning sunrise. We struck gold very early with a South Polar Skua and a Brown Noddy (very rare for North Carolina) before we reached the Gulf Stream. The highlight came later that day when a Fea's Petrel, the first documented from North America, came winging by. The bird became a signature species for my trips and set into motion events that would culminate with the second pivotal date. On Saturday, May 29, 1993, I was leading a group offshore specifically to search for Fea's Petrel. About 11:00 o'clock that morning, we found a large dark bird sitting on the water. The bird permitted us to approach to within point-blank range. It was a juvenile Brown Skua, a species not previously documented from North America. Two hours later, there was a shout that beaked whales had been seen. Expecting Cuvier's, which are regular, I was surprised to see a dolphin-like gray head rise out of the water, followed by another. Immediately I realized that these were Mesoplodonts, but the question was, which ones? I knew that these animals represented the rarest group of whales in the world and the most difficult to identify, including some that had never been identified alive in the wild. I also knew they had a reputation for being very shy of boats, so I expected them to dive deep and eliminate any possibility of identifying them. Fortunately I was wrong. Moments later, the captain shouted that they were ahead of the bow and I scrambled forward to see. For ten minutes we stayed with them and were eventually able to identify them as True's Beaked Whales, a species previously known *only* from some two dozen beach-washed dead animals worldwide. Of the twenty-six other birders on board, few knew much about whales, but my excitement became infectious and soon everyone was as interested as they would have been over a rare bird. Unfortunately, the only whale references on board were a couple of coffee-table books I had brought. They provided some help but left a lot to be desired as field identification aids. It was at that moment that the idea for this guide was conceived. In the intervening years, I have been reminded many times that the sea brings different interests together. Bird-watchers who otherwise have little interest in mammals become fascinated when a whale is sighted, and whale watchers will divert their focus to gaze at a sea turtle or a seal or a bird. There is a commonality among all these marine creatures that is shared with its venturesome observers: they are all at sea together.

ACKNOWLEDGMENTS

It is difficult to thank all the people who helped in the creation of this book. As all field guide authors know, a great measure of thanks must go to those untold hundreds or thousands of people who pioneered the field to a point where the possibility of and the need for a field guide was even realistic. As my home base is North Carolina, I must offer special recognition and thanks to Paul DuMont and Bob Ake, who pioneered pelagic birding off Hatteras and with whom I took my first organized pelagic trips. Debi Shearwater helped focus my interest in whales, particularly beaked whales, which ultimately paid off with my True's Beaked Whale sighting in 1993.

In the compilation of all the descriptions and information, I owe much to those who directly and indirectly helped me. However, any errors that may occur are my responsibility alone.

Thanks goes to the following field collaborators, a very partial list of those who shared many a day at sea with me: Lynn Barber, Bill Blakesley, Alan Brady, Ned Brinkley, Derb Carter, Buck and Linda Cooper, Ricky Davis, Bill Drummond, Steve Dinsmore, Paul DuMont, Shawneen Finnegan, John Fussell, Paul Guris, Todd Hass, Annie and Nita Heilman, John Janowski, Cam Kepler, Ted and Kris Koundakjian, Bruce Lantz, Harry LeGrand, Paul Lehman, Guy McCaskie, Todd McGrath, Roger McNeill, Peter Milbourne, Mike O'Brien, Paul O'Brien, Brian Patteson, Butch Pierce, Jeff Pippen, Macklin Smith, Paul Sykes, Russ Tyndall, R. Haven Wiley, Angus Wilson, and John Wright.

Many others helped with compiling data or offering helpful suggestions, especially Charles Avenengo, Wes Biggs, David Boertmann, Alan Brady, Ned Brinkley, Charles Buhrman, Kees Camphuysen, David Curtis, Tim Cole, Ricky Davis, Steve Dinsmore, Donna Dittman, Jon Dunn, Paul Guris, Todd Hass, Paul Hess, Jack Huttmann, Greg Lasley, Andrew Lassey, Harry LeGrand, Paul Lehman, Tony Marr, Anthony McGeehan, Ian

McLaren, James Mead, Dale Middleton, John Nicholas, Blair Nikula, Brian Patteson, Wayne Peterson, Jack Peachy, Todd Pusser, Antonio Sandoval Rey, Don Robeson, Andrew Schiro, Dan Shaltanis, Steve Stedman, Emmalee Tarry, Dylan Walker, Haven Wiley, Amy Williams, and Alec and Frank Zino.

I also thank Captains Alan Foreman and Spurgeon Stowe for their mastery in locating and staying with untold numbers of seabirds and marine mammals. Without their spectacular boats, *Country Girl* and *Miss Hatteras,* I would have been a frustrated landlubber and this book would not have been possible.

Finally, thanks to the staff at the University of Texas Press for believing in the project and helping me see it through to completion.

INTRODUCTION

This book is a comprehensive guide to the field identification of the air-breathing pelagic marine wildlife found in the Atlantic Ocean north of the Tropic of Cancer. The term "pelagic" means "open-ocean wanderer" and refers to those species that spend most or all of their lives at sea. Additionally, I coin the term "semipelagic" to refer to those species in which some individuals occur pelagically while others do not.

Wildlife observers who regularly venture offshore are well aware of the remarkable diversity of wildlife that can be found. Traditional field guides normally focus on one group of organisms (e.g., birds). However, unlike the land, where observers can afford to specialize, the ocean is a different story. Almost without exception, an organized seabird-watching trip will become completely sidetracked with the appearance of a whale. Sadly, although well equipped to identify the birds, these observers suddenly find themselves at a loss because nobody remembered to bring a whale identification guide.

To be of practical use, such a guide must fit within two constraints: (1) cover a geographical area large enough to be useful but not too large to be overly confusing, and (2) cover enough species in sufficient detail to be of value to advanced observers but at a level of simplicity that does not overwhelm a beginner.

In the former case, the area selected was the Atlantic Ocean from the Tropic of Cancer to the Arctic Circle. Several factors made this choice a logical one. First, the boundaries are more than arbitrary because the continental masses and ocean circulation rather effectively define this body of water. Second, over 90 percent of the species that occur in this area may be found in both its eastern and western halves. Third, the vast majority of observational activity in the Atlantic occurs in this region. In the latter case, the question of what species to include or leave out involved only birds. While it made sense to include every pelagic species that had occurred during the past 50 years, I decided to limit coverage of semipelagic species to only those that routinely occur beyond the sight of land.

Readers are cautioned that the identification of wildlife at sea is considerably more challenging than on land. To begin with, the motion of a boat makes focusing for extended periods of time more difficult. Furthermore, distances at sea are deceptively difficult to judge. Thus the apparent size of something may be drastically different from the actual. In cases where size is an important consideration, extreme caution should be applied. Finally, most marine organisms are combinations of gray, black, brown, and white. These colors, against a blue-gray sea, make for a low-contrast environment. Discernible field marks may not be as evident as illustrated, particularly if the light is less than ideal. There is no shame in concluding that something was, under the circumstances of viewing, unidentifiable.

Ocean Habitats and Ecology

Compared with the land, there is far less habitat diversity on and in the ocean. However, distinct ecological zones do exist, although they may be difficult for an observer in a boat to discern. To understand the oceans, it is important to look at not just the water masses, but the water in relation to the land. Nearly 71 percent of the earth's surface is water, but the distribution of land and water is not uniform. Where the Southern Hemisphere is dominated by water, including a broad circumglobal zone unimpeded by land, the Northern Hemisphere consists of three discrete ocean basins bounded by continents that comprise two-thirds of the earth's landmass. These ocean basins are the Atlantic, bounded by North America to the west, Greenland and Iceland to the north, and Europe and Africa to the east; the Pacific Ocean (the largest ocean basin), bounded by Asia to the west and north and by North America to the north and east; and the Indian Ocean (the smallest), bounded by Africa and the Middle East to the west and by Asia to the north and east.

Unlike the Southern Hemisphere, the northern ocean basins represent discrete entities with no direct mixing of adjacent waters. Geologically, they were formed by a series of expanding plates in the earth's crust that for the last 600 million or so years have been moving the continents around. In particular, the Atlantic Ocean is the direct product of this continental drift, resulting from the separation of the American from the Euro-African landmasses starting roughly 200 million years ago. To this day, the tectonic activity at the Mid-Atlantic Rift continues.

Ecologically, the ocean is very complex and beyond the scope of a field guide. However, since this is a guide to air-breathing oceanic wildlife, an overview of the major ecological factors that affect the distribution of those organisms is warranted.

Water Surface

The most obvious ecological distinction is above the water versus under the water. While birds occupy the former and whales, dolphins, seals, and sea turtles occupy the latter, all are tied to both ecozones. Seabirds must feed on organisms that live under the surface and all air-breathing marine animals must routinely come to the surface to breathe.

Latitude

A second important distinction is latitude, or a north-south position relative to the earth's Equator and poles. For simplicity, I recognize six ecozones in the northern Atlantic.

The Tropic Zone lies roughly south of 20° North. It is typified by constant warm temperatures, light easterly tradewinds (called the "doldrums" by ancient mariners) and an absence of prolonged periods of violent weather. Except for the northern Caribbean, the Tropic Zone is south of the Tropic of Cancer and is outside the scope of this text.

The Subtropic Zone lies roughly between 20° and 30° North. Similar to the Tropics, it shows minimal seasonality and is generally warm and mild all year. However, it also comprises the "hurricane highway" during summer and fall.

The Warm Temperate Zone lies roughly from 30° to about 35° North in the west and to about 40° North in the east. The region is decidedly warm during summer but cool to moderately cold during winter. The prevailing winds also vary depending on longitude. In the west, the prevailing winds are from the west or northwest, coming off the North American landmass. Farther east, they swing to the southeast and become northeast near the African and southern European landmasses.

The Cold Temperate Zone continues from the Warm Temperate Zone to about 40° North in the west and 50° North in the east. Tradewind circulatory patterns resemble those of the Warm Temperate Zone. These waters are generally cool in summer and moderately cold to very cold during winter, but they are not normally ice-covered during winter.

The Subarctic Zone extends from the Cold Temperate Zone to about 40° North in the west and to above the Arctic Circle in the east. Mild summers and harsh winters are typical here, with prevailing winds from the west. However, the asymmetrical distribution means that the eastern half

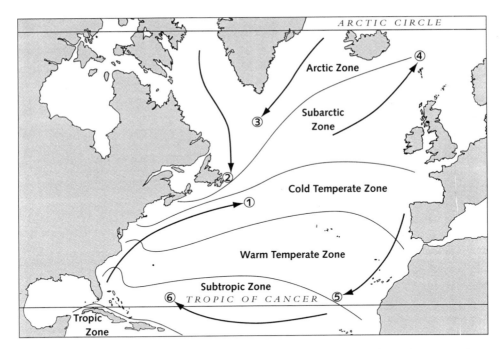

Figure 1. Map of the region of coverage showing principal ecological zones and major circulatory currents: (**1**) Gulf Stream, (**2**) Labrador Current, (**3**) Irminger Current, (**4**) Norway Current, (**5**) Canary Current, (**6**) North Equatorial Current.

of the northern Atlantic is milder in winter than the western. Additionally, great changes in seasonal daylight occur, particularly in the northeastern Atlantic where this zone reaches the Arctic Circle. Coastal waters may develop sea ice, especially during colder winters.

The Arctic Zone is that area which lies north of the Subarctic Zone. The short summers with nearly perpetual daylight are replaced by long, harsh winters of perpetual darkness. Pack ice generally covers these waters during winter, effectively separating the water from the air, making the water uninhabitable to many animals at this time.

Ocean Depth and Distance from Shore

Another important distinction is ocean depth. With the invention of depth finders, oceangoing observers have the luxury of seeking out specific submarine topographic features. Depth has a very significant impact on the available food chain. For example, in shallow water sunlight can penetrate to the bottom, permitting a very different bottom (benthic) community to flourish than in the inky blackness of a bottom that lies a mile below the surface. These different communities offer different food resources, affecting the composition of seabirds, marine mammals, and sea turtles that occur.

Closely related to water depth is the distance from shore. To a large extent, this is because the edges of the continental landmasses are below sea level. Therefore, close to shore, there is an extension of "land" under the ocean's surface that does not exist far at sea. For simplicity, I recognize five zones:

Inshore or Coastal Water is the most silty, due in part to the mixing of wave action. In addition, the outflow of rivers may result in a significant decrease in salinity as large volumes of fresh water are dumped into the sea. Where these rivers also carry large volumes of sediment, there will be a large region of turbidity and possibly a shallow bar or shoal extending several miles out to sea.

Shallow Offshore Water refers to that region of the ocean beyond the direct influence of the coast but still over the continental landmass. Throughout much of its extent, the depth of this zone is rather uniform, showing minimal topography. In the Tropics and some of the Subtropics, these waters may lie over coral reefs. Elsewhere their continuity may be broken by steep-walled submarine canyons.

The Continental Shelf is the break of the continental landmass, sometimes ending so abruptly that the water depth will increase tenfold over the course of a few dozen boat lengths. Deep sea currents striking this slope create upwellings that bring deep-ocean nutrients to the surface, effectively allowing the above-water organisms to access the deep, below-water ones.

Submarine Canyons may also serve as areas of dramatic depth changes along the continental shelf edge. As with continental shelf walls, these areas bring shallow and deep-water environments into close proximity and often have upwelling currents.

Deep Offshore Water refers to the open ocean beyond the edge of the continental shelf. In the northern Atlantic, these waters tend to be rather featureless at the surface owing to the great and consistent depth of the sea floor below. As a result, the abundance and diversity of air-breathing wildlife is relatively low.

Oceanic Currents

The surface waters of the ocean are in constant circulatory motion. In the Northern Hemisphere, these circulatory systems, called gyres, move Subtropical and Temperate water in a clockwise direction and move Subarctic and Arctic water counterclockwise. In the Southern Hemisphere, the circulatory patterns are reversed. The motion and direction of gyre flow is influenced by the rotation of the earth, a phenomenon called the Coriolis effect.

On a more localized level, the effect of these currents flowing past continental landmasses is to create rather distinct habitat zones. Where these boundary currents flow rapidly, the effect can be visible to the eye in the form of current lines or color changes from one side of the current to the other. These edge zones have greater wildlife diversity than the adjacent waters. The effect is comparable to land-based ecotones—such as where a forest meets a field, resulting in greater diversity of wildlife along the edge than in either the forest or in the field.

In the Northern Hemisphere, the western boundary currents are relatively narrow and flow rapidly to the north, while the eastern boundary currents are broad and flow slowly to the south. Currents with more concentrated flow-energy have better-defined edge zones and consequently greater diversity than currents with weak flow.

In the northern Atlantic, there are six distinct oceanic currents:

The Gulf Stream is a Subtropical western boundary current that originates in the Gulf of Mexico south of Florida. It flows northward at a speed of two to five knots as a "river" some 30 to 40 miles wide. It travels north along the coast of the United States, roughly paralleling the continental shelf to about 35° north latitude where it collides with the Labrador Current. This collision causes the Gulf Stream to deflect eastward, crossing the Atlantic to Great Britain as part of the North Atlantic Gyre. This influx of warm water into the northeastern Atlantic is the reason for the asymmetrical distribution of the Subarctic Zone. Ecologically, the Gulf Stream is the most significant oceanic current in the Atlantic.

The Labrador Current originates in the high Arctic between Canada and Greenland and flows south along the North American coastline. In the vicinity of Cape Hatteras, North Carolina, where it meets the Gulf Stream, the interface causes both to deflect eastward. So abrupt is this change that the line of contact is often visible as an obvious color change (greenish and cold versus deep blue and warm) and occasionally may seem to "boil." This intersection also creates a strong downwelling/upwelling mixing zone. In part, because the Gulf Stream is a deep-flowing current (ca. 1,000 feet deep), where the two intersect, the slower-moving, cold-water Labrador Current dives under the Gulf Stream. This creates a downwelling (downward flow) of the Labrador, carrying the rich organic sediments from the Subarctic Zone under the warm Gulf Stream. This downward flow returns to the surface as upwellings a short distance later. Moreover, this convergence occurs along the steepest section of continental shelf for eastern North American. The result of this combination is to produce the richest localized diversity in the northern Atlantic. In fact, over 85 percent of the species covered in this guide have occurred in this one area.

The Irminger Current originates in the high Arctic and flows southwest between Greenland and Iceland. Its flow is responsible for the movement of icebergs that form in Greenland and move southward into the Atlantic. It was one of these that was responsible for the sinking of the *Titanic*.

The Norway Current is a flow from the northeastern Atlantic through the North Sea between northern England and Iceland. This current sets up a counterclockwise circulation that is part of the Subpolar North Atlantic Gyre.

The Canary Current flows to the southeast parallel to the coast of northwestern Africa from the Canaries to the Cape Verde Islands. It is an eastern boundary current and represents the southward return of the Subtropical Gyre. Compared with the Gulf Stream, which transports water at a speed of 25 to 75 miles per day (40 to 120 km/day), the Canary transports water at a speed of only 2 to 4 miles per day (3 to 7 km/day). However, the Canary Current is much wider than the Gulf Stream and thus carries the same volume of water per day.

The North Equatorial Current is roughly continuous with the Canary Current and crosses the Atlantic to the west parallel to the Tropic of Cancer. This is the returning current of the Subtropical North Atlantic Gyre.

Birds

Because of their strong attachment to the above-water habitats and ability to travel considerable distances in a relatively short time, seabirds are the most habitat-specific group covered in this guide. Tropical species such as frigatebirds, tropicbirds, boobies, and Tropical terns typically do not migrate far from the Tropics or Subtropics. Conversely, most species in the Subarctic migrate substantial distances away from their breeding grounds during the winter months, frequently crossing from Subarctic into Subtropical or even Tropical waters, with some migrating between hemispheres. For example, Arctic Terns breed in the Arctic and winter in the Antarctic. Other species, such as Greater and Sooty Shearwaters, Wilson's Storm-petrel, and South Polar Skua, have an opposite pattern. The occurrence of these species in northern Atlantic waters during our summer months actually represents their "wintering" cycle.

Seabirds that are truly pelagic spend their entire lives at sea, save for the actual nesting process. The petrels and shearwaters represent the classic example. After they leave the nest, they put to sea for one to several years and do not return to land until they are ready to breed. For this book, these are the bird species of emphasis because seeing them generally requires an offshore excursion. Semipelagic species are those that spend a great deal of time far at sea but frequently return to land throughout the year, sometimes daily. Most of the gulls and terns fit this pattern. Coastal birds are those which really do not have a pelagic existence but are commonly seen from shore or in nearshore waters. While some venture into near offshore waters, particularly between adjacent landmasses (such as in the English Channel), they are not really offshore dwellers and are excluded from coverage. Specifically, these groups include loons, grebes, cormorants, pelicans, and sea ducks.

Cetaceans (Whales and Dolphins)

This is the book's only group with no attachment to land. Cetaceans are born in the ocean and live their entire lives at sea. Most are highly social and exhibit very specific and occasionally complex migratory behavior. Many species, particularly the larger ones, may travel great distances during the course of a year. They might spend the summer months in the colder northern waters where they mate and later move into Tropical waters to give birth. Some species such as the Humpback Whale have segregated wintering grounds. For example, during winter, immature males congregate exclusively in shallow inshore waters of the middle Atlantic states of North America.

Some groups are rather rare and poorly known. Paramount among these are the beaked whales. In fact, one species, True's Beaked Whale, had never been documented alive in the wild prior to 1993 (photographed by the author). Another species, Gervais' Beaked Whale (a.k.a. Gulf Stream Beaked Whale), whose normal range is the Tropical waters of the Caribbean, was first discovered as a dead animal floating in the English Channel.

Unlike birds, entire families of which may be categorized as "Tropical" or "Subarctic," cetaceans do not lend themselves to familial categorization. Rather, within each family of whales or dolphins, different species occupy different ecological zones. Therefore, while birds may be categorized at the family level by ecological labels, cetaceans may not.

Seals

Within this guide, this is the group most closely tied to the land, and in many cases, pack ice. With the single exception of the Monk Seals, all members occupy Subarctic to Arctic habitats. Most do not venture far from their breeding grounds, and when they do, it is generally in coastal waters. However, unlike coastal seabirds (not covered), seals venture offshore to feed and only occur on the beach when breeding or hauled out to rest.

Sea Turtles

This is the only "cold-blooded" (heterothermic) group covered by this guide. Because of their heterothermic metabolism, they are normally restricted to warmer Subtropical and Tropical waters, where they live their entire lives except when the adult females crawl ashore to lay their eggs. At sea, they are most often found in the shallower waters above the continental shelf or coral reefs.

Seasonal Changes

As already noted, seasonal differences can have significant impact on habitats, particularly in the less Equatorial regions. Where temperature and diurnal (day/night) cycles vary considerably, the faunal composition may change dramatically from winter to summer. Species respond to seasonal changes in one of three ways: they may migrate in or out, they may remain as permanent residents, or they may exhibit a combination of the two behaviors.

Often the terms "migration" and "dispersal" are used interchangeably, but they actually represent very different phenomena. Migration refers to the seasonal departure of a population from one geographic area for another. Implicit within this definition is the notion that such movement is predictable in terms of timing and destination and that most, if not all, of the population is included. Dispersal refers to the less directional diffusion away from a region of concentration and may be limited to members of a particular age or sex class. Generally speaking, Tropical and Subtropical species are more prone to dispersal while Arctic and Subarctic species are more prone to migration. This is because the need to travel for survival is less where food and other resources are more universally available. For example, Tropical terns tend to remain in close proximity with their breeding grounds year round. However, nonbreeders, presumably to escape competition with established adults, tend to disperse widely and may show up in locations far from the remainder of the population. Others, such as petrels, disperse seaward, away from their breeding grounds, and are not seen until they return. Conversely, species such as the Arctic Tern or Northern Right Whale breed in the Arctic and Subarctic Zones and migrate far to the south, with the tern wintering in the Antarctic, the whale off Florida and the Caribbean.

Some species neither migrate nor disperse widely. Arctic-breeding species that do not leave their cold-water haunts include Bowhead Whale, Narwhal, and Walrus. Similarly, Tropical species such as Magnificent Frigatebird and Red-footed Booby rarely if ever leave their Tropical environs. A few species exhibit complex patterns. For example, during the summer months, Humpback Whales are common in waters around the Gulf of Maine and Bay of Fundy. During winter, the population migrates south but not as a unit. Adult and immature females winter in the Caribbean, but the immature males congregate along the coast of the middle Atlantic states. Adult males remain offshore.

Comfort Considerations

Among the most important aspects of preparing to travel offshore is adequately preparing for weather and sea conditions. This would be easy if every trip occurred during mild weather and on calm seas. Obviously, this is not the case. For a truly enjoyable trip, it is essential to have the proper clothing and to avoid seasickness.

Choices of Clothing

The combination of wind, sun, sea conditions, and air temperature makes the selection of dress different from what would be appropriate on shore.

Bright Sun: On sunny, calm days, the surface of the ocean reflects the most intense rays of the sun. Sunburn is far more likely at sea than on land given similar exposure. Because the relatively cool water lessens the apparent temperature, it seems less hot. This false sense of being able to stay out for long periods in the sun intensifies the problem. Adequate protection includes sunscreen, a hat, and sunglasses. The sunscreen should have a high SPF, such as 30. The sunglasses should have 100 percent UV filtration coatings because the ultraviolet light is also reflected by the water. Without UV filtration, the dark lenses cause your pupils to dilate, allowing your eyes to receive more ultraviolet radiation than they would otherwise. Hats should fit snugly and have a retaining strap that is attached to your belt or around your neck so that when the hat blows off your head, it will not end up in the sea.

Overcast or Rainy Days: On these days, the primary consideration is to remain warm and dry. Without sun, offshore temperatures can be much colder than on shore, particularly if the wind is blowing. Not only does wind produce wind chill, so does the forward motion of the boat. Rain or sea spray further intensify the chill potential. To remain comfortable, dress in multiple layers. The outermost layer (pants and jacket) should be lightweight and waterproof. Should weather conditions change from cold and rainy to sunny and hot, you can easily remove the outer layers to remain comfortable.

Cold Winter Days: Near-freezing to freezing temperatures can be difficult to protect against because the cold wind and spray seem to cut through everything. Down-filled jackets are not advised because down loses its insulation capacity when wet. Although expensive and cumbersome to wear, a Navy or Coast Guard–type survival suit offers the best overall protection. It is warm and waterproof and even makes an effective life jacket. The next best is a good outdoorsman's suit with jacket-and-pants combination. Water-resistant outer pants are better than thermal underwear because the former is easier to remove if needed. Being overdressed is no better than being underdressed—it is just as uncomfortable (and risky) to get wet from sweat as rain or sea spray.

About Seasickness

Unquestionably the single most discouraging (and feared) aspect of offshore travel is seasickness. There is a joke that describes three stages of seasickness. In Stage One, you're afraid you're going to get sick. In Stage Two, you're afraid you're going to die; and in Stage Three, you're afraid you're *not* going to die. Seasickness, however, is actually nothing more than your body's way of indicating that it is out of balance. Regardless of how debilitating the seasickness may seem at the time, most people recover within thirty to sixty minutes after entering conditions that are calmer than their sickness threshold.

Within each ear are three hollow, looped, tubular structures called semicircular canals. Each lies in a different plane or axis of orientation (i.e., length, or x-axis; width, or y-axis; and depth, or z-axis). They are filled with a fluid that sloshes back and forth when your head moves. This fluid movement bends tiny hairs connected to nerves that go to the brain and provide information on your orientation. This allows you to keep your balance while moving from place to place without falling down or bumping into objects. However, when you get into choppy sea conditions, the signals keep changing, and these perpetually changing signals are confusing. Your brain interprets this disorientation as a sign that you ate something toxic, so it sends a signal to your stomach to get rid of everything. That is how you get seasick.

Everyone has a different threshold for sickness as related to three factors: (1) the relative wave amplitude—how big the waves are in relation to your boat; (2) the suddenness of change of motion as determined by wave steepness and boat speed—the steeper the waves or the faster your boat and the wave intersect, the more sudden the motion change; and (3) the axes of movement. For example, if there are small, rounded waves moving with the boat, the movement is gentle and in one direction, producing a rhythmic up and down. If the waves are large and come at the boat from the side, there are two axes of motion, up and down plus side to side. If the waves are steep, there may be a rhythmic up motion, followed by a sudden and violent drop. If there is also a cross-chop, the boat may also twist back and forth, adding a third axis. Needless to say, the bigger the amplitude of motion, the more sudden the changes and the more axes of motion involved, the easier it is to get sick.

Individual thresholds for seasickness are also affected by daily factors and experience. Lack of sleep, stress, or consumption of caffeine, alcohol, or greasy or spicy foods all lower the threshold. Experience also affects susceptibility. The more often someone goes offshore, the more conditioned they become. This is called getting "sea legs." On a day-to-day basis, an average person will gain sea legs after a few hours. Most people who get sick do so within the first few hours of the trip unless the sea conditions worsen significantly during the day.

Effective seasickness prevention should start well in advance of the first symptoms. Contrary to popular belief, it is never too late to combat seasickness, although it is much easier to prevent the symptoms than reverse them. There are three general categories of prevention: drug therapy, nondrug therapy, and behavioral therapy. Nothing is universally effective, nor is the same method equally effective for the same person every time. The use of multiple strategies is often better than one alone, provided that such mixing *never* involves combining drugs with alcohol or other drugs.

Drug Therapy: Two classes of drugs are used to prevent seasickness: prescription drugs and over-the-counter drugs. The vast majority of drugs are essentially antihistamines, so the common side effects, particularly drowsiness, are to be expected. As with any drug, the nature and severity of the side effects vary with the individual and the drug. You should always consult a medical professional for the most appropriate strategy before trying something new.

There are several different drugs available. Some are designed to last four hours, some up to twenty-four. Some promise fewer side effects. As a general rule, those that last longer and minimize drowsiness are preferable. Since antihistamines are not addictive, it is generally safe to take them, as recommended, on consecutive days. Most manufacturers recommend taking the first dose about one hour before beginning an activity. However, starting the treatment twenty-four to forty-eight hours in advance is often advised because the common side effects, like drowsiness, may be diminished and the overall anti-nausea effect builds.

Oral drugs *must* be taken well in advance of any symptoms. As soon as the stomach becomes upset, it "clamps down" and the pill cannot pass into the intestines for absorption. Anti-nausea transdermal patches or suppositories are not subject to this problem, although the latter would be somewhat awkward to deal with on a pitching boat. Injectable antinausea drugs also exist, but these are not appropriate for prevention.

Nondrug Therapy: Nondrug alternatives include eating ginger or wearing acupressure wristbands. Some users report great success with these methods, even when drug therapies have failed. Any of these approaches should be compatible with a drug therapy, and collectively they may provide the necessary protection when one alone does not suffice.

Behavioral Therapy: Much of what you do, both prior to and after getting on the boat, will have a lot to do with whether you get sick. First, be sure that you *do* eat prior to departure. An empty stomach is more tense and more easily upset than one containing some food. But for at least twenty-four hours prior to departure, avoid food that is greasy, acidic, spicy, or heavy. Also avoid alcohol and "recreational" drugs. Any mild, bulky, or starchy food is preferable, such as bread, doughnuts, and the like. For those who can tolerate them, salty foods such as crackers or pretzels are even more effective (avoid potato chips, which are greasy). You should also have something to drink, but avoid filling your stomach with large volumes of liquid. Most colas and coffee contain caffeine, which can cause stomach upset. While some people find that drinking carbonated beverages can settle their stomachs, others report that the carbonation worsens the problem. In truth, it is the constant sipping of a palatable liquid and the constant nibbling of snacks that helps. Acidic drinks, such as citrus juices, can cause stomach upset. The best choice of drink is a sports drink. It not only lacks the negative attributes of some other beverages but also will rapidly replenish needed electrolytes should you become dehydrated from seasickness or overexposure to the sun.

Getting a good night's sleep prior to departure makes a big difference. Once on the boat, if you experience discomfort, stay outside and toward the back of the boat on the lowest deck possible. Avoid diesel fumes and cigarette smoke. Finally, stay active. It is no coincidence that trips which encounter wildlife early have fewer seasick passengers.

If everything fails and you feel sick, do what you need to do as soon as possible. Don't fight it. Often someone will experience one or two attacks of nausea and then recover for the rest of the day. It is even possible to enjoy much of the trip if the seasickness continues because there may be periods of comfort between the bouts of nausea. Find something exciting to watch during these recovery periods and you may find that you make fewer trips to the rail. Finally, experience is an important factor. The reason that boat captains don't get sick is that they are offshore daily and have adjusted.

Understanding Weather

Weather plays an important role in the success of an offshore trip with regard to not only how comfortable you are but also how much wildlife you see. If you are looking for whales or sea turtles, the animals will be most easily visible under slick, calm conditions. If you are looking for birds, some wind and sea is preferable because when conditions become too calm, birds sit on the water and are harder to locate.

Although a detailed discussion of meteorological conditions is beyond the scope of a wildlife field guide, a few basic concepts can go a long way to predicting sea conditions and the likelihood of success based on weather.

Weather patterns occur because the earth's atmosphere, like ocean currents, is in constant motion. This means that different masses of air—some originating in colder climates, others in warm climates—eventually collide with each other, creating inclement weather. These parcels of air may be characterized by their atmospheric pressure and temperature.

Atmospheric pressure is a measure of the relative density of a parcel of air. As warm air expands, its density lessens; conversely, as cold air contracts, its density increases. Although warm air parcels often result in low-pressure systems and cold parcels result in highs, the nature of weather is more complex than that.

The terms "high pressure" and "low pressure" refer to the relative pressure of a given parcel of air compared with its surrounding air masses. Meteorologists refer to lines of equal atmospheric pressure as isobars. When drawn on a map, they resemble topographic lines of elevation. If drawn in 3-D, a high-pressure system would look like a hill, with the center of the high representing the top of the hill. The more isobar lines there are, the taller the hill would be. The closer the lines are together, the steeper the sides. Low-pressure systems look like valleys but otherwise work the same way.

The boundary where unlike air masses meet is called a front. Dramatic, even violent weather systems may develop along frontal boundaries. The strength of the front is related to the difference of the colliding air masses.

Fronts are characterized as either warm or cold (Figure 1). Generally speaking, warm fronts move Tropical air masses from south to north, and cold fronts move Arctic air from north to south. Since most weather systems also move from west to east, both types of fronts share this direction of movement.

Calm weather generally prevails under large parcels of slow-moving or stationary air. When fronts move through and replace these parcels, the resultant wind shift and intensification can cause rough conditions offshore. As a general rule, the passage of a cold front results in stronger winds and rougher seas than the passage of a warm front.

The wind direction ahead of and following the passage of a front may

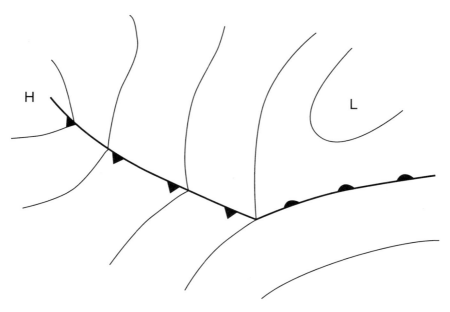

Figure 2. Stylized weather front. This is an example of a generic weather system showing a cold front (solid triangles on heavy black line) associated with a high (H).

be predicted from the isobars on either side of the frontal boundary. As a rule, the frontal boundary will lie roughly perpendicular to the isobars and the wind direction will be roughly parallel with them. In the Northern Hemisphere, the circulatory flow around a high is clockwise, around a low, counterclockwise. At the surface, however, friction with the land or the ocean surface causes the winds to deflect slightly away from true parallel. Around highs, the deflection is outward, and around lows, inward (Figure 2).

For example, if a cold front passes with a low to the north of your position, the wind ahead of the front may be out of the southeast to southwest and will swing to the north or northwest after its passage. A few hundred miles farther north, with the center of the low south of your position, the wind may be southwest ahead of the front and east to northeast after it passes. A high would reverse these tendencies.

Warmer air has a greater capacity to hold water vapor than cold air. As this water vapor cools, it condenses into clouds. If a moisture-laden low forms and then collides with cold, dry air, the result is the formation of massive cloud banks that may include thunderstorms. The local winds generated by thunderstorms may be considerably stronger and even of a different direction than those which occur regionally. Isolated thunderstorms can and should be avoided whenever possible. When a continuous string of these storms forms, it is called a squall line and may produce a wide band of rather violent weather with severe thunderstorms, hail, or tornados. A tor-

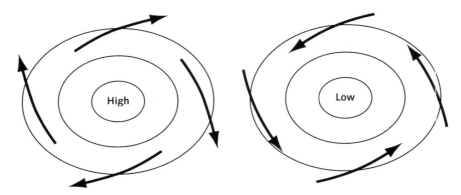

Figure 3. Circulation patterns around pressure cells are clockwise around a high and counterclockwise around a low.

nado spawned over the water is called a waterspout. Although waterspouts are generally weaker than their land-based cousins, they are still dangerous and should be given a wide berth.

Of special concern are concentrated, low-pressure systems where high wind and squalls create particularly violent if not dangerous weather. Such storms may develop over warm or cold water, but two patterns that originate in Tropical waters bear specific mention.

The first involves lows that form in the Gulf of Mexico and move up the Atlantic coast. Ahead of the storm there may be strong southeast winds that strengthen and shift to the northeast as the storm passes. Called northeasters ("nor'easters"), they occur most commonly during winter and spring. The second pattern involves lows that develop off Tropical Africa during summer and fall. These systems typically move west with the tradewinds. Fueled by the warm water, they strengthen into very large and concentrated low-pressure systems with sustained wind speeds that are often well in excess of 100 miles an hour. Where the maximum sustained wind speed is less than 75 miles an hour, the system is called a tropical storm. When the maximum sustained wind speed exceeds 75 miles an hour, it is a hurricane. Highly unpredictable, most tropical storms and hurricanes move westward through the Caribbean into the Gulf of Mexico or track the Gulf Stream north past the North American coast. As they reach colder waters, they weaken but may not die before reaching New England or Canada. These storms are extremely dangerous and under *no* circumstances should anyone venture near the coast, much less offshore, within forty-eight hours of the approach of one. However, they may blow seabirds far inshore or drive them hundreds of miles north of their normal range, giving birders an opportunity to observe seabirds on inland lakes or even in parking lots!

More than anything else, the advisability of going offshore is based on waves. Waves are generated by wind, both locally and from a long distance away. Large storms, especially tropical storms and hurricanes, can generate sizable waves while still hundreds of miles distant. Waves that are generated at a distance are called ground swell. They consist of widely spaced, rounded, parallel waves moving in a unified direction away from the wind source. Their direction and amplitude are completely unrelated to local conditions. If the local wind is light, then the ground swell will be simple and generally result in conditions that are not too uncomfortable. But if local wind and weather conditions are not calm, the effects of the local weather will be superimposed on the former and very rough conditions might prevail.

Waves generated by local wind conditions are asymmetrically shaped. Because they are being pushed by the wind, the waves are steeper on their running (leeward) side than on their back (windward) side. Sailing into the wind is considerably rougher than running with the wind, not only because the boat meets the steep side of the wave but because it is running against the wave's direction of movement. Running with the wind is smoother because the boat's movement complements the wave movement and the wave is not as steep. Finally, the presence of current has an effect. The current flow creates an additional force. Where current flow and wind direction are opposite, wave amplitude (height) is greater and period (spacing) is shorter than with calm water or with the wind and current moving in the same direction (see Figure 3).

When deciding to go offshore, there are several factors to consider.

1. The wind generated from a weather front may not diminish during the course of the day and, in many cases, may strengthen.

2. If you go offshore with the wind at your back, your trip out will be far easier and faster than your returning trip.

3. Consider the length of your boat. Wave heights less than one-twentieth of the boat's length are comfortable in most circumstances (for example, two-foot waves and a forty-foot boat). Wave heights greater than one-tenth of the boat's length are moderately rough (four-foot waves and a forty-foot boat); greater than one-seventh, very rough (six-foot waves and a forty-foot boat).

4. If your itinerary takes you into an oceanic current, particularly the Gulf Stream, consider the wind direction in relation to the current flow. If the wind direction opposes the flow of the current, the waves may be much larger. In fact, it is possible to be in four- to six-foot seas just outside the current and yet see eight- to twelve-foot seas in the current only a few hundred yards away.

5. The open ocean, where the wind has the opportunity to build its

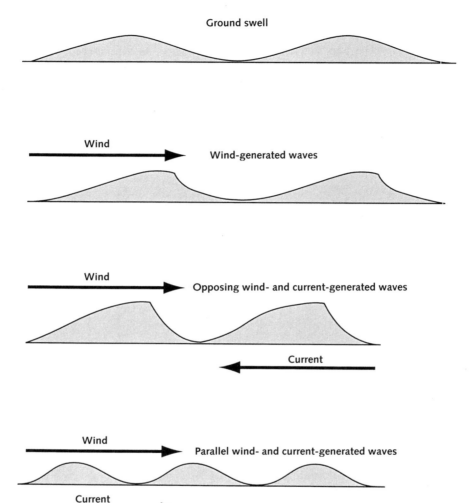

Figure 4. Relative effects of wind and current on the size, shape, and spacing of waves.

effects, will be rougher than "sheltered" waters—where a peninsula or a cape shields the water from the long-distance effects of the wind on the sea. This may be true even if that projection of land is a few miles away.

For centuries, mariners have used the Beaufort scale to categorize the severity of sea and weather conditions. It is reproduced in Table 1, with adaptations to fit the scope of this text.

If you are going offshore in a sport-fishing boat (generally 35–60 feet in length) or a "head boat" (75–120 feet in length), your trip will be comfortable at Beaufort 3 and under; at Beaufort 4, conditions will be relatively comfortable for most passengers if they have taken precautions against seasickness; Beaufort 5 will be bearable for some and rough for many; at Beaufort 6, only the weather-hardy will find the conditions bearable; at Beaufort 7 and above, none of these boats should be offshore. If you are on a large, oceangoing ship, Beaufort 5 and below should be easy, Beaufort 6–8 moderately comfortable for many. Even Beaufort 9–10 may be surprisingly manageable with some ships. Ultimately, trust the boat captain to know what weather conditions are unsafe. If your captain is reluctant to go offshore, pressing the issue is unwise. Similarly, if you are concerned about rough conditions, ask what might be expected.

For observing wildlife, whales, seals, and sea turtles are most easily seen with Beaufort 3 or less. Birds, on the other hand, may be more easily seen with Beaufort 3–5 conditions because the wind and waves encourage the birds to fly, making them more visible. On smaller boats, Beaufort 6 and above conditions would make viewing so difficult that being offshore is pointless, regardless of the strength of your constitution. Conversely, on very large vessels (ca. 250 feet and up), observations from a safely enclosed upper bridge or viewing facility may be surprisingly good even up to Beaufort 10 seas. However, as a general rule, there is no valid reason to be at sea during storm conditions.

Veteran oceangoing observers pay close attention to weather reports, not only those on television that display the weather maps but also marine forecasts broadcast by NOAA over special-frequency airwaves reserved for that purpose. Occasional offshore venturers may get a good grasp of weather from local televised forecasts. Even without isobars, one can still estimate the wind direction based on the orientation and movement of the frontal boundary.

Another way to estimate the relative strength of a system is to look at the temperature change on opposite sides of the front. The greater the change, the stronger the system. If the temperature change is more than a few degrees, it is a safe bet that the wind behind the front will be brisk or strong. Also consider the speed of the advancing front. A rapidly moving front will generally have stronger winds behind it than a weak front.

Finally, pay attention to the weather system behind the front because depending on what follows, strong wind and rough conditions may persist for as little as a few hours or as much as several days. For example, a rapidly advancing front may produce more violent weather as it passes, but it will be gone sooner than one which is less severe but creeps along.

TABLE 1

BEAUFORT NUMBER	WIND SPEED (mph)	WAVE HEIGHT (feet)	SEA CONDITIONS	WILDLIFE OBSERVABLE
0	<1	0	flat calm; mirror-like	great for whales, fair for birds
1	1−3	.5−1	calm; slight swell, rippled surface	great for whales, fair for birds
2	4−7	1−2	slight swell with small wavelets	good for whales, good for birds
3	8−11	1−3	small waves; occasional whitecaps	great for birds, good for whales
4	12−18	2−4	scattered whitecaps; occasional chop	great for birds, good for whales
5	19−24	4−8	numerous whitecaps; moderately rough	good for birds, poor for whales
6	25−30	8−12	rough; boats under 100 feet will have waves break over their bows	poor for birds from small boats, good from large ships
7	31−37	12−16	very rough; impossible observation conditions except from large ships	fair for birds
8	38−45	16−20	gale-force winds; seas unsafe for typical day-excursion boats	poor for viewing wildlife
9	46−53	18−25	strong gale	poor for viewing wildlife
10	54−63	20−40	whole gale	poor for viewing wildlife
11	64−74	30−60	near hurricane	poor for viewing wildlife
12	>75	>40	hurricane-force winds	poor for viewing wildlife

A Word on Nomenclature

Most species get two names, one scientific and one common. Scientific names are used by the professional community because they are more precise and are universally recognized (always binomial, in Latin). However, for the lay person, they are complex, often hard to pronounce, and sometimes even harder to remember. Hence, species also receive common or popular names. Compared with the scientific names, common names can differ with different geographic regions and can change frequently without any corresponding change in the status of the organism as a species. For example. *Pterodroma feae,* whose common name in the 1980s was "Gon-Gon," became "Cape Verde Petrel" in the early 1990s. Within a couple of years, its name in Europe was changed to "Fea's Petrel" while in North America it became "Cape Verde Islands Petrel." Only one year later the European name was universally adopted and it is now "Fea's Petrel." Several species have more than one acceptable common name. Of these, three patterns exist:

1. Name differences resulting from regional (North American versus European) preferences. Where both are given, the North American common name (indicated by the superscript NA) is listed first in this book, followed by the name used in Europe and Britain (indicated by E). Both names are listed in the species accounts and on the plates. However, because the range abundance charts are location-specific, only the regionally appropriate names appear there (e.g., "Dovekie" on North American charts and "Little Auk" on the European).

2. Cases where a name other than the currently accepted common name is preferred by the author. In these cases, both names are listed, the currently accepted name first, followed by the alternate name. These dual listings occur only in the species accounts.

3. Old common or colloquial names are provided as a reference. These alternate names occur only in the species accounts and are listed on a separate line beneath the main species heading (as "also . . .").

1 Albatrosses and Allies

2. **BLACK-BROWED ALBATROSS** (*Thalassarche melanophris*).
   a. Adult Dorsal View. Yellow bill, black "eyebrow," blackish back and upperwings.
   b. Adult Ventral View. Broad dark underwing borders, especially on leading edge.
   c. Immature Ventral View. Dark bill with black tip, neck collar, sooty underwings.

4. **SOUTHERN GIANT PETREL** (*Macronectes giganteus*). Accidental occurrence.
   Adult (based on single occurrence record). Massive yellow bill. Predominately dark brown with paler, "dirty" head.

1. **WANDERING ALBATROSS** (*Diomedia exulans*). Accidental occurrence.
   a. Immature Ventral View (based on single occurrence record). Pink bill, white face; brown underparts, often darkest on chest band; white underwings with dark tips.
   b. Adult Dorsal View (based on single occurrence record). White head and back; blackish upperwings with white patches.

3. **YELLOW-NOSED ALBATROSS** (*Thalassarche chlororhynchos*). Accidental occurrence.
   a. Immature Ventral View. Blackish bill, white head; white underwings with narrow black borders.
   b. Subadult Ventral View. Grayish head, white underwings.
   c. Adult Dorsal View. Black bill with yellow ridge; dark gray back and upperwings.

32. **NORTHERN GANNET** (*Sula bassana*). See also Plates 8, 9. For comparison.
   Immature. Note long, wedged-shaped tail.

55. **GREAT BLACK-BACKED GULL** [NA] **OR GREATER BLACK-BACKED GULL** [E]
   (*Larus marinus*). See also Plate 18. For comparison.
   Adult. Note white tail and border on upperwing.

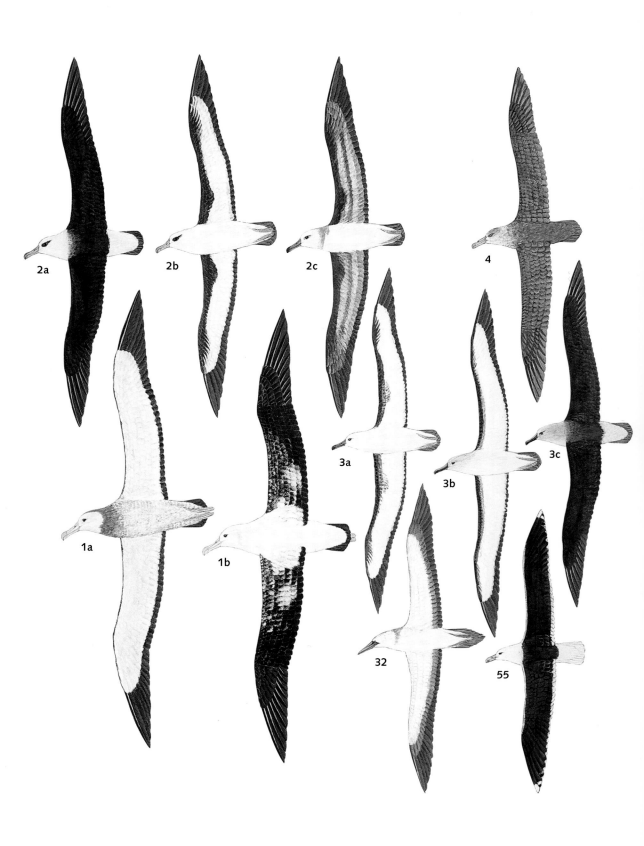

Plate
2 Common Petrels

5. **NORTHERN FULMAR** (*Fulmarus glacialis*). See also Plate 4.
   a. Light Morph Ventral View. Large head and straw-colored bill; very white underparts.
   b. Light Morph Dorsal View. Pale gray to brownish gray back and upperwings; variable white wing-flash, frosty rump and tail.
   c. Gray Morph Dorsal View. As 5b, but darker and more uniformly colored above.

6. **BLACK-CAPPED PETREL** (*Pterodroma hasitata*). See also Plate 3.
   a. Ventral View. Black cap through eye; white collar; white underwings with diagonal black midwing bar.
   b. Dorsal View. Narrow white neck collar, broad white rump.

17. **GREATER SHEARWATER**[NA] **OR GREAT SHEARWATER**[E] (*Puffinus gravis*). See also Plate 5. For comparison.
   Adult Dorsal View. Distinguished from Black-capped Petrel by dark forehead, browner back, narrow white rump, and short, rounded tail rather than long, wedge-shaped tail.

3 Rarer Petrels

10. **FEA'S PETREL** (*Pterodroma feae*).
    a. Dorsal View. Grayish back with dark M-shaped pattern; contrasting pale rump and tail.
    b. Ventral View. Hooded appearance, sometimes with black eye-patch; blackish underwings.

11. **ZINO'S PETREL** (*Pterodroma madeira*).
    Dorsal View. Distinguished from Fea's Petrel by proportionately shorter and broader wings (more so than illustrated) and less obvious back pattern and pale midwing panel.

8. **MOTTLED PETREL** (*Pterodroma inexpectata*). Accidental occurrence.
    Ventral View (based on single occurrence record). Blackish underbody; white underwings with black diagonal bar.

7. **BERMUDA PETREL** (*Pterodroma cahow*).
    a. Ventral View. Hooded appearance; white underwings with dark borders; "thumbprint" spots on greater primary coverts.
    b. Dorsal View. Uniformly grayish above with pale base to rump.

6. **BLACK-CAPPED PETREL** (*Pterodroma hasitata*). See also Plate 2.
    Dark Morph Dorsal View. Blackish cap tends to be discernible; rump white, even if narrow. Compared with Bermuda Petrel, appears stockier and not as long-winged.

9. **HERALD PETREL** (*Pterodroma arminjoniana*). See also Plate 4.
    Light Morph Ventral View. Mostly dark head; white underbody; underwings variable with broad white midwing band.

4 Dark Petrels and Shearwaters

5. **NORTHERN FULMAR** (*Fulmarus glacialis*). See also Plate 2.
   a. Dark Morph Ventral View. Solidly dark gray; large head and straw-colored bill.
   b. Dark Morph Dorsal View. Uniformly dark gray with pale bill.

19. **SOOTY SHEARWATER** (*Puffinus griseus*).
    a. Ventral View. Blackish brown head and body; white underwing coverts.
    b. Dorsal View. Uniformly dark with dark bill.

13. **WHITE-CHINNED PETREL** (*Procellaria aequinoctialis*). Accidental occurrence.
    Ventral View. Uniformly dark with straw-colored bill; white chin visible only at very close range. Distinguished from Fulmar by much longer, albatross-like wings.

21. **MEDITERRANEAN SHEARWATER** (*Puffinus mauretanicus*).
    Dark Morph Ventral View. "Dirty" brown underparts; grayish white underwings; feet project beyond tail.

9. **HERALD PETREL** (*Pterodroma arminjoniana*). See also Plate 3.
   a. Dark Morph Ventral View. Uniformly dark with white underwing-flash.
   b. Dark Morph Dorsal View. Uniformly dark above. Distinguished from Sooty Shearwater by proportionately shorter head and shorter, heavier bill.

14. **BULWER'S PETREL** (*Bulweria bulwerii*). See also Plate 7.
    Dorsal View. Much smaller than others; very long wings and tail; pale upperwing bar.

5a

5b

19a

19b

13

21

9a

9b

14

5 Larger Shearwaters

17. **GREATER SHEARWATER**[NA] **OR GREAT SHEARWATER**[E] (*Puffinus gravis*). See also Plate 2.
    a. Ventral View. Dark brown cap; white underparts with brownish oval belly patch; underwings with dark diagonal pattern.
    b. Dorsal View. Dark cap separated from back by white neck collar; white crescent separates rump from tail. Juveniles are very scaly-backed.

18. **BULLER'S SHEARWATER** (*Puffinus bulleri*).
    Dorsal View (based on single occurrence record). Gray back contrasts with black cap and tail; bold M-shaped back pattern; underparts white.

16. **CAPE VERDE SHEARWATER** (*Calonectris edwardsii*). Newly recognized species.
    Dorsal View. Like diminutive Cory's but darker above with dusky yellow bill.

15. **CORY'S SHEARWATER** (*Calonectris diomedea*).
    a. Ventral View. Grayish hood; yellow bill with black subterminal ring; underbody and underwings clean white.
    b. Dorsal View. Brownish upperparts sometimes showing darker M-shaped back pattern; rump often with narrow white margin.

Plate

6

Small "Black and White" Shearwaters

20. **MANX SHEARWATER** (*Puffinus puffinus*).
    a. Dorsal View. Blackish above; crown separated from shoulder bar by narrow white crescent.
    b. Ventral View. Underwings and underbody white (including undertail coverts); wings appear sharply pointed.

21. **MEDITERRANEAN SHEARWATER** (*Puffinus mauretanicus*). See also Plate 4.
    a. Dorsal View. Distinctly brownish above; wings more rounded; feet project visibly beyond tail.
    b. Ventral View. Highly variable. Often with chest band. Distinguished from Manx by dark flanks and dirtier appearance.

23. **AUDUBON'S SHEARWATER** (*Puffinus lherminieri*).
    a. Dorsal View. Dark brown above; tail long and wedge-shaped.
    b. Ventral View. Dark cap continuous with shoulder bar; underparts white with dark undertail coverts.

22. **LITTLE SHEARWATER** (*Puffinus assimilis*).
    a. Dorsal View. Grayish above with frosty midwing panels; wings short and rounded.
    b. Ventral View. Face and neck extensively white; underwings white with narrow dusky borders; blue feet project beyond tail.

20a

21a

23a

22a

20b

21b

23b

22b

Plate
7 Storm-petrels

24. **WILSON'S STORM-PETREL** (*Oceanites oceanicus*).
a. Dorsal View. Dark brown with rounded white rump patch; short broad wings with pale, half-moon-shaped carpal bar.
b. Pattering View. Pale underwing area may mimic European Storm-petrel. Long legs; yellow webs between toes.

26. **EUROPEAN STORM-PETREL** (*Hydrobates pelagicus*).
a. Dorsal View. Very dark with square-shaped white rump; upperwing with faint carpal bar; wings proportionately slender and rounded.
b. Pattering View. Underwings with white midwing bar; short legs; feet entirely dark.

27. **BAND-RUMPED STORM-PETREL** (*Oceanodroma castro*).
Dorsal View. Dark blackish brown above with sharply defined white rump; dark tail about twice as long as rump (proportions of Wilson's are more equal); wings long and falcon-like with grayish carpal bar.

28. **LEACH'S STORM-PETREL** (*Oceanodroma leucorhoa*).
a. Typical Morph Dorsal View. Distinctly brown with long, slender, pointed wings. Tan carpal bar widens toward wrist; white of rump elongated, often bisected with dark line; tail forked.
b. Dark Morph Dorsal View. As Typical but with mostly dark rump. Very rare in Atlantic and should be compared with Swinhoe's Storm-petrel.

29. **SWINHOE'S STORM-PETREL** (*Oceanodroma monorhis*).
Dorsal View. Uniformly blackish except for pale carpal bars. Compared with Leach's, wings are broader, tail is less forked.

25. **WHITE-FACED STORM-PETREL** (*Pelagodroma marina*).
a. Dorsal View. White face with dark cap and eye-patch.
b. Pattering View. White underbody and underwings; very long legs, feet with yellow webs; distinctive flight (see text).

14. **BULWER'S PETREL** (*Bulweria bulwerii*). See also Plate 4.
Dorsal View. Uniformly dark except for pale carpal bar. Wings and tail very long; tail wedge-shaped, not notched.

Plate

8 White Sulids

32. **NORTHERN GANNET** (*Sula bassana*). See also Plates 1, 9.
    a. Adult Ventral View. Cream-colored head, gray bill.
    b. Adult Dorsal View. White back, inner wings, and tail; outerwing black, "dipped in ink."
    c. Subadult Dorsal View. Head whiter than adult; secondaries and tail black. Back usually mottled.

34. **MASKED BOOBY** (*Sula dactylatra*). See also Plate 9.
    a. Adult Ventral View. Yellow bill; broad black facial area.
    b. Adult Dorsal View. Black primaries, secondaries, and greater coverts (subadult gannet has mostly white secondary coverts); tail black.

35. **RED-FOOTED BOOBY** (*Sula sula*). See also Plate 9.
    a. White Morph Adult Ventral View. White head, blue bill with red facial skin; red feet often visible against white tail.
    b. White Morph Adult Dorsal View. Most easily distinguished from Masked Booby by blue bill and white tail.

9 Brown Sulids

32. NORTHERN GANNET (*Sula bassana*). See also Plates 1, 8.
a. Immature Ventral View. Brownish head, dusky bill; underparts variably white or dark; lesser underwing coverts white, remainder dark.
b. Immature Dorsal View. Uniformly dark brown, sometimes with pale crescent at base of rump.

34. MASKED BOOBY (*Sula dactylatra*). See also Plate 8.
a. Immature Ventral View. Dark brown head sharply demarcated from white underparts; bill dusky to yellow with black facial skin.
b. Immature Dorsal View. Dark head and back divided by white neck collar. Upperwing coverts paler than remainder.

35. RED-FOOTED BOOBY (*Sula sula*). See also Plate 8.
a. Immature Ventral View. Uniformly dark grayish brown, often with discernibly darker head and chest band; bill pinkish gray with dark tip, becoming bluish gray with age.
b. Dark Morph Adult Ventral View. Uniformly dark brown; bill blue with red base; legs and feet bright red.

36. BROWN BOOBY (*Sula leucogaster*).
a. Immature Ventral View. Head and neck solid dark brown; underparts mottled brown. Underwing linings white, remainder of underwing dark; feet yellowish.
b. Adult Ventral View. Head and neck solid brown, sharply contrasting with white chest; bill yellow with no black at the base. Distinguished from Masked Booby by ab–sence of white neck collar.

33. BLUE-FOOTED BOOBY (*Sula nebouxii*). Accidental occurrence.
a. Immature Dorsal View. Head and upperparts brown with three white patches: neck, midback, rump; bill dark gray.
b. Adult Ventral View. Head lightly streaked brown; body and underwing linings white with dark midwing bar and box-like underwing patch; powder blue feet not always visible.

Plate

10 Frigatebirds

37. **MAGNIFICENT FRIGATEBIRD** (*Fregata magnificens*).
a. Adult Male Dorsal View. Uniformly blackish; scapulars have purple sheen at close range.
b. Displaying Adult Male Ventral View. Red gular sac is characteristic of all adult male frigatebird species; inflated during courtship.
c. Subadult Male Ventral View. Uniformly dark as adult male but with variable white mottling on midbelly and axillars.
d. Adult Female Ventral View. Dark head; white neck, chest, and upper belly; white lower belly with dark triangular wedge projecting forward.
e. Subadult Female Ventral View. As adult female but with mottled chin and wedge.
f. Stage 1 Immature Ventral View. White head and neck separated from white belly by incomplete chest band.
g. Stage 2 Immature Ventral View. Head, chest, and upper belly uniformly white; white "wedge" projects backward.

37X. **GREAT FRIGATEBIRD** (*Fregata minor*). Unrecorded; shown for comparison.
a. Adult Male Dorsal View. Distinguished from Magnificent by pale carpal bars and greenish sheen on scapulars; otherwise not reliably separable from Magnificent.
b. Adult Female Ventral View. Dark head, grayish chin, red eyering surprisingly visible; white chest and upper belly; dark box-shaped projection from lower belly.
c. Immature Ventral View. Resembles adult female Magnificent but with tan rather than blackish head.

38. **LESSER FRIGATEBIRD** (*Fregata ariel*). Accidental; single occurrence record.
a. Adult Male Ventral View. Much smaller than Magnificent. Prominent white axillary bars.
b. Adult Female Ventral View. Resembles diminutive female Great but with less extensively dark head and blackish chin.
c. Immature Ventral View. Resembles diminutive immature Great: tawny head; white underparts with dark wedge from lower belly.

46. **LONG-TAILED JAEGER**[NA] **OR LONG-TAILED SKUA**[E] (*Stercorarius longicaudus*). See also Plates 13, 14. For comparison.
Alternate Adult Ventral View. Black cap set off from white chin to midbelly; much smaller bird with different-shaped wings; elongated tail feathers at center, not outer edges.

37a

37b

37c

37d

37e

37f

37g

37Xa

37Xb

37Xc

46

38a

38b

38c

Plate

11 Phalaropes

---

39. **RED PHALAROPE**[NA] **OR GREY PHALAROPE**[E] (*Phalaropus fulicarius*).
a. **Alternate (breeding) Plumage Male Dorsal View.** White face, dark gray crown; reddish underparts; yellow bill.
b. **Molting Fall Juvenile Dorsal View.** Note that most juvenile birds depart the breeding grounds after starting to molt. Upperparts (juvenile plumage) blackish, becoming pale gray as molt progresses, starting with the back. Bill stout, larger than Red-necked and lacking back stripes.
c. **Fall Adult Dorsal View.** Head and crown white with restricted black nape and eye-patch; upperparts becoming pale gray with molt; broad white wing-stripes; no back stripes.
d. **Alternate (breeding) Plumage Female Swimming.** Black crown, white face; bright cinnamon-colored underparts; yellow bill with black tip.
e. **Winter Adult Swimming.** As fall adult but without residual feathers of summer plumage. Upperparts pale gray and very uniform.

40. **RED-NECKED PHALAROPE** (*Phalaropus lobatus*).
a. **Alternate (breeding) Plumage Male Dorsal View.** Upperparts brownish with tawny to golden V-shaped back stripes and scapular edges; face white with reddish stripe on side of neck; bill thin and dark.
b. **Juvenile Dorsal View.** Crown and back of neck brownish gray; dark eye-patch more prominent than Red; back with pale V-shaped pattern.
c. **Fall Adult Dorsal View.** Crown and back of neck dark without white collar separating them from the back; upperparts grayish with pale "ghost" stripes. Distinguished from Red Phalarope by smaller size, slenderer bill, and narrower white wing-stripe.
d. **Alternate (breeding) Plumage Female Swimming.** Dark gray head with black face mask, white chin; cinnamon-colored throat and sides of neck; dark gray back with golden back and scapular stripes.
e. **Winter Adult Swimming.** Crown and center of hindneck dark blackish, back pale gray with "ghost" stripes. Distinguished from Red Phalarope by more extensively dark crown and eye line.

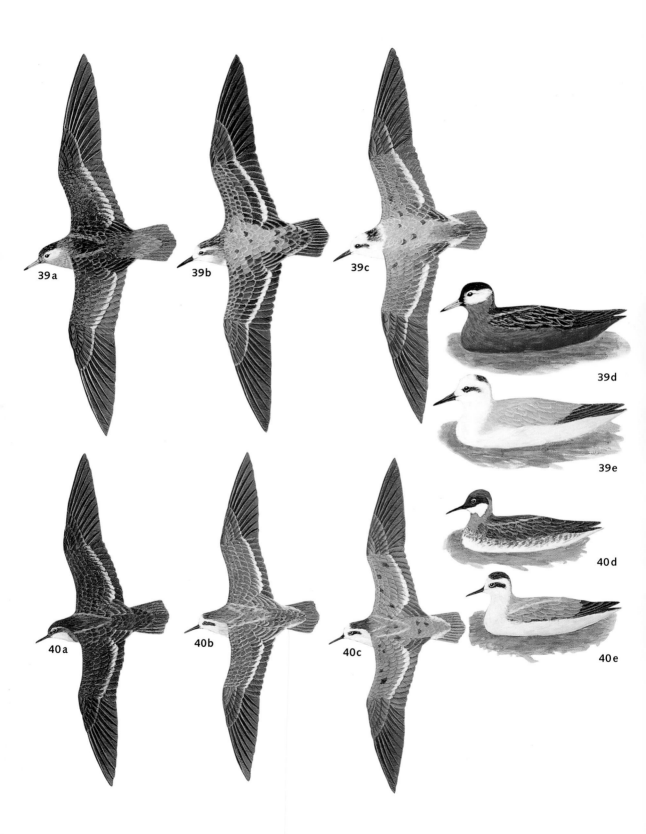

39a

39b

39c

39d

39e

40a

40b

40c

40d

40e

Plate

12 Skuas

41. GREAT SKUA (*Catharacta skua*).
a. Dark Morph Dorsal View. Upperparts blackish brown with hint of cinnamon tones; crown blackish and variable, separated from back by golden neck streaks. White wing-flash broader than South Polar Skua.
b. Light Morph Dorsal View. Upperparts brown, mottled with cinnamon and golden coloration; crown and face black, contrasting with pale nape and neck; golden color of neck and upper back very streaky; secondaries contrastingly paler than upperwing.
c. Dark Morph (Juvenile) Ventral View. Uniformly blackish with cinnamon tones; white underwing-flash twice the width of upperwing-flash. Distinguished from darkest South Polar Skuas by proportionately broader wings and shorter tail.
d. Light Morph Ventral View. Dark cap and cinnamon-colored underparts, sometimes set off by darker chest.

43. SOUTH POLAR SKUA (*Catharacta maccormicki*).
a. Dark Morph Dorsal View. Head brownish, hindneck diffusely washed with yellow; back darker, grayish brown, and lacking pale streaks or mottling; white wing-flash distinct but narrow.
b. Light Morph Dorsal View. Most of head pale yellowish or tan; upperparts contrastingly dark grayish brown and unstreaked. Otherwise upperparts lack contrasting parts except for white wing-flash.
c. Juvenile Ventral View. Distinctly grayish (although strong lighting and sun-bleached plumage can give the appearance of warmer tones); head and neck without contrasting paleness but body coloration will appear slightly paler than back and underwings; underwing-flash less extensive than in dark-morph Great Skuas.
d. "Typical" Morph Ventral View. Head separated from body by distinct yellowish neck collar that lacks streaking. Underwings show stronger contrast between secondaries and coverts than Great Skua.
e. Very Light Morph Ventral View. Head and entire underbody pale yellow to white; underwings dark with white wing-flash and paler gray secondaries.

42. BROWN SKUA (*Catharacta lonnbergi*). Accidental occurrence.
a. Adult Light Morph Dorsal View. Crown and face variably dark brown set off by heavily mottled hindneck and upper back. Underparts may be mottled as well; extent of underpart mottling typically parallels extent of upperpart mottling. Lacks cinnamon tones of Great Skua; wings proportionately much broader than South Polar Skua.
b. Dark Morph (Juvenile) Ventral View. Uniformly chocolate brown, sometimes with pale wash of yellow on neck; white underwing-flash twice the width of upperwing-flash.

42X. SOUTHERN SKUA (*Catharacta antarctica*). Unrecorded; shown for comparison.
Dorsal View. Resembles Brown Skua but with distinct black cap.

49. HERRING GULL (*Larus argentatus*). See also Plate 18. For comparison.
Immature Dorsal View. Same size as Great Skua but paler, grayish brown, and lacking white wing-flash that is diagnostic of group.

44. POMARINE JAEGER[NA] OR POMARINE SKUA[E] (*Stercorarius pomarinus*). See also Plates 13, 14. For comparison.
Dark Morph Adult Ventral View. Much smaller than skuas with proportionately longer wings and tail.

41a

41b

41c

41d

43a

43b

43c

43d

43e

42a

42b

42X

49

44

Plate

13 Adult Jaegers

44. POMARINE JAEGER [NA] **OR POMARINE SKUA** [E] (*Stercorarius pomarinus*). See also Plates 12, 14.
a. Alternate (breeding) Plumage Dorsal View. Blackish crown extends below eye; upperparts uniformly dark except for white primary shafts on outer 8–10 primaries; elongate central tail feathers spoon-shaped and twisted.
b. Light Morph Alternate Plumage Ventral View. Black cap surrounded by pale yellow on neck; chest band of variable width but dark, well defined, and often "ragged." Double white underwing-flash with primary flash over half the length of the primaries.
c. Typical Basic Plumage Ventral View. As alternate but with short, blunt, rounded tail feathers.
d. Basic Plumage Variant Ventral View. Rarely observed plumage. Head and neck uniformly dark; otherwise as typical basic plumage.

45. PARASITIC JAEGER [NA] **OR ARCTIC SKUA** [E] (*Stercorarius parasiticus*). See also Plate 14.
a. Alternate (breeding) Plumage Dorsal View. Crown brownish extending to level of eye, white spot in front of bill. Upperparts uniformly gray-brown with outermost 4–6 primary shafts white. Elongated central tail feathers about equal to length of tail and sharply pointed.
b. Very Light Morph Alternate Plumage Ventral View. Crown dark brown extending to level of eye. Underparts white, undertail coverts dark. Breastband may be partial or entirely absent.
c. Light Morph Alternate Plumage Ventral View. As preceding but with grayish brown breastband, the leading edge of which is ill defined. Single underwing-flash covers about half the length of the primaries.
d. Basic Plumage Ventral View. As typical alternate but with darker, more clearly defined breastband and shorter central tail feathers.

46. LONG-TAILED JAEGER [NA] **OR LONG-TAILED SKUA** [E] (*Stercorarius longicaudus*). See also Plates 10, 14.
a. Alternate (breeding) Plumage Dorsal View. Sharply defined black cap; sides of neck straw-colored. Grayish back and wing coverts contrast with darker outerwing. Elongated, streamer-like central feathers sometimes over half of body length. White primary flash usually restricted to outermost 2 primary shafts.
b. Basic Plumage Dorsal View. Upperparts dark brown without obvious contrast to outerwings; sides of neck cream to dirty white.
c. Alternate Plumage Ventral View. Sharply defined black cap and yellowish sides of neck; chin to midbelly white without chest band. Underwings without obvious white flash.
d. Basic Plumage Ventral View. White underparts broken by bold chest band; sides of neck washed with tan to dirty white; underwings without obvious wing-flash; undertail coverts strongly barred.
e. Basic Plumage Ventral View. True "winter" plumage rarely if ever observed in northern Atlantic. As preceding but with uniformly dark head and neck.

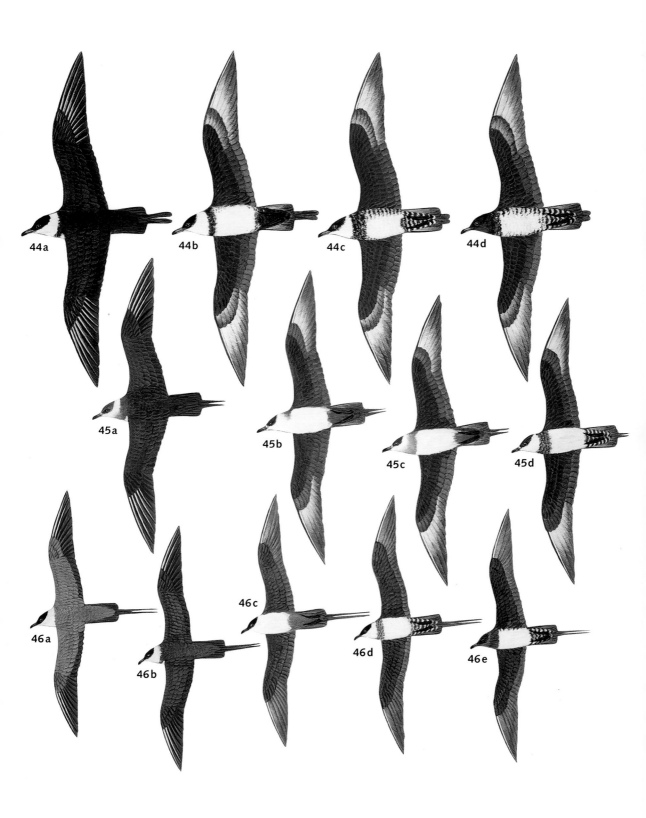

44a

44b

44c

44d

45a

45b

45c

45d

46c

46a

46b

46d

46e

Plate
14 Immature and Dark-bellied Jaegers

44. POMARINE JAEGER^{NA} **OR POMARINE SKUA**^E (*Stercorarius pomarinus*). See also Plates 12, 13.
a. Juvenile Dorsal View. Dark grayish brown above. White shafts visible on 8--10 primaries; central tail feathers distinctly rounded.
b. Juvenile Ventral View. Underparts barred; underwings with double wing-flash.
c. Dark-Phase Basic Adult Ventral View. Uniformly blackish brown, often with golden hue to neck defining blackish cap. Double wing-flash; central tail feathers rounded to spoon-shaped.
d. Subadult Ventral View. Variable. Throat and neck dirty white to mottled brown. Broad chest band defines white belly. Double wing-flash; central tail feathers blunt.

45. PARASITIC JAEGER^{NA} **OR ARCTIC SKUA**^E (*Stercorarius parasiticus*). See also Plate 13.
a. Juvenile Dorsal View. Upperparts brown to cinnamon brown, white base of bill. White feather shafts visible on outermost 4−6 primaries. Fresh juvenile plumage has obvious white tips on flight and tail feathers; center tail feathers sharply pointed.
b. Juvenile Ventral View. Underparts brown to reddish brown, finely barred appearing solidly colored at distance. Single underwing-flash.
c. Basic Adult Dark-Phase Ventral View. Uniformly blackish except for single white underwing-flash and white at base of bill.
d. Subadult Ventral View. Dark crown and chest band define light throat and neck collar. Belly white. Underwings and undertail barred. Single white underwing-flash. Central tail feathers pointed.

46. LONG-TAILED JAEGER^{NA} **OR LONG-TAILED SKUA**^E (*Stercorarius longicaudus*). See also Plates 10, 13.
a. Dark-headed Morph Juvenile Dorsal View. Dark brownish gray above. Compared with larger cousins, head is more rounded and wings longer and narrower. White feather shafts generally restricted to outermost two primaries. Center tail feathers blunt.
b. Pale-headed Morph Juvenile Ventral View. Head dirty white; underparts grayish brown and barred; underwings barred with single wing-flash.
c. Dark-headed Morph Juvenile Ventral View. As pale-headed morph but with dark head and darker underparts.
d. Subadult Ventral View. Head with dark cap, tan throat and neck, and dark chest band. Underparts white with barring on the flanks and undertail coverts. Underwings may lack any white wing-flash. Center tail feathers may be blunt or pointed.

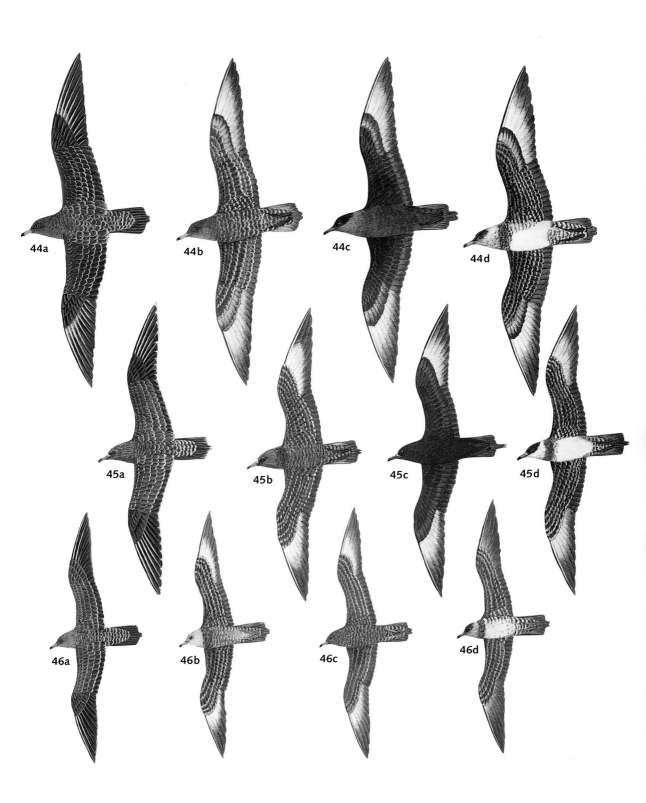

44a 44b 44c 44d

45a 45b 45c 45d

46a 46b 46c 46d

Medium-sized Gulls with Black Wingtips

62. **BLACK-LEGGED KITTIWAKE** (*Rissa tridactyla*). See also Plate 17.
a. Basic (winter) Adult Dorsal View. Back and upperwings medium gray, becoming white just before black "dipped-in-ink" wingtips. Head with grayish collar and dark crescent-shaped spot behind eye.
b. Alternate (summer) Adult Ventral View. Black "dipped-in-ink" wingtips. Bill yellow; eye dark; legs and feet black.
c. Subadult Dorsal View. As adult but with black wingtip less sharply defined.

47. **RING-BILLED GULL** (*Larus delawarensis*).
a. Basic (winter) Adult Dorsal View. Light gray back; outerwings with black wedge. Head streaked brown, becoming white by March or April. Yellow bill with black subterminal ring; yellow eye; yellow feet (not shown).
b. Immature Dorsal View. White head with brown streaks; pink bill with black tip; gray back; upperwings mottled gray-brown and white. Outer primaries blackish, inner primaries are paler. Rump lightly mottled; tail banded and mostly dark.

58. **MEDITERRANEAN GULL** (*Larus melanocephalus*). See also Plate 19.
Immature Dorsal View. Head white with black earspot; pale gray back and midwing panel; outer wings and secondaries contrastingly dark; rump and tail white with black subterminal band.

48. **COMMON GULL** (*Larus canus*).
a. Basic (winter) Adult Dorsal View. Head white with brown streaks, often forming collar; bill yellow, sometimes with gray subterminal ring. Gray upperparts with black wingtips; large white spots on outermost two primaries.
b. Alternate (summer) Adult Ventral View. Distinguished from Kittiwake by shape of black wingtips, large white spots on outermost primaries, and yellow feet.
c. Immature Dorsal View. Gray back; upperwings evenly brown contrasting little with darker outer primaries; white rump and tail with black tail-band encircled by white border.

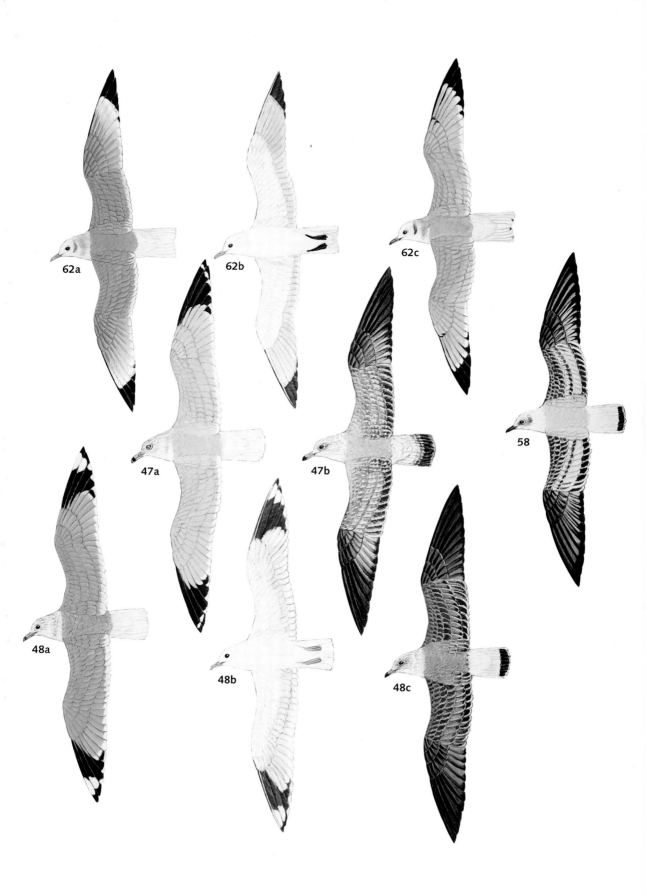

62a

62b

62c

47a

47b

58

48a

48b

48c

Plate

16 Small Gulls with Black Heads
(Summer Plumage)

56. **LAUGHING GULL** (*Larus atricilla*).
a. Basic (winter) Dorsal View. Dusky ear-patch. Back and upperwings gray, becoming blackish on outerwing. No obvious wing pattern. White tail.
b. Alternate (summer) Adult Ventral View. As basic adult but with black head, red bill.
c. Immature Dorsal View. Head variably hooded with brown. Upperparts brown, becoming gray (with molt) starting with the back. Black tail.

63. **SABINE'S GULL** (*Larus sabini*). See also Plate 17.
a. Alternate (summer) Adult Dorsal View. Head gray with black margin separating white neck collar. Upperwings with bold triangular regions of black, gray, and white forming M-shaped pattern. Tail notched.
b. Basic (winter) Adult Ventral View. As alternate plumage but with white head and black neck collar. Underwing pattern white with black upperwing wedge visible as ghost image.

57. **FRANKLIN'S GULL** (*Larus pipixcan*). Accidental occurrence.
a. Basic Adult Dorsal View. Dark gray hood around and back of eye. Upperparts gray with obvious bands of white on both sides of black at wingtips. Wings rounded.
b. Immature Dorsal View. Dark gray hood; gray back; brown upperwings; white tail with neat black tail-band.

60. **BONAPARTE'S GULL** (*Larus philadelphia*). See also Plate 17.
a. Basic (winter) Adult Dorsal View. White head with black earspot; black bill; light gray upperparts with triangular white wedge on outerwings.
b. Alternate (summer) Adult Ventral View. As basic adult but with black head. Underwing pattern entirely white with narrow black border.

59. **BLACK-HEADED GULL** (*Larus ridibundus*). See also Plate 17.
a. Basic (winter) Adult Dorsal View. White head with black earspot; red bill. Upperparts gray (darker than Bonaparte's) with triangular white wedge on outerwings.
b. Alternate (summer) Adult Ventral View. As basic adult but with dark brown head. Underwing pattern mostly dark with white bands on outermost primaries.

64. **ROSS'S GULL** (*Rhodostethia rosea*). See also Plate 17.
a. Basic (winter) Adult Dorsal View. White head with black earspot; back and upperwings evenly gray with narrow black leading edge of primary; white wedge-shaped tail.
b. Alternate (summer) Adult Ventral View. Pink head and body, separated by narrow black collar. Underwing pattern dark gray with triangular white trailing margin.

61. **LITTLE GULL** (*Larus minutus*). See also Plate 17.
a. Basic (winter) Adult Dorsal View. White head with black earspot; back and upperwings evenly gray; wingtips distinctly rounded.
b. Alternate (summer) Adult Ventral View. As basic adult but with black head. Underwing pattern evenly blackish with white trailing border.

17 Small Gulls with W-shaped Back Patterns and Dark Tail-Bands

63. **SABINE'S GULL** (*Larus sabini*). See also Plate 16.
   a. Juvenile Dorsal View. Head distinctly hooded. Hood, back, and upperwing warm brown with distinctly scaly back. Upperwings with bold triangular regions of black, white, and brown forming M-shaped pattern. White tail with black tail-band.
   b. Immature Ventral View. As juvenile but with hood becoming reduced to grayish neck collar. Underwing pattern white with black upperwing wedge visible as ghost image. Black feet.

62. **BLACK-LEGGED KITTIWAKE** (*Rissa tridactyla*). See also Plate 15.
   a. Immature (fall and winter) Dorsal View. White head with black earspot and neck collar; black bill. Back and upperwings gray with bold black M-shaped pattern. Tail white and slightly notched with black tail-band.
   b. Immature (spring and summer) Ventral View. As immature fall and winter but with bill becoming yellow. Underwing pattern mostly white with narrow black borders to outerwing. Black feet.

59. **BLACK-HEADED GULL** (*Larus ridibundus*). See also Plate 16.
   a. Immature Dorsal View. White head with black earspot. Bill orangeish with black tip. Gray back; upperwings with ill-defined M-shaped pattern of brown on innerwing and white on outerwing. White tail with black band.
   b. Immature Ventral View. Underwing pattern white and gray, becoming darkest toward outerwing. Outermost primaries dark gray with white stripes. Orangeish feet.

60. **BONAPARTE'S GULL** (*Larus philadelphia*). See also Plate 16.
   a. Immature Dorsal View. White head with black earspot. Light gray back; upperwings with brown M-shaped pattern and prominent white in outerwings. White tail with black band.
   b. Immature Ventral View. Underwing pattern white with narrow black trailing margin. Orangeish feet.

64. **ROSS'S GULL** (*Rhodostethia rosea*). See also Plate 16.
   Immature Dorsal View. White head with black earspot. Back and upperwings gray with dark M-shaped pattern. Tail wedge-shaped with black terminal band.

61. **LITTLE GULL** (*Larus minutus*). See also Plate 16.
   a. Immature Dorsal View. White head with blackish crown and earspot. Back and upperwings gray with dark M-shaped pattern. Wingtips rounded; tail squared with black terminal band.
   b. Immature Ventral View. Underwing pattern white with narrow dark trailing margin.

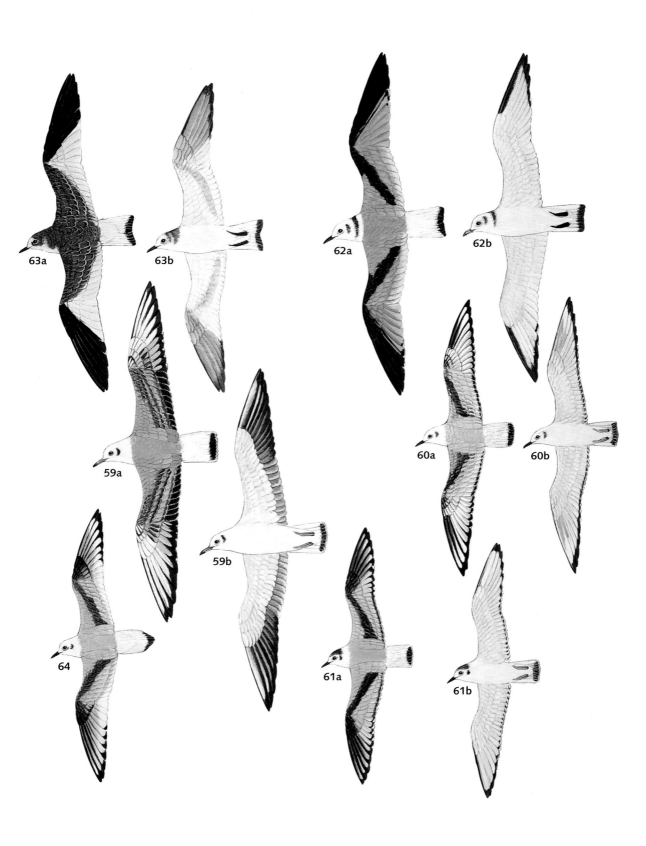

Plate

18 Large Gulls with Dark Wingtips

49. **HERRING GULL** (*Larus argentatus*). See also Plate 12.
a. Basic Adult. Yellow bill and eye; pink feet. Upperparts pale gray with black wingtips above and below. Head streaked well through winter, becoming white in late winter or early spring.
b. Immature (first winter). Fall and early winter birds mostly brown. Upperwings blackish with pale region on inner primaries. Tail mostly dark or sometimes with white base. Head and body pale progressively throughout winter and into spring.

51. **THAYER'S GULL** (*Larus thayeri*).
a. Basic Adult. Yellow bill; dark eye; pink feet. Upperparts slightly darker gray than Herring Gull with limited black or dark gray wingtips. Underwings white. Head streaking retained through winter, becoming white in late winter or early spring.
b. Immature (first winter). Head and body finely patterned grayish brown, often with dark "punched in the eye" pattern. Upperwings gray-brown and evenly colored, including outer primaries. Underwings grayish tan with white primaries. Tail dark brown.

50. **YELLOW-LEGGED GULL** (*Larus cachinnans*).
a. Basic Adult. Lemon yellow bill, eye, and feet. Upperparts gray, darker than Herring Gull. Wingtips black above and below with large white spots in outer primaries. Head streaking minimal or absent from autumn onward, but different geographic populations may vary (see text).
b. Immature (first winter). Head and rump white and lightly streaked with gray-brown; body darker. Upperwings with pale inner primaries. Tail mostly dark.

55. **GREAT BLACK-BACKED GULL** [NA] **OR GREATER BLACK-BACKED GULL** [E]
(*Larus marinus*). See also Plate 1.
a. Basic Adult. Bill yellow; eye pale to dusky; feet pink; upperparts black. Larger than Herring Gull. Head streaking is minimal or absent.
b. Immature (first winter). Head and rump white with minimal dark streaking. Underbody more heavily mottled. Upperwings checkered with dark outerwings and secondaries. Tail white with dark terminal band.

54. **LESSER BLACK-BACKED GULL** (*Larus fuscus*).
a. Basic Adult, Form *fuscus*. Yellow bill, eye, and feet; black upperparts. Smaller than Herring Gull. Head streaking minimal.
b. Basic Adult, Form *graellsii*. As *fuscus* but with medium gray upperparts and black wingtips. Head streaking moderate, especially around eye through winter.
c. Immature (first winter). Head white and streaked with gray-brown, particularly around eye and draping across top of head. Upperparts dark blackish brown with white margins neatly defining secondaries and greater coverts. Rump mostly white, tail black.

49a

51a

50a

55a

54a

54b

49 b

51b

50b

55b

54c

Plate

19 White-winged Gulls

53. **GLAUCOUS GULL** (*Larus hyperboreus*).
    a. Basic Adult Dorsal View. White head, large bill. Upperparts pale gray, becoming white at wingtips. Largest of all white-winged gulls.
    b. Immature (first winter). Bill pink with black "dipped-in-ink" tip. Entire plumage "coffee-stained" white to nearly pure white.

52. **ICELAND GULL** (*Larus glaucoides*).
    a. Basic Adult, Form *glaucoides* Dorsal View. Like smaller version of Glaucous but with proportionately smaller bill and broader wings.
    b. Basic Adult, Form *kumlieni* Dorsal View. As above but with dark gray markings on outermost primaries.
    c. Immature Dorsal View. Bill mostly or entirely black. Otherwise like smaller version of Glaucous with proportionately broader wings.

65. **IVORY GULL** (*Pagophila eburnea*).
    a. Adult Dorsal View. Pure white with coal black eye. Bill gray with yellow tip.
    b. Immature Dorsal View. Pure white except for dark face and black spots at feather tips, particularly flight and tail feathers.

58. **MEDITERRANEAN GULL** (*Larus melanocephalus*). See also Plate 15.
    a. Subadult Dorsal View. White head with dark earspot. Bill dark or dusky with reddish cast. Upperparts pale gray. Black bars on outermost wingtips. Wingtips become pure white with increasing age.
    b. Alternate Adult Dorsal View. The only white-winged gull with black head and red bill.

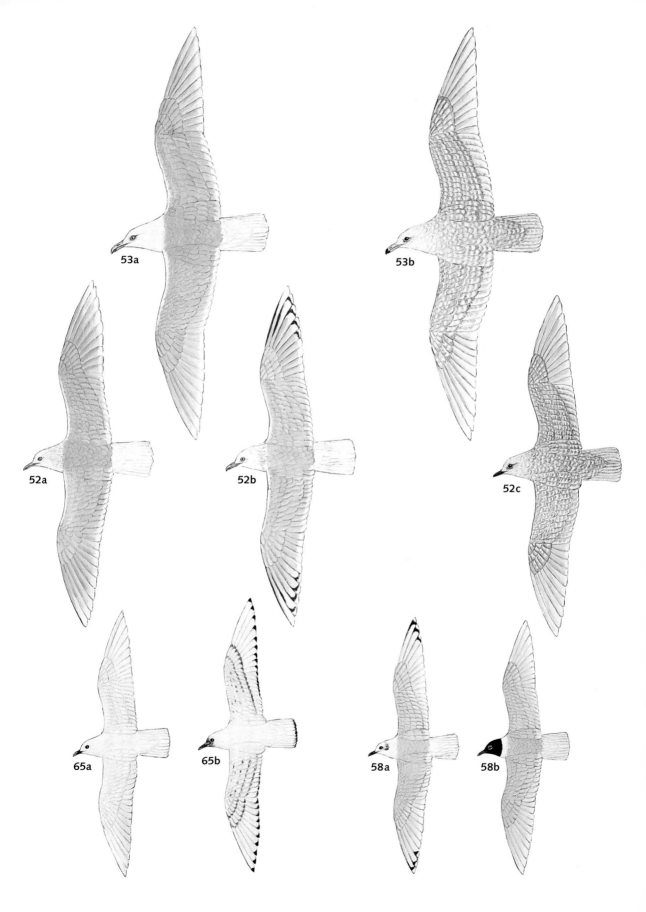

Plate
20 Tropicbirds and Large Terns

30. **RED-BILLED TROPICBIRD** (*Phaethon aethereus*).
a. Immature Dorsal View. Upturned black eye-stripe; yellow bill. Back and upperwings barred, tertials contrastingly blacker. Black wedge on outerwing includes greater primary coverts.
b. Adult Dorsal View. Bright red bill. Back and upperwings finely barred with gray. Black wedge on outerwing includes greater primary coverts. Central tail feathers extremely long and streamer-like.

31. **WHITE-TAILED TROPICBIRD** (*Phaethon lepturus*).
a. Immature Dorsal View. Straight black eye-stripe; yellow bill. Back and upperwings coarsely barred black. Black wedge on outerwing does *not* include greater primary coverts.
b. Adult Dorsal View. Bill yellow to orange. Back white; upperwings with two diagonal black bars. Central tail feathers long but proportionately shorter than Red-billed.

70A. **SANDWICH TERN** (*Sterna sandvicensis*). For comparison.
Dorsal View. Black cap; black bill with yellow tip.

70B. **GULL-BILLED TERN** (*Sterna nilotica*). For comparison.
Dorsal View. Black cap; stout black bill.

69. **ROSEATE TERN** (*Sterna dougallii*). See also Plate 21. For comparison.
Adult Dorsal View. Black cap; slender black bill. Long outer (not central) tail feathers. Upperwings unmarked.

70C. **ROYAL TERN** (*Sterna maxima*). For comparison.
Dorsal View. Broad black eyeline wraps around nape. Orange bill. Back and upperwings gray and unmarked.

30a

30b

31a

31b

70A

70B

69

70C

21 White Terns

67. **COMMON TERN** (*Sterna hirundo*).
a. Adult (spring, early summer) Dorsal View. Bill red with black tip. Upperparts pale gray with darker wedge in outer primaries. Longer head and bill than Arctic Tern.
b. Adult (late summer, fall) Ventral View. Bill red, often lacking black tip. Otherwise as spring adult. Underwing pattern white with wide gray trailing margin of primaries.
c. Immature Dorsal View. Black crown limited to eye-patches and rear crown. Back and upperwings darker than adult. Leading edge of wing with dark bar.

68. **ARCTIC TERN** (*Sterna paradisaea*).
a. Adult Dorsal View. Red bill. Upperparts pale gray, sometimes appearing frosty. Bill and head distinctly shorter and tail longer than Common Tern.
b. Adult Ventral View. Underwings white with narrow, well-defined dark trailing edge to primaries.
c. Immature Dorsal View. Distinguished from Common Tern by shorter head and bill, paler upperparts, and less obvious dark bar on leading edge of wing.

69. **ROSEATE TERN** (*Sterna dougallii*). See also Plate 21.
a. Adult Dorsal View. Long, black bill. Upperparts pale, frosty gray with narrow black leading edge to primaries. Wings shorter and tail much longer than Common Tern.
b. Alternate Adult Ventral View. Underbody sometimes develops bright pink flush. Underwing pattern white with dark leading (not trailing) edge to primaries.
c. Immature Dorsal View. Distinguished from Common Tern by longer bill, dusky forehead, paler upperparts, and narrower dark leading edge to wing.

70D. **FORSTER'S TERN** (*Sterna forsteri*). For comparison.
Basic (winter) Plumage Dorsal View. Head white with black eye-patch. Back and upperwings gray, outerwings white.

67a

67b

67c

68a

68b

68c

69a

69b

69c

70D

22 Dark Terns

72. **SOOTY TERN** (*Sterna fuscata*).
a. Adult Dorsal View. White forehead; black upperparts, including collar. White eyebrow stripe short, not extending past eye. Tail black with narrow white stripes on sides.
b. Adult Ventral View. Underwings two-toned: white linings with dark gray trailing half.
c. Immature Ventral View. Entirely black except for white underwing linings and vent area.

71. **BRIDLED TERN** (*Sterna anaethetus*).
a. Adult Dorsal View. White forehead, black crown, white collar. Dark gray upperparts. White eyebrow stripe extends well past eye. Tail dark gray with broad white stripes at sides.
b. Adult Ventral View. Underwings white with less contrastingly dark trailing half.
c. Immature Dorsal View. White head with dark eye-stripe. Dark brown back and upperparts. Brown tail with frosty or white sides.

66. **BLACK TERN** (*Chlidonias niger*).
a. Alternate Adult Ventral View. Superficially like immature Sooty Tern but much smaller, with proportionately shorter head and tail.
b. Basic Plumage Dorsal View. Dark hood across crown and past eye. White collar. Grayish upperparts, including rump and tail.

73. **BROWN NODDY** (*Anous stolidus*).
a. Adult Dorsal View. Solid brown with frosty white forehead and forecrown. Wedge-shaped tail. At close range, flight feathers slightly darker than remainder of plumage.
b. Immature Ventral View. As adult but lacking white forehead and forecrown.

74. **BLACK NODDY** (*Anous minutus*).
Dorsal View. Solid blackish brown with white forehead and forecrown. Distinguished from Brown Noddy by longer bill, whiter forehead, and lack of contrast on upperwings.

72a

72b

72c

71a

71b

71c

66a

73a

73b

74

66b

Plate
23 Small to Medium Alcids

82. **ATLANTIC PUFFIN** (*Fratercula arctica*).
a. Alternate Adult. Large, brightly colored bill of red and blue-gray with yellow stripes. Grayish white face. Dark chest band, white underparts.
b. Basic Adult. Bill slenderer and washed with gray. "Dirty" face.
c. Adult Swimming. Head and bill distinctive.
d. Immature Swimming. Bill half the thickness of an adult and mostly dark. Face grayish white but "dirty."

79. **BLACK GUILLEMOT** (*Cepphus grylle*).
a. Immature. Salt-and-pepper head and body, darker on back, whiter on underparts. Upperwings dark with large oval white patches.
b. Alternate Adult. Brownish black with large white upperwing patches and white underwing linings.
c. Alternate Adult Swimming. Solidly dark with large white oval wing patches.
d. Basic Adult Swimming. Salt-and-pepper, mostly white head, darker back. Wings dark with large white patches.

75. **DOVEKIE**[NA] **OR LITTLE AUK**[E] (*Alle alle*).
a. Alternate Plumage. Black head and neck, sharply contrasting with white underparts. Tiny size. Whirring wings in flight.
b. Basic Plumage. Dark crown and mask. Throat and sides of neck white.
c. Alternate Swimming. Chubby little bird with big, seemingly beakless head. Mostly dark above the waterline.
d. Basic Swimming. White of throat and sides of neck highlight black back and crown combination.

81. **LONG-BILLED MURRELET** (*Brachyramphus perdix*). Accidental occurrence.
a. Basic Plumage. Small, evenly two-toned, dark above, white below. White stripe along scapulars.
b. Basic Plumage Swimming. Dark of crown extends to below eye and continues down neck to back. White band across scapulars.

80. **ANCIENT MURRELET** (*Synthliboramphus antiquus*). Accidental occurrence.
a. Basic Plumage. Distinguished from Basic Plumage Dovekie by pale bill and white underwings.
b. Basic Plumage Swimming. Straw-colored bill; gray back (not black).

82b

82a

82c

82d

79b

79c

79a

79d

75a

75b

75c

75d

81a

80a

81b

80b

Plate
24 Larger Black and White Alcids

78. **COMMON MURRE**[NA] **OR GUILLEMOT**[E] (*Uria aalge*).
a. Alternate Plumage. Dark brown head, neck, and back. White belly. Distinguished from Thick-billed Murre by slenderer bill and neck.
b. Basic Plumage. Head white except for dark crown and eye-stripe. Otherwise as alternate plumage. Underwings rather dusky.
c. Alternate Plumage (spectacled form) Swimming. Uniformly dark brown above waterline. Some birds of NE range have white "spectacles." Bill slender and solidly black.
d. Basic Plumage Swimming. Head white with dark crown and eye-stripe connecting at the eye. Bill slender and unmarked. Flanks along waterline white, often with dark streaks.

77. **THICK-BILLED MURRE**[NA] **OR BRUNNICH'S GUILLEMOT**[E] (*Uria lomvia*).
a. Alternate Plumage. Black head, neck, and back. Bill with horizontal white stripe. Blacker and more "bull-necked" than Common Murre.
b. Basic Plumage. Similar to alternate but with white chin and throat. White bill stripe less obvious. Underwings rather dusky.
c. Alternate Plumage Swimming. Uniformly black above waterline. Bill pointed but stout with white stripe.
d. Basic Plumage Swimming. White throat, black crown and hindneck. Flanks along waterline bright white.

76. **RAZORBILL** (*Alca torda*).
a. Alternate Plumage. Black head, neck, and back. Bill broad and squarish with horizontal and vertical white bars. Smaller but chunkier than Thick-billed Murre.
b. Basic Adult. Sides of head and neck white. Bill stout with vertical white stripe. Underwings white, not as dusky as murres.
c. Alternate Plumage Swimming. Black head, neck, and back. Bill broad with horizontal and vertical white stripes.
d. Immature Plumage Swimming. Face and crown dark, but white on throat and sides of neck extensive. Bill stout and blunt but lacking white stripes of adults. Distinguished from Thick-billed Murre by more extensive white face, stouter bill, and habit of cocking longer tail upward while swimming.

78b

78a

78c

78d

77b

77a

77c

77d

76b

76c

76a

76d

25 Surfacing Patterns of Large Whales

83. **BLUE WHALE** (*Balaenoptera musculus*). See also Plate 26.
a. Head Outline. Top of head broad U-shaped with single ridge.
b. Blow/Roll Sequence. Blow tall, columnar. Head and back bluish. Blowhole submerges long before dorsal fin appears. Fin small. Shows flukes. Flukes triangular, bluish.

84. **FIN WHALE** (*Balaenoptera physalus*). See also Plate 26.
a. Head Outline. Top of head rounded V-shaped with single ridge.
b. Blow/Blow Sequence. Blow tall, columnar. Head and back brownish black with pale chevrons behind head. Blowhole submerges shortly before dorsal fin appears. Fin prominent and distinctly falcate.

85. **SEI WHALE** (*Balaenoptera borealis*). See also Plate 26.
a. Head Outline. Top of head V-shaped with single ridge.
b. Blow/Roll Sequence. Blow tall, somewhat bushy. Head and back dark gray. Blowhole submerges at same time dorsal fin appears. Fin usually tall, triangular.

86. **BRYDE'S WHALE** (*Balaenoptera edeni*). See also Plate 26.
a. Head Outline. Top of head V-shaped with three ridges.
b. Blow/Roll Sequence. Blow tall, somewhat bushy, and with distinctive "side branches." Head and back dark gray. Blowhole submerges at same time dorsal fin appears. Fin tall, usually falcate to hooked.

87. **MINKE WHALE** (*Balaenoptera acutorostrata*). See also Plate 28.
a. Head Outline. Top of head narrow, pointed, V-shaped.
b. Blow/Roll Sequence. Blow bushy, often indistinct. Head and back blackish. Dorsal fin appears before blowhole submerges. Fin tall, falcate.

88. **HUMPBACK WHALE** (*Megaptera novaeangliae*). See also Plates 26, 27, 28.
Blow/Roll Sequence. Head with rows of knobs. Blow bushy. Head and back black. Blowhole submerges as dorsal fin emerges. Dorsal fin usually reduced to rounded hump, arched steeply out of the water before diving. Shows flukes. Flukes with rough trailing edge and unique black and white markings.

91. **SPERM WHALE** (*Physeter macrocephalus*). See also Plate 27.
Blow/Roll Sequence. Head squared. Blow bushy, projects asymmetrically to the left. Head to dorsal hump usually above the water at same level. Dorsal hump arched on dives. Shows flukes. Flukes dark and broadly triangular.

89. **NORTHERN RIGHT WHALE** (*Eubalaena glacialis*). See also Plate 27.
Blow/Roll Sequence. Top of head with callosites. Blow distinctive, V-shaped, in two separate columns. Head and back black. Back smooth and lacks dorsal fin. Shows flukes. Flukes black, elongate.

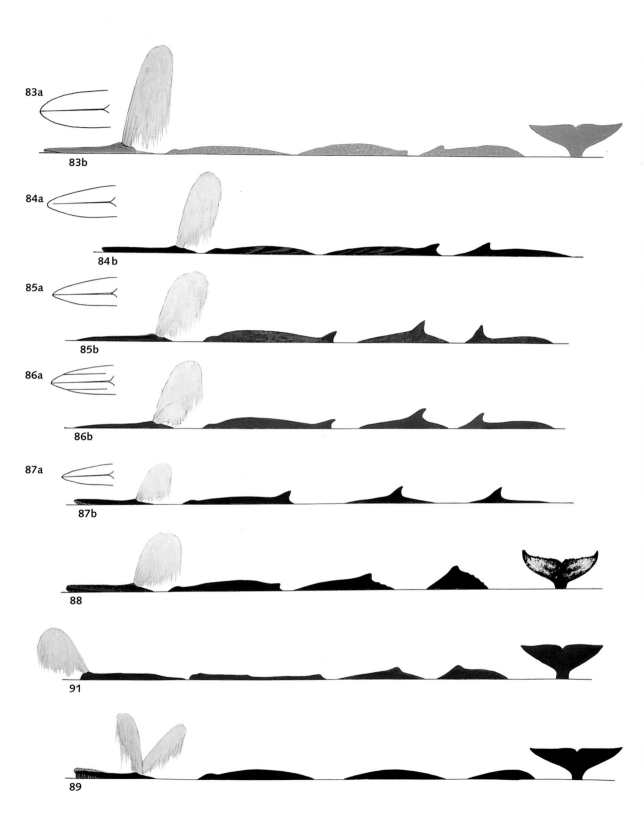

83a

83b

84a

84b

85a

85b

86a

86b

87a

87b

88

91

89

Plate
26 Large Whales with Dorsal Fins

83. **BLUE WHALE** (*Balaenoptera musculus*). See also Plate 25.
Profile. Massive size. Bluish coloration. Tiny dorsal fin.

84. **FIN WHALE** (*Balaenoptera physalus*). See also Plate 25.
a. Right Side Profile. Brownish black head and back. Right side of throat white. Chevron patterns on back. Dorsal fin prominent, usually falcate.
b. Left Side Profile. Left side of throat dark.

85. **SEI WHALE** (*Balaenoptera borealis*). See also Plate 25.
Profile. Head and back dark gray. Tip of rostrum decurved. Single ridge on top of head. Dorsal fin tall, usually triangular.

86. **BRYDE'S WHALE** (*Balaenoptera edeni*). See also Plate 25.
Profile. Head and back dark gray. Tip of rostrum decurved. Central ridge on top of head flanked by lateral ridges. Dorsal fin tall, falcate to hooked.

88. **HUMPBACK WHALE** (*Megaptera novaeangliae*). See also Plates 25, 27, 28.
Profile. Head with distinctive knobs. Head and body black. Pectoral fins extremely long, mostly white. Dorsal fin precedes distinct knucklelike bumps.

X. **WHALE SHARK** (*Rhincodon typhus*). For comparison.
Profile. Size of whale but has white spots, two broad triangular dorsal fins, and a vertically oriented tail fin.

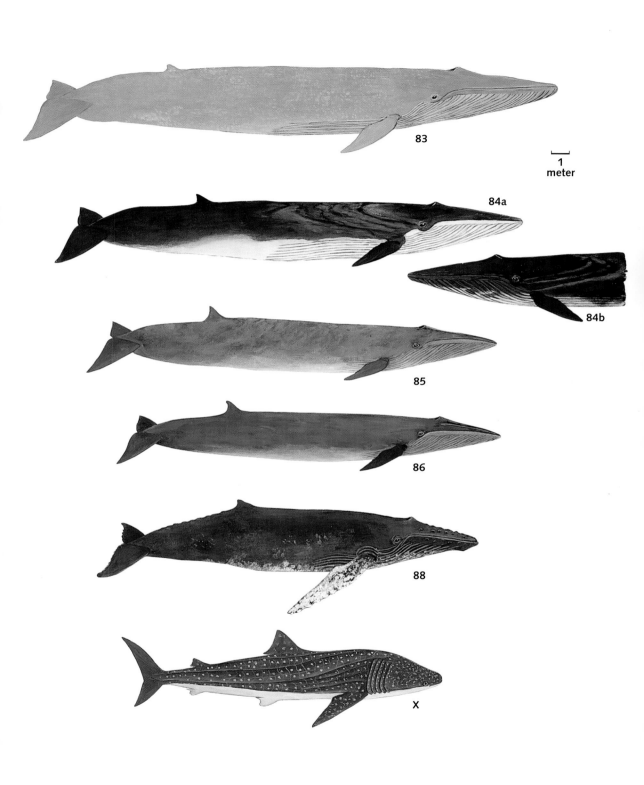

83

1
meter

84a

84b

85

86

88

X

27 Whales with Dorsal Hump or Lacking Dorsal Fin

89. **NORTHERN RIGHT WHALE** (*Eubalaena glacialis*). See also Plate 25.
    a. Profile. Robust black whale lacking dorsal fin. Huge head and steep-arched lower jaw. Callosites on rostrum and sides of lower jaw.
    b. Flukes. Elongate, triangular with straight trailing edge. Solid black.

90. **BOWHEAD WHALE** (*Balaena mysticetus*).
    Profile. Similar to Right Whale but with white on lower jaw and without callosites. High Arctic only.

88. **HUMPBACK WHALE** (*Megaptera novaeangliae*). See also Plates 25, 26, 28.
    a. Profile. Mostly black. Head tapered with knobs on rostrum. Dorsal fin often reduced to dome-shaped hump. Pectoral fins extremely long, mostly white.
    b. Flukes. Trailing edge ragged and tips usually curled backward. Underside pattern extremely variable, ranging from nearly white to black. Patterns are as unique to individuals as fingerprints.

91. **SPERM WHALE** (*Physeter macrocephalus*). See also Plate 25.
    a. Profile. Evenly brownish gray. Massive box-shaped head with skinny underslung lower jaw. Head separated from back by step-like depression. Skin of back distinctly wrinkled. Dorsal fin reduced to fleshy hump, followed by series of knucklelike bumps.
    b. Flukes. Broad, triangular, uniformly dark.

119. **NARWHAL** (*Monodon monoceros*).
     a. Female/Immature Profile. Pale gray to off-white with variable profusion of dark gray spots and blotches, especially concentrated around the head. Back smooth without dorsal fin. Flukes with rounded trailing edge seem "backwards."
     b. Adult Male Profile. As female except for very long, spiral tusk.

118. **BELUGA** (*Delphinapterus leucas*).
     Profile. Uniformly white to creamy white. Forehead bulbous. Head can be turned from side to side, unlike other whales. Back lacks dorsal fin but may show dorsal ridge or slight hump.

130. **WEST INDIAN MANATEE** (*Trichechus manatus*). See also Plate 37. For comparison.
     Profile. May superficially resemble small, finless whale, although swimming behavior and habitat are different. Brown with small cow-like head and rounded, paddle-shaped tail.

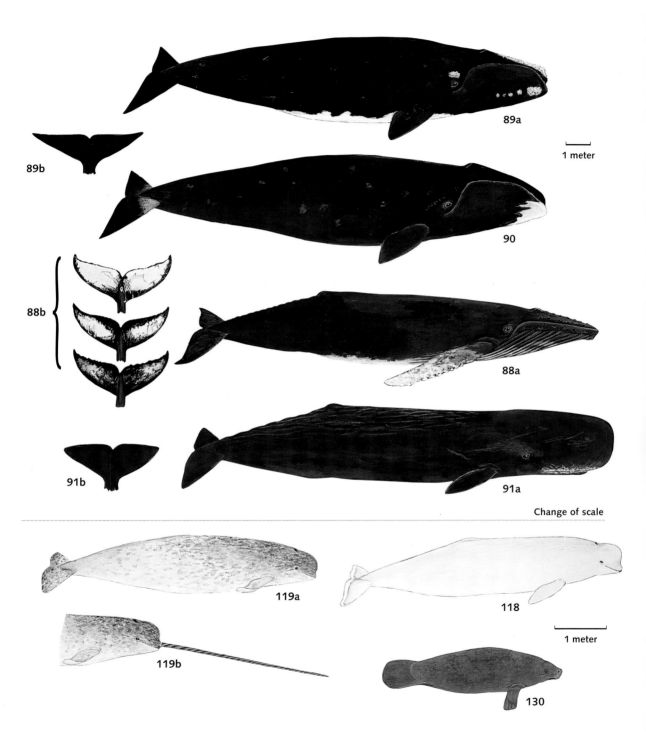

89a

89b

1 meter

90

88b

88a

91b

91a

Change of scale

119a

118

1 meter

119b

130

28 Medium Whales with Dorsal Fin

87. MINKE WHALE (*Balaenoptera acutorostrata*).
Profile. Head and rostrum sharply pointed. Head and back dark with white blaze on pectoral fin and side of body behind pectoral. Dorsal fin tall and falcate.

88. HUMPBACK WHALE (*Megaptera novaeangliae*).
Profile. Young animals frequent inshore waters of North America. Head tapered with knobs on top of rostrum. Long, mostly white pectoral fins. Dorsal fin usually reduced to prominent hump.

95. NORTHERN BOTTLENOSE WHALE (*Hyperoodon ampullatus*). See also Plate 29.
a. Adult Male Profile. Steep, bulbous forehead with well-defined beak. Coloration grayish brown with pale blaze across blowhole. Dorsal fin tall and falcate.
b. Adult Female, Immature Profile. Forehead more sloping and less bulbous than adult male. Smaller overall but otherwise similar.

94. CUVIER'S BEAKED WHALE (*Ziphius cavirostris*). See also Plates 29, 30.
Female Profile. Variable brown to gray. Forehead steep and sloping but lacking sharp demarcation with beak. Forehead often scarred. Dorsal fin triangular to falcate.

100. KILLER WHALE (*Orcinus orca*).
Female Profile. Black with bold white ear-patch, lower jaw and belly with finger-like patch above vent. Head dome-shaped. Dorsal fin large, centrally placed, and triangular. Variable white to grayish blaze behind dorsal fin.

X. BASKING SHARK (*Cetorhinus maximus*). For comparison.
Profile. Size and color of medium whale. Distinguished by presence of two dorsal fins (second one rather small) and large, vertically oriented tail.

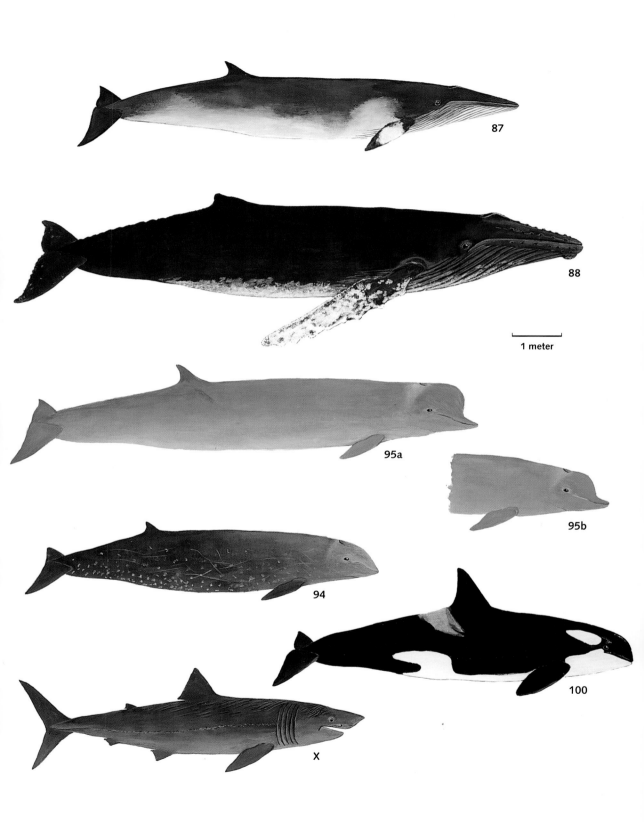

87

88

1 meter

95a

95b

94

100

X

Plate
29 Surfacing Patterns of Beaked Whales

95. NORTHERN BOTTLENOSE WHALE (*Hyperoodon ampullatus*). See also Plate 28. **Blow/Roll Sequence.** Dome-shaped head emerges but beak is not lifted above water. Head submerges before dorsal fin. Fin is tall and falcate. May show flukes, which lack median notch.

94. CUVIER'S BEAKED WHALE (*Ziphius cavirostris*). See also Plates 28, 30.
a. Blow/Roll Sequence Female. Gray to brownish head raised above water. Back slightly darker than head. Head submerges well before dorsal fin appears. Prominent fin falcate.
b. Blow/Roll Sequence Adult Male. Creamy white head emerges from water. Roll changes from white to brown before dorsal fin emerges.

96. TRUE'S BEAKED WHALE (*Mesoplodon mirus*). See also Plate 30.
Blow/Roll Sequence. Beak and head emerge at low angle, roll forward to expose black eye-patch. Line of jaw nearly straight. Head submerges as dorsal fin appears. Black fin contrasts sharply with grayish back. Fin is the last to submerge.

97. GERVAIS' BEAKED WHALE (*Mesoplodon europaeus*). See also Plate 30.
Blow/Roll Sequence. Surfacing behavior similar to True's. Overall coloration much darker.

98. SOWERBY'S BEAKED WHALE (*Mesoplodon bidens*). See also Plate 30.
Blow/Roll Sequence. Long, slender rostrum thrust from water at steep angle. Line of jaw straight for most of extent but arched at corner of mouth. Head rolls forward to submerge as dorsal fin shows. Head and back grayish, becoming slightly darker toward midback.

99. BLAINVILLE'S BEAKED WHALE (*Mesoplodon densirostris*). See also Plate 30.
Blow/Roll Sequence. Beak emerges at moderate angle, sometimes forcibly slapped downward on forward roll. Jaw strongly arched to above level of eye. Coloration distinctly brownish. Dorsal fin may be darker than back but contrast not as clean-cut as True's.

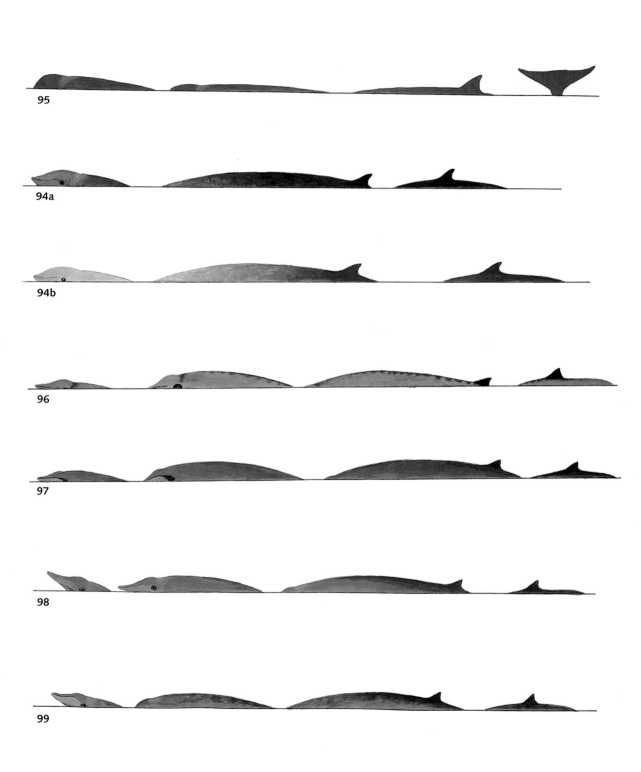

95

94a

94b

96

97

98

99

Plate

30 Beaked Whales

94. **CUVIER'S BEAKED WHALE** (*Ziphius cavirostris*). See also Plates 28, 29.
a. Adult Male Profile. Head and upper back creamy white with heavy scarring. Forehead slopes toward small, indistinct, pointed beak. Body color warm brown. Dorsal fin tall and falcate.
b. Adult Female Profile. Darker, sometimes much grayer than males. Forehead slope gentler.

97. **GERVAIS' BEAKED WHALE** (*Mesoplodon europaeus*). See also Plate 29.
a. Adult Female Profile. Domed forehead with slender, well-defined beak. Jawline slightly arched. Black eye-patch elongate and continuous with jawline. Lower jaw paler than upper. Back dark gray without obvious markings.
b. Adult Male Head. Melon and beak small. Head dark gray with lighter jaw. Black eye-patch elongate, continuous with jaw. Single teeth erupt from each side of forward third of lower jaw.

96. **TRUE'S BEAKED WHALE** (*Mesoplodon mirus*). See also Plate 29.
a. Adult Female Profile. Domed forehead with well-defined bottle-like beak. Jawline relatively straight. Large, rounded black eye-patch contrasts against gray head. Black dorsal line from blow to dorsal fin. Black fin contrasts sharply with gray back.
b. Adult Male Head. Dome-shaped melon, bottle-like beak. Gray head with large black circular eye-patch. Single pair of teeth erupt from tip of lower jaw.

98. **SOWERBY'S BEAKED WHALE** (*Mesoplodon bidens*). See also Plate 29.
a. Adult Female Profile. Forehead proportionately small, beak long and slender. Jawline straight on forward two-thirds, then arched. Black eye-patch minimal or absent. Head and body coloration evenly grayish. Dorsal fin same color as back or slightly darker.
b. Adult Male Head. Very long pencil-like beak. Small rounded melon. Single pair of teeth erupt from each side of middle of lower jaw.

99. **BLAINVILLE'S BEAKED WHALE** (*Mesoplodon densirostris*). See also Plate 29.
a. Adult Female Profile. Small rounded forehead, seemingly "caved-in." Jawline very strongly arched rising to above eye level. Small, black, ovoid eye-patch. Head and back distinctly brown. Off-white lower jaw. Flanks often with white blotches. Dorsal fin darker than back but lacking sharp contrast.
b. Adult Male Head. White lower jaw arched above top of upper. Broad, triangular teeth emerge from top of arches, resembling paired "fins."

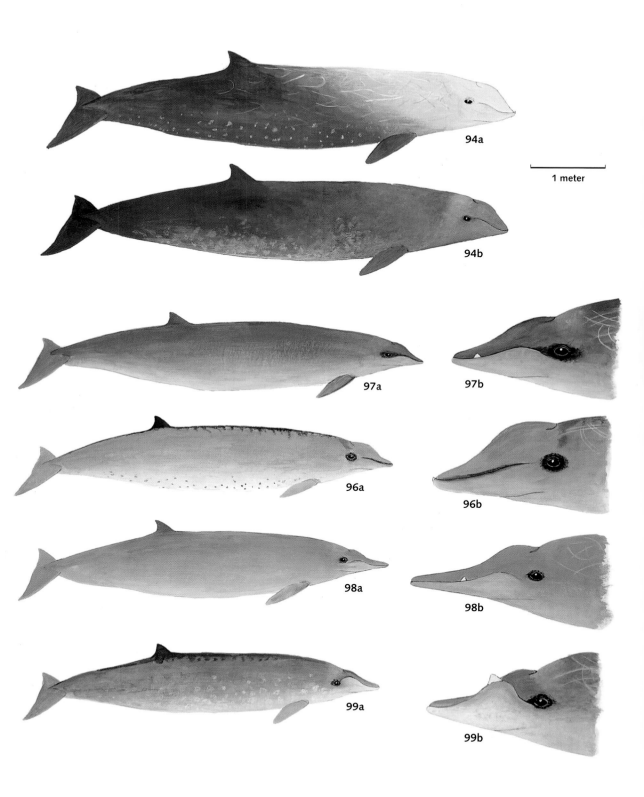

94a

94b

1 meter

97a

97b

96a

96b

98a

98b

99a

99b

31 Surfacing Patterns of Medium to Small Black Whales

100. **KILLER WHALE** (*Orcinus orca*). See also Plates 28, 32.
a. Blow/Roll Sequence Female. Head and back black; white oval on side of head. Dorsal fin very tall, triangular to falcate.
b. Blow/Roll Sequence Adult Male. Huge vertical dorsal fin waivers blade-like.

104/ **PILOT WHALES** (*Globicephala* spp.). See also Plate 32. (*Note:* Separating Long-finned
105. from Short-finned not reliable except by range unless pectoral fins are seen.)
a. Blow/Roll Sequence Female. Rounded black forehead first to emerge, followed by broad black dorsal fin.
b. Blow/Roll Sequence Adult Male. As female but dorsal fin much broader, emerges jackknife-like.

101. **FALSE KILLER WHALE** (*Pseudorca crassidens*). See also Plate 32.
Blow/Roll Sequence. Cigar-like black head and body may clear the water. Dorsal fin proportionately small and falcate, generally rounded. Active swimmer, frequently porpoising.

103. **PYGMY KILLER WHALE** (*Feresa attenuata*). See also Plate 33.
Blow/Roll Sequence. Much smaller than pilot whales, false killer whale. Actively porpoising. Head distinctly rounded. Broadly white lips. Dorsal fin tall, straight on leading edge, and generally pointed.

102. **MELON-HEADED WHALE** (*Peponocephala electra*). See also Plate 33.
Blow/Roll Sequence. Similar to Pygmy Killer Whale. Head more pointed, lips narrowly white. Dorsal fin smaller, more rounded, and triangular.

93. **DWARF SPERM WHALE** (*Kogia simus*). See also Plate 33.
Blow/Roll Sequence. Small size. Squared head emerges, followed by prominent triangular dorsal fin. Often floats log-like on water. Compare with Pygmy Sperm Whale.

92. **PYGMY SPERM WHALE** (*Kogia breviceps*). See also Plate 33.
Blow/Roll Sequence. Nearly identical to Dwarf Sperm Whale but slightly larger with distinctly smaller dorsal fin. Notch at blowhole.

120. **HARBOR PORPOISE** (*Phocoena phocoena*). See also Plate 33.
Blow/Roll Sequence. Very small, unobtrusive. Only top of head and back emerge from water. Dorsal fin low and triangular.

108. **BOTTLENOSE DOLPHIN** (*Tursiops truncatus*). See also Plates 34, 35.
Blow/Roll Sequence. Grayer than others. When not porpoising, rounded top of head precedes sizable dorsal fin. Dorsal fin falcate with convex leading edge.

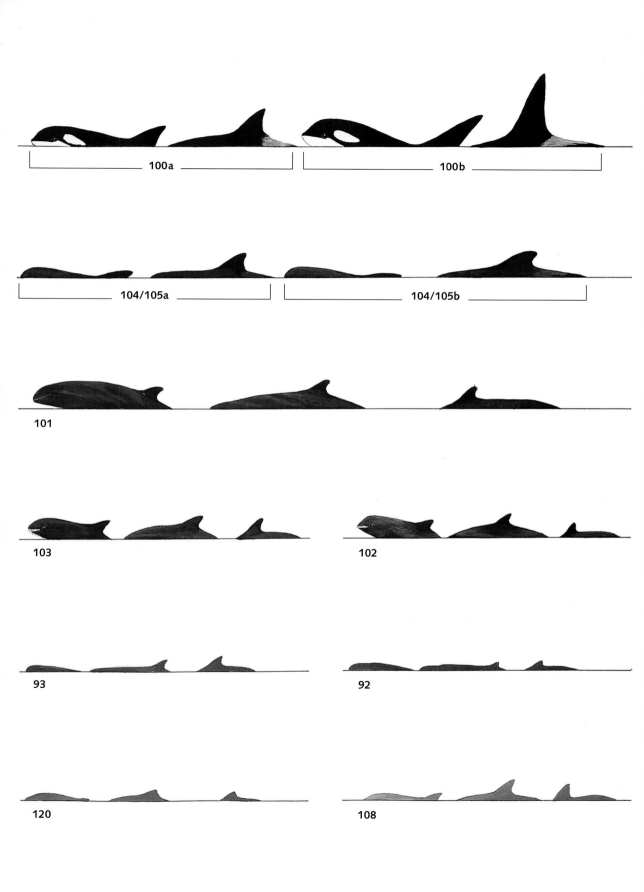

100a

100b

104/105a

104/105b

101

103

102

93

92

120

108

32 Killer and Pilot Whales

100. KILLER WHALE (*Orcinus orca*). See also Plates 28, 31.
a. Female Profile. Unique black and white pattern. White oval behind eye, white "bent finger" above vent. Dorsal fin very large and falcate. Grayish wispy pattern behind dorsal. Pectoral fins broad, paddle-shaped.
b. Adult Male Profile. As female but with huge erect dorsal fin. Pectoral fins proportionately much larger. Tail flukes curled downward.

101. FALSE KILLER WHALE (*Pseudorca crassidens*). See also Plate 31.
Profile. Narrow, cylindrical, cigar-like head and body. Dorsal fin proportionately small, falcate, and rounded at tip. Pectoral fins small and "kinked."

104. LONG-FINNED PILOT WHALE (*Globicephala melas*). See also Plate 31.
a. Adult Male Profile. Bulbous forehead. Dorsal fin much wider than tall. Pale wisp behind eye. Pectoral fins very long.
b. Female Profile. As male but more gently sloping forehead, more "traditional" dorsal fin. Lacks pale wisp on head.

105. SHORT-FINNED PILOT WHALE (*Globicephala macrorhynchus*). See also Plate 31.
a. Adult Male Profile. Nearly identical to Long-finned, distinguished by distinctly shorter pectoral fins.
b. Female Profile. As female Long-finned but with much shorter pectoral fin.

106. RISSO'S DOLPHIN (*Grampus griseus*). See also Plate 34.
a. Female Profile. Mostly dark gray. Forehead rounded and steep. Head and back heavily scarred. Dorsal fin tall and pointed.
b. Adult Male Profile. Head pale gray to white, heavily scarred. Forehead bulbous. Dorsal fin taller than female.

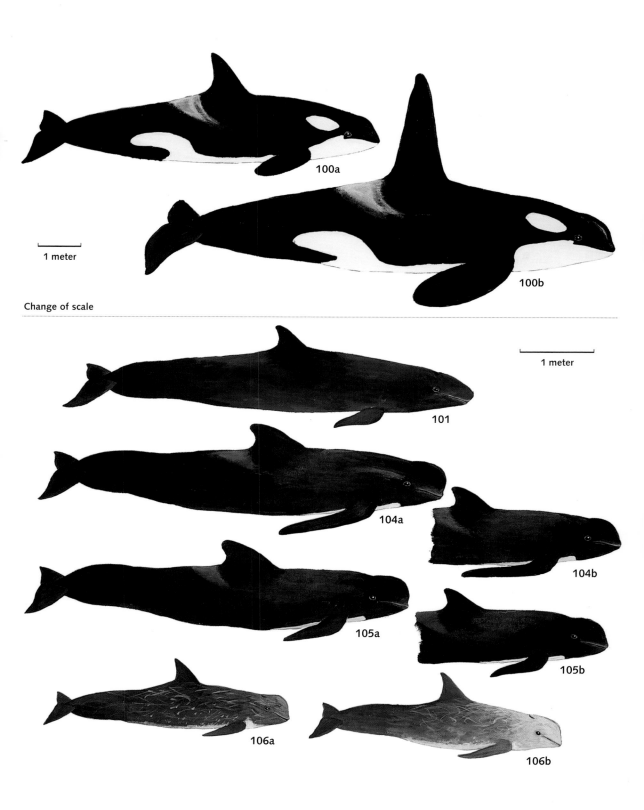

100a

100b

1 meter

Change of scale

101

104a

104b

105a

105b

106a

106b

1 meter

Plate

33 Small Black Whales

92. **PYGMY SPERM WHALE** (*Kogia breviceps*). See also Plate 31.
Profile. Squared head with "gill" stripe. Tiny underslung jaw. Indentation at blowhole. Tiny dorsal fin.

93. **DWARF SPERM WHALE** (*Kogia simus*). See also Plate 31.
Profile. Squared head with "gill" stripe. Tiny underslung jaw. No indentation at blowhole. Prominent falcate dorsal fin.

102. **MELON-HEADED WHALE** (*Peponocephala electra*). See also Plate 31.
Profile. Forehead somewhat flat, comes to blunt point at tip of jaws. Lips narrowly white. Dorsal fin rounded, pectoral fins pointed.

103. **PYGMY KILLER WHALE** (*Feresa attenuata*). See also Plate 31.
Profile. Forehead rounded, projecting slightly ahead of mouth. Lips broadly white. Dorsal fin slender and pointed. Pectoral fins rounded.

120. **HARBOR PORPOISE** (*Phocoena phocoena*). See also Plate 31.
Profile. Small. Forehead slopes to tip of jaws; jawline "smiling." Dorsal fin broad and triangular. Underparts (seldom seen) pale with dark line from eye to pectoral fin.

X. **REQUIEM TYPE SHARK** (*Carcharinus* spp.). For comparison.
Profile. Has five functional gill slits ("gill" line of Kogias is pigmentation only). Two dorsal fins; vertically oriented tail fin.

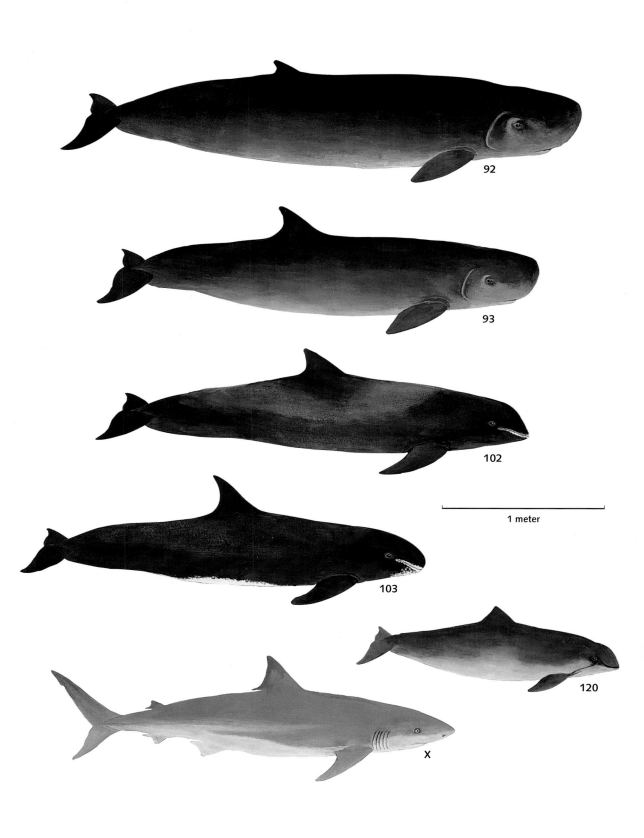

92

93

102

1 meter

103

120

X

Plate

34 Surfacing Patterns of Dolphins

108. BOTTLENOSE DOLPHIN (*Tursiops truncatus*).
Common Surface Exposure. Head and back emerge from water. Distinct melon and beak. Large dorsal fin. Uniformly gray body coloration.

106. RISSO'S DOLPHIN (*Grampus griseus*).
Common Surface Exposure. Head and back emerge from water. Head heavily scarred. Dorsal fin tall and pointed.

107. ROUGH-TOOTHED DOLPHIN (*Steno bredanensis*).
Common Surface Exposure. Head and back emerge from water. Sloping forehead without clearly defined beak. White suspender-like back stripes.

109. ATLANTIC SPINNER DOLPHIN (*Stenella longirostris*).
Common Surface Exposure. Bounds high out of the water. Melon rounded, beak slender. Body with three even bands of color (middle band lacks hourglass pattern).

111. PANTROPICAL SPOTTED DOLPHIN (*Stenella attenuata*).
Common Surface Exposure. Bounds clear of the water. White lips. Two-toned body. Spotting sparse except on lower body.

112. ATLANTIC SPOTTED DOLPHIN (*Stenella frontalis*).
Common Surface Exposure. Head and back emerge from water. White head stripe. Back heavily spotted.

114. COMMON DOLPHIN (*Delphinus delphis*).
Common Surface Exposure. Porpoises clear but remains close to the water surface. Body with three bands of color; middle band forms strong hourglass pattern in which leading half is cream or straw-colored.

110. CLYMENE DOLPHIN (*Stenella clymene*).
Common Surface Exposure. Porpoises clear of water. Black lips and tip of rostrum. Body with three bands of color; middle band forms evenly gray hourglass pattern.

117. ATLANTIC WHITE-SIDED DOLPHIN (*Lagenorhynchus acutus*).
Common Surface Exposure. Animated with head and back emerging from water. Dorsal fin relatively straight on leading edge. Tail stock with obvious straw-colored patch.

116. WHITE-BEAKED DOLPHIN (*Lagenorhynchus albirostris*).
Common Surface Exposure. Head and back emerge from water. Beak white, forehead dark gray. Black dorsal fin contrasts with pale gray upper back and white lower back.

115. FRASER'S DOLPHIN (*Lagenodelphis hosei*).
Common Surface Exposure. Porpoises close to water surface. Forehead without distinct beak. Three-toned body with black middle stripe. Small dorsal fin.

113. STRIPED DOLPHIN (*Stenella coeruleoalba*).
Common Surface Exposure. Bounds high out of water. Sides of body medium to light gray with thin black line from beak to anus.

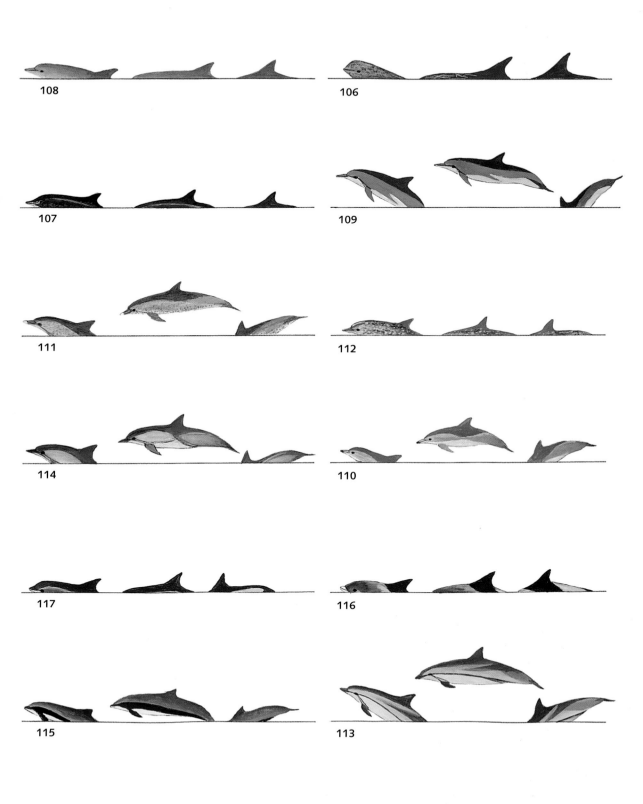

108

106

107

109

111

112

114

110

117

116

115

113

Plate

35 Mostly Gray Dolphins

108A. **OFFSHORE BOTTLENOSE DOLPHIN** (*Tursiops truncatus*). See also Plates 31, 34. **Profile.** Large. Rounded melon, well-defined beak. Head and body coloration grayish to brownish gray with variable wash of paler coloration on sides of body. Dorsal fin large and falcate. Underbelly frequently pink.

108B. **COASTAL BOTTLENOSE DOLPHIN** (*Tursiops truncatus*). See also Plates 31, 34. **Profile.** Nearly identical to Offshore Bottlenose but considerably smaller on average. Underbelly more often white to pale gray.

111. **PANTROPICAL SPOTTED DOLPHIN** (*Stenella attenuata*). See also Plate 34. **a. Immature Profile.** Rounded melon, well-defined beak with white tip. Top of head and back dark, contrasting with paler gray sides. Gray band on sides sweeps up in broad blaze behind dorsal fin. Lacks spotting. **b. Adult Profile.** As immature but with more distinct white tip to beak, dark line from eye to pectoral, and fine dark spotting, mostly concentrated on lower half of body. Slenderer than Atlantic Spotted Dolphin.

112. **ATLANTIC SPOTTED DOLPHIN** (*Stenella frontalis*). See also Plate 34. **a. Immature Profile.** Superficially resembles Bottlenose Dolphin. Forehead with white central stripe. Dark line from eye to pectoral fin. **b. Adult Profile.** Bold white median stripe on top of head. Majority of head and body heavily spotted with large spots, dark and light. Larger and far more profuse spots than Pantropical Spotted Dolphin.

109. **ATLANTIC SPINNER DOLPHIN** (*Stenella longirostris*). See also Plate 34. **Profile.** Rounded melon with long, slender beak. Dark gray back, medium gray sides, white underparts; the three colors form mostly uniform bands rather than hourglass pattern.

107. **ROUGH-TOOTHED DOLPHIN** (*Steno bredanensis*). See also Plate 34. **Profile.** Forehead continuous with beak, lacking obvious transition. Lips white speckled with dark brown. Body dark brown with pale suspenders-like stripe.

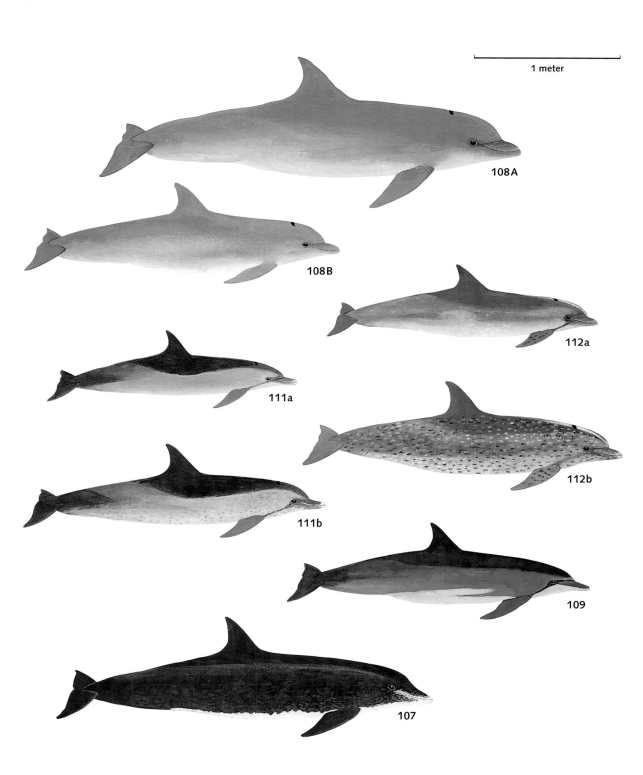

1 meter

108A

108B

112a

111a

112b

111b

109

107

36 Strongly Patterned Dolphins

114. **COMMON DOLPHIN** (*Delphinus delphis*). See also Plate 34.
Profile. Melon rounded with well-defined beak. Head and back dark gray. Strong "hourglass" pattern on sides with straw-colored leading half.

110. **CLYMENE DOLPHIN** (*Stenella clymene*). See also Plate 34.
Profile. Melon rounded with well-defined beak. Three-tone coloration: dark gray above, medium gray on sides, white below. Gray sides form "hourglass" pattern, with leading half gray, not straw-colored.

113. **STRIPED DOLPHIN** (*Stenella coeruleoalba*). See also Plate 34.
Profile. Melon rounded with small but well-defined beak. Head and sides gray with thin black line from mouth to anus. Pectoral fins strongly "kinked."

117. **ATLANTIC WHITE-SIDED DOLPHIN** (*Lagenorhynchus acutus*). See also Plate 34.
Profile. Melon separated from beak by crease but otherwise without sharp angle. Broad white "paint stripe" along middle of body, straw-colored "paint stripe" across tail stock.

115. **FRASER'S DOLPHIN** (*Lagenodelphis hosei*). See also Plate 34.
Profile. Forehead and beak continuous. Gray back, white belly, separated by broad black band from eye to anus. Dorsal fin small.

116. **WHITE-BEAKED DOLPHIN** (*Lagenorhynchus albirostris*). See also Plate 34.
Profile. Forehead and beak ill defined except by color. White beak, black forehead. Mostly gray with bold black oval patch between pectoral and dorsal fins. Dorsal fin and adjacent area black. Lower back behind dorsal fin frosty gray to white.

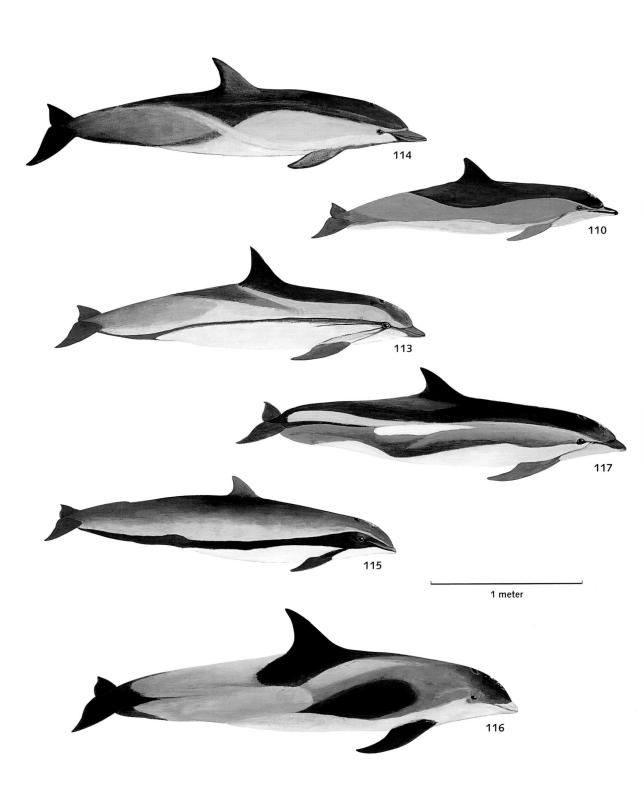

114

110

113

117

115

1 meter

116

Plate
37 Uniformly Colored Seals and Manatee

129. **MEDITERRANEAN MONK SEAL** (*Monachus monachus*).
   a. Profile. Squared muzzle, mostly white. Head and back brown and mottled. Underbelly usually with white central patch.
   b. Head. Small, rounded crown, mottled dark brown. Muzzle well delineated from forehead. Muzzle square, largely white, but coloration variable.

127. **"BLUE-BACK" HOODED SEAL** (*Cystophora cristata*). See also Plate 38.
   Profile. Small. Black crown, face, and upper muzzle. Blue-gray upperparts. White lower jaw, throat, and underparts.

122. **CALIFORNIA SEA LION** (*Zalophus californianus*). Feral or escapee.
   a. Profile. Head and neck broad. Muzzle slender and pointed. Coloration uniformly dark brown. Flippers long and pointed. Hind-flippers rotate forward under body.
   b. Head. Large, rounded crown. Forehead slopes into otherwise narrow, pointed muzzle. External ear flaps (pinnae).

126. **BEARDED SEAL** (*Erignathus barbatus*).
   a. Profile. Head small. Uniform brown coloration with occasional darker blotches.
   b. Head. Forehead slopes into muzzle without obvious break. Head rather small. Muzzle large, square, and brown. Whiskers (vibrissae) white and very long.

128. **GRAY SEAL** [NA] **OR GREY SEAL** [E] (*Halichoerus grypus*).
   a. Female Profile. Large "horsehead" with little neck evident. Color usually gray with darker blotches.
   b. Male Profile. "Horsehead." Color usually dark brown with light blotches.
   c. Male head. Top of head and forehead muzzle are continuous, creating "horsehead" appearance.

121. **WALRUS** (*Odobenus rosmarus*).
   Profile. Large, reddish brown head and body. Prominent ivory tusks erupt from upper jaw. Heavily wrinkled skin.

130. **WEST INDIAN MANATEE** (*Trichechus manatus*). See also Plate 27.
   Profile. Small "cowhead" with squared muzzle. Forelimbs are small flippers. Tail is rounded paddle.

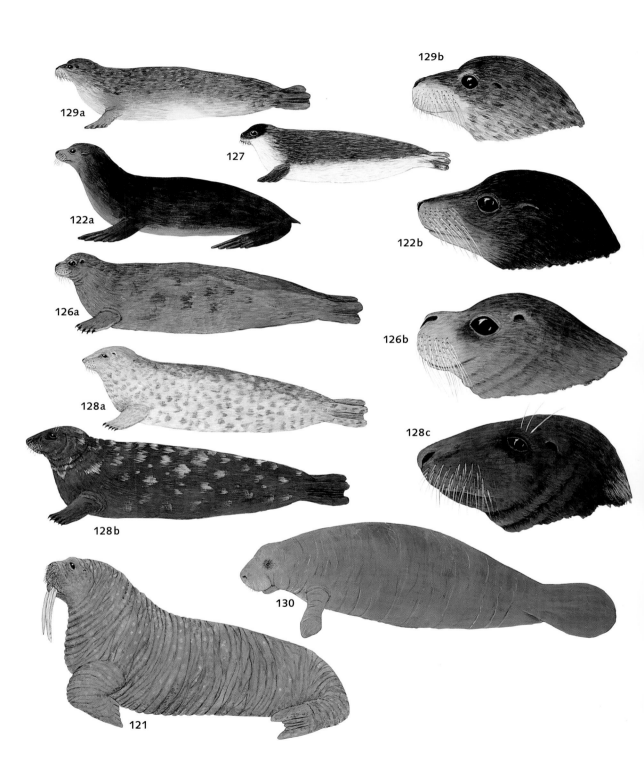

129a

129b

127

122a

122b

126a

126b

128a

128c

128b

130

121

Plate
38 Strongly Patterned Seals

123. **HARBOR SEAL** (*Phoca vitulina*).
a. Profile. Small head, with Cocker Spaniel–like muzzle. Plump body. Coloration tawny brown with variable profusion of dark blotches.
b. Head. Forehead rounded. Muzzle short, squarish, and somewhat cocker spaniel–like. Large eyes. Nostrils form V-shaped pattern.

124. **RINGED SEAL** (*Phoca hispida*).
a. Profile. Superficially similar to Harbor Seal but much plumper and gray, not tan. Pale ring patterns on dark background.
b. Head. Gray with dark rounded spots and pale rings.

125. **HARP SEAL** (*Phoca groenlandica*).
a. Immature Profile. Face dark; crown and back "eggplant" gray. Underparts white. Entire body covered with large black patches. Fore-flippers gray, same as back.
b. Immature Head. Muzzle tapered and pointed. Coloration variable, typically dark gray face and central muzzle region from tip of snout to eye. Top of head and sides of neck grayish to "eggplant" gray with white band.
c. Adult Profile. Black head, white body, except for black U-shaped pattern on back (the harp).
d. Adult Head. Head and face mostly black. Muzzle tapered and pointed. Throat generally white.

127. **HOODED SEAL** (*Cystophora cristata*). See also Plate 37.
a. Female Profile. Head black. Body pale gray to white with large, black blotches. Fore-flippers dark.
b. Female Head. Muzzle rounded and blunt. Face and muzzle black. Hindcrown and neck white with large black blotches.
c. Displaying Male Profile. As female but with inflatable nasal sacs, one black, one reddish.
d. Male Head. As female but with flaccid skin of nasal sac (when deflated) overhanging lips.

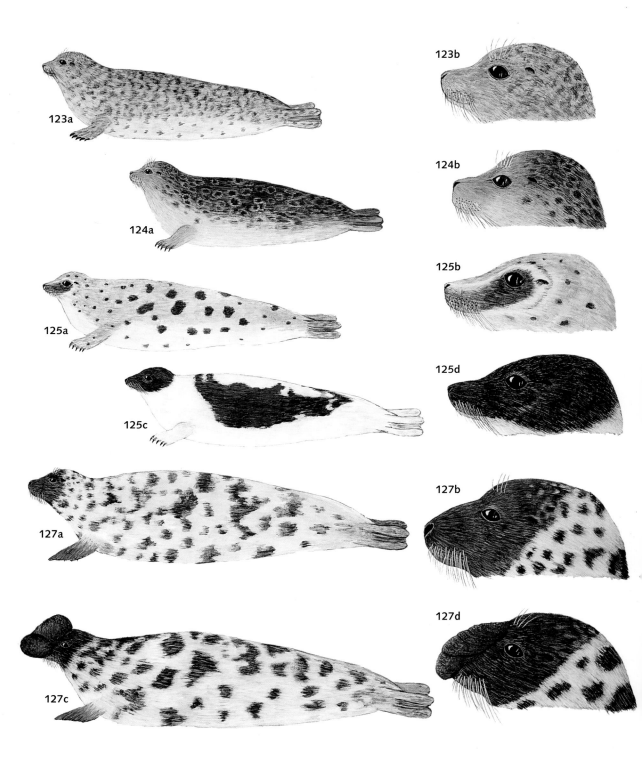

123a

123b

124a

124b

125a

125b

125c

125d

127a

127b

127c

127d

Plate
39 Sea Turtles

131. **LOGGERHEAD TURTLE** (*Craetta caretta*).
Profile. Head with obvious beak. Skin yellowish. Two pair prefrontals between eyes. Nuchal touches first costal. Carapace reddish brown. Five or more costal scutes.

132. **GREEN TURTLE** (*Chelonia mydas*).
Profile. Head rounded, skin of neck pale. One pair prefrontals between eyes. Nuchal never touches first costal. Carapace reddish brown.

136. **LEATHERBACK TURTLE** (*Dermochelys coriacea*).
Profile. Massive salt-and-pepper head. Back with longitudinal ridges but no plates. Black with white flecks and spots.

133. **HAWKSBILL TURTLE** (*Eretmochelys imbricata*).
Profile. Head yellowish with hawk-like beak. Two pair prefrontals between eyes. Nuchal never touches first costal scute. Carapace brown with fine zigzag yellow and orange markings (tortoise shell). Central keel on back.

134. **ATLANTIC RIDLEY TURTLE** (*Lepidochelys kempi*).
Profile. Olive coloration. Carapace nearly circular. Five costals, the first touching the nuchal.

135. **OLIVE RIDLEY TURTLE** (*Lepidochelys olivacea*).
Profile. Olive coloration. Carapace nearly circular. Six to nine costals, the first touching the nuchal.

131

133

132

134

135

136

SPECIES ACCOUNTS

This book covers four distinct groups: birds, whales and dolphins, seals, and sea turtles. Traditionally these have been treated by four separate field guides. Each species account includes up to four headings: **Identification** describes the important distinguishing characteristics including body length (L), wing spread (W) for birds or weight (Wt.) for whales, dolphins, seals, and sea turtles. **Flight behavior** (birds) and **Surfacing behavior** (whales and dolphins) describe important behaviors useful for identification. **May be confused with** contrasts each species with look-alikes. **Range/distribution** summarizes the principal geographic range and movements of each species.

BIRDS

Birds are small to large organisms whose bodies are covered with feathers (plumage) and whose forelimbs are modified into wings capable, in most cases, of sustained flight. All have toothless mandibles modified into a beak. The most important features of seabird identification involve the size and shape of the bird (especially in flight), the shape of the beak, and the pattern of coloration of the plumage. Some species may exhibit considerable plumage variation. When such variation is rather continuous between two extremes, the variants are called color morphs. Distinct variants without continuous variation are color phases. Although many popular guides commonly refer to dark and light "color phases," in most cases, these variants are better considered color morphs.

Many species also have distinct age and season-related plumages. In some groups, such as jaegers and gulls, a single individual might pass through more than a half-dozen different plumages before achieving their distinctive "high breeding" plumage. Some simple terminology regarding the age and molt cycle will be useful. The first plumage that a bird has once leaving the nest is called the juvenile plumage. It is often distinctive in that each feather, particularly on the back and upperwing, are precisely outlined with a pale contrasting color. After the first few months, the first molt produces what is often popularly called a "first winter" plumage. However, this does not always coincide with the actual winter season and creates confusion when viewing Southern Hemisphere birds in their "winter" during our summer. Therefore, the term "first basic plumage" is preferred. In the late winter or spring, a second, partial molt produces the "first summer" or "first alternate plumage." From that point on, a "summer" plumage is considered "alternate" and "winter" is "basic." Once the bird achieves its full adult plumage, the age designation—first, second, and so on—is exchanged with the generic term "adult" (e.g., adult basic).

TOPOGRAPHY OF A SEABIRD

Dorsal View

1. Bill
2. Eye
3. Forehead
4. Ear-patch
5. Crown
6. Nape
7. Shoulder
8. Shoulder bar
9. Back or mantle
10. Rump
11. Uppertail coverts
12. Tail
13. Lesser secondary coverts
14. Median secondary coverts
15. Greater secondary coverts
16. Wrist
17. Primary coverts
18. Primaries
19. Secondaries
20. Tertials

Ventral View

21. Head
22. Neck
23. Chin
24. Throat
25. Breastband
26. Chest
27. Axillars
28. Secondary underwing coverts
29. Primary underwing coverts
30. Primaries
31. Secondaries
32. Tertials
33. Belly
34. Flank
35. Undertail coverts
36. Feet

Order PROCELLARIIFORMES: Large, diverse group of highly pelagic species usually characterized by tubular nostrils positioned above the ridge of the upper beak. Most species have long, narrow wings and short tails. Worldwide, there are four families and about 100 species. Three families and 29 species have been recorded from the northern Atlantic.

Family DIOMEDEIDAE (Albatrosses): Very large seabirds with exceptionally long, narrow wings. Flight is outstandingly graceful, often with effortless gliding without flapping. Of 16 species worldwide, 13 occur in the Southern Hemisphere and 3 in the northern Pacific; 3 Southern Hemisphere species have occurred in the northern Atlantic.

1. **WANDERING ALBATROSS** (*Diomedea exulans*)
Plate 1.
Identification: L. 43−45 in (110−155 cm); W. 110−130 in (280−330 cm). Gigantic, predominantly white and black seabird with extraordinarily long wingspan. Maturation requires several years, each with its own plumage variation. Plumage changes are progressive throughout life, with birds becoming whiter as they age. Descriptions here are limited to the few Northern Hemisphere records.
Adult. Head and crown white, possibly with wash of pink on side of head. Bill bright pink. Back and rump white. Upperwings blackish with variable white patches, mostly close to the body. Tail black. Entire underbody and underwings white with narrow black margin to the wing.
Immature. Brown hood highlights white face and pink bill. Back and upperwings blackish. Underbody mottled brown. Underwings as adult.
Flight behavior: Typical albatross flight. Glides with apparent effortlessness on long, bowed wings. Rarely flaps. Dynamically soars by catching updrafts off windward side of waves. Will rest on the water, unwilling to fly when calm.
May be confused with: Size, pink bill, and white underwing are diagnostic. Only the Royal Albatross (*D. epomophora*) is similar, but that species is unrecorded in the Northern Hemisphere. Field separation of the two is complex and beyond the scope of this guide. However, any "Great Albatross" with brown body markings or white upperwing patches would be Wandering.
Range/distribution: Common in the Southern Hemisphere. One record from the northern Atlantic was an immature from Portugal. Other Northern Hemisphere records include an immature from Sicily, an adult from California, and possible occurrence off Japan.

2. **BLACK-BROWED ALBATROSS** (*Thalassarche melanophris*)
    Plate 1.
    Identification: L. 35 in (89 cm); W. 95 in (240 cm).
    Adult. Head and neck white. Eye surrounded by black, crescent-shaped eye-patch. *Bill orangey yellow with reddish tip.* Back and upperwings blackish with white primary shafts. Rump white and tail dark gray. Underparts entirely white. *Underwings white with broad black margins,* thickest on the leading edge.
    Immature. As adult except for dusky bill with black tip. Reduced black eye-patch, dark collar at side of neck, and sooty underwings.
    Flight behavior: See Wandering Albatross.
    May be confused with: Yellow-nosed Albatross is smaller with blackish bill and, more extensively, white underwings with narrow black margins. Northern Gannet is slightly smaller with proportionately shorter wings and longer, wedge-shaped tail. Great Black-backed Gull is smaller with shorter wings and white tail.
    Range/distribution: Abundant in the southern oceans. Very rare, but regular from late spring through early fall in the eastern Atlantic north to Scotland where possible breeding attempts have occurred. Accidental in the western Atlantic north to possibly Newfoundland, Canada.

3. **YELLOW-NOSED ALBATROSS** (*Thalassarche chlororhynchos*)
    Plate 1.
    Identification: L. 30 in (76 cm); W. 77 in (195 cm). Superficially similar to Black-browed Albatross but smaller, with *white underwing with narrow black border.*
    Adult. Head pearly gray, bill black with bright yellow upper ridge and reddish tip.
    Immature. Bill black. Head white.
    Flight behavior: See Wandering Albatross.
    May be confused with: See Black-browed Albatross.
    Range/distribution: Abundant in the southern oceans but with more northerly distribution than Black-browed. No confirmed sightings in the eastern half of the northern Atlantic. Accidental in the western Atlantic north to Quebec, Canada. Of the few western Atlantic records of albatrosses, the majority are Yellow-nosed.

Family PROCELLARIIDAE (Fulmars, Petrels, Shearwaters): Large
to small seabirds superficially resembling long-winged gulls. Most fly with rising and falling arcs or weaving through the waves on stiffly held wings. About 65 species worldwide, 20 from the northern Atlantic.

Genus *Macronectes* (Giant Petrels): These albatross-size petrels have massive, pale-colored bills. Two species worldwide, both of the southern oceans. One species has been recorded as a vagrant in the northern Atlantic.

4. **SOUTHERN GIANT PETREL** (*Macronectes giganteus*)
Plate 1.
Identification: L. 35 in (89 cm); W. 79 in (200 cm). Plumage variable with light- and dark-morph adult plumages and a different immature plumage. *Light-morph adult.* Unrecorded in Northern Hemisphere. Pure white with dark flecking.
Dark-morph adult. Head mottled gray and white. Bill massive, straw-colored with greenish tip. Upperparts mottled grayish brown to gray. Underparts grayish brown with off-white mottling.
Immature. Uniformly dark brown. Bill as adult's.
Flight behavior: Somewhat albatross-like but less graceful, more stiff-winged.
May be confused with: Adult plumage superficially resembles Northern Fulmar, but Giant Petrels are twice the size with wings proportionately longer. Immatures resemble White-chinned Petrel but are smaller with wings proportionately longer. The bill of White-chinned is far less massive. At extremely close range, the white chin-patch is distinctive. The very closely related Northern Giant Petrel (*M. halli*) has a reddish bill tip rather than greenish and is unrecorded from the Northern Hemisphere.
Range/distribution: Abundant in the Southern Hemisphere, even in harbors and inland waterways. Single sight report of a dark-morph adult from France and an unconfirmed report from East Yorkshire, England.

Genus *Fulmarus* (Fulmars): Medium-size, stocky seabirds with proportionately large heads and pale-colored bills. Two species worldwide, one breeds in the northern Atlantic.

5. **NORTHERN FULMAR** (*Fulmarus glacialis*)
Plates 2, 4.
Identification: L. 19 in (48 cm); W. 42 in (107 cm). *Large-headed seabird with heavy, straw-colored bill.* Light and dark morphs exist with much variation. Some observers further differentiate the light and dark morphs by adding "double-light" and "double-dark" morphs to the descriptive possibilities. From an identification perspective, such descriptions tend to be a bit overly analytical; three basic variations are described here.
Light morph. Head white, back and upperwings pale to medium gray or grayish brown. Head and rump white, tail gray. Wings often with bold white

flashes at bases of primaries. Typically the palest individuals have the largest white wing-flashes.

Gray morph. Similar to light morph but with head and rump grayish to the same color as the back.

Dark morph. Entire bird uniformly dark gray to blackish gray. White wing-flash may be reduced or lacking. Dark-morph birds are rare in the northern Atlantic, representing only 2−3 percent of individuals.

Flight behavior: Rapid and direct with stiffly held wings, alternating glides with stiff, rapid wingbeats. Flight path often close to the water, then suddenly vaulting upward to considerable height and remaining at higher elevation for several seconds before gradually returning toward the sea surface.

May be confused with: Light and gray morphs: Plumage superficially gull-like. Combination of large head, white wing-flash, and stiff-winged flight is diagnostic. Dark morph: Sooty Shearwater is longer and narrower-winged, has a small head, dark bill, and frosty underwing linings. The rare Herald Petrel is longer-winged, dark-billed, and has white flash on underwing, not upperwing. See also White-chinned Petrel.

Range/distribution: Abundant breeder in Canada, Greenland, Iceland, Britain, and northern coastal Europe. Disperses southward and offshore during winter. Prevalent in shallow to deep offshore waters. Most winter in Cold Temperate waters, although many remain in ice-free northern waters.

Genus *Pterodroma* (Gadfly Petrels): Medium-sized, highly pelagic seabirds characterized by short, strongly hooked bills and dramatic arcing, "roller-coaster" flight on long, falcon-like wings. Approximately 30 species worldwide (taxonomy highly unsettled with some), 7 known from the northern Atlantic. Most species are dark above, white below, with black ulnar bar, or predominantly dark above and below.

6. **BLACK-CAPPED PETREL** (*Pterodroma hasitata*)
   Plates 2, 3.
   Identification: L. 18 in (46 cm); W. 40 in (102 cm). Plumage strikingly dark above and white below. Head white with blackish cap extending through eye, usually separated from back by white neck collar, although some birds lack the collar. Back and upperwings dark brownish black, occasionally showing an indistinct dark M-shaped back pattern. Uppertail coverts white, tail black. The relative extent of these marks is variable. Some birds may have narrow white rumps while others may have broad ones. Underparts pure white. Underwing linings white with black diagonal bar.

   Flight behavior: Flight active and acrobatic with steep, rapid, arcing, "roller-coaster" flight. The steep arcing describes a sinusoidal flight path of rise and fall where the birds may attain a fully perpendicular orientation with the water. In stronger wind, they often twist and weave throughout the arcs. Sometimes they approach ships but do not follow them.

May be confused with: Greater Shearwater similar above but with dark cap, including forehead; Black-capped has white forehead. Greater has browner back, narrow white crescent separating rump from tail. Greater's underwing has partial ulnar bar formed of brown spots. There is a distinctive brown smudge on center of belly. Very rare Bermuda Petrel is smaller and distinctly hooded, not capped, and lacks the white collar. The base of the uppertail coverts are grayish white and may appear as a narrow pale crescent or may not be evident at all. Bermuda Petrel's wing shape is comparatively long and narrow, and the underwing has a broader dark bar that borders the wing.

Range/distribution: Breeds on Caribbean Islands, dispersing into the western northern Atlantic, mostly associated with deep Gulf Stream waters, particularly along the edge of the continental shelf. Greatest abundance is off Cape Hatteras, North Carolina.

7.   **BERMUDA PETREL** (*Pterodroma cahow*)
(also Cahow)
Plate 3.
Identification: L. 15 in (38 cm); W. 35 in (89 cm). Small petrel, dark gray above, white below. Head with hooded appearance, the dark extending to below the eye but separated from the bill by white forehead. Nape, back, and upperwings dark gray to brownish gray with little contrast except for darker, indistinct M-shaped pattern across back and upperwing. Base of rump with frosty gray to white crescent. Entire underparts white. Underwings white with broad dark borders. Black underwing bar hugs the leading edge for most of its extent. At close range, underwing shows black "thumbprint" marks near the tips of the greater primary coverts. Wings are notably long, narrow, and somewhat rounded at the tips.

Flight behavior: Generally as Black-capped but with shallower arcs that tend to remain more horizontally oriented. Some individuals (young birds?) may engage in "helicopter flight," which is utterly unique. At the top of an arc, the bird will stall, remaining motionless or with quick, downward flicks of the outerwing rise vertically to a new stationary position.

May be confused with: See Black-capped Petrel. Fea's and Zino's have uniformly dark gray underwings and are browner-backed. Both have a pale rump and tail that contrasts with the darker back. Bermuda Petrel appears mostly or entirely dark above.

Range/distribution: Breeds only on Nonsuch Island, Bermuda. Distribution at sea largely unknown, although some evidence suggests daily dispersal of breeding birds to the northeast, where they may congregate before coming to the nests at night. A handful of sightings in the deep Gulf Stream waters off the Carolinas also suggests widespread dispersal of nonbreeders to the west.

8. **MOTTLED PETREL** (*Pterodroma inexpectata*)
Plate 3.
Identification: L. 14 in (35 cm); W. 29 in (74 cm). Crown dark gray to blackish, separated from bill by white forehead. Back and upperwings gray with dark M-shaped pattern. Rump pale, contrasting with darker tail. Chin, throat, and upper chest white. *Lower chest and belly smudged and barred dark gray.* Underwings white with diagonal black bar.
Flight behavior: Dramatic, high-arcing flight.
May be confused with: Fea's and Zino's have similar upperparts but browner. Underparts completely different.
Range/distribution: Normal range restricted to Pacific and southern Indian Oceans. Single northern Atlantic record from New York State.

9. **HERALD PETREL OR TRINIDADE PETREL** (*Pterodroma arminjoniana*)
Plates 3, 4.
Identification: L. 16 in (40 cm); W. 40 in (102 cm). Includes two generally distinct color morphs.
Light morph. Head and upperparts uniformly dark brown to black. Chin mottled white, sometimes separated from body by neck collar. Body white. Underwings with broad, blackish diagonal bar separating white greater primary and secondary coverts from mottled black and white forewing. Flanks and undertail coverts often barred or mottled dark brown.
Dark morph. Upperparts as light morph. Underparts medium brown to black. Underwing mostly dark with jaeger-like white flash at base of primaries and sometimes extending as narrow white line along base of secondaries.
Flight behavior: In light winds, rather shearwater-like with alternating flaps and glides and minimal arcing. Wings are often held more fully extended and shearwater-like than is typical of other gadfly petrels. In strong winds, may arc steeply. Regularly approaches boats but generally does not follow.
May be confused with: Sooty Shearwater is narrower-winged with head and tail projecting equally from the plane of the wings. Herald Petrel has tail projection twice that of head. Underwing of shearwater is dark with frosty white underwing linings. Northern Fulmar (dark morph) has larger head,

shorter wings, and bright straw-colored bill, not dark. A dark-morph petrel photographed at Hawk Mountain in eastern Pennsylvania and identified as Kermadec Petrel (*P. neglecta*) was possibly an aberrant Herald Petrel. Kermadec Petrel is nearly identical to Herald but has a distinct, skua-like white upperwing-flash at the base of the primaries. The occasional suggestion that Kermadec has a more extensively white underwing pattern than Herald is an unsafe distinction in the field.

Range/distribution: Breeds on South Trinidade Island off Brazil. Possibly distinct from the Herald Petrel of the southern Pacific and Indian Oceans. In the North Atlantic, occurs regularly May–September in deep Gulf Stream waters off Cape Hatteras, North Carolina. Accidental elsewhere along the North American coast.

10. FEA'S PETREL (*Pterodroma feae*)
(also Cape Verde Petrel, Gon-Gon)
Plate 3.
Identification: L. 15 in (38 cm); W. 38 in (97 cm). Head with grayish face and black mask, which may blend with a dark crown. Back gray. Upperwings brownish gray with dark brown M-shaped pattern across back and wings. Rump and tail contrastingly pale gray with white border. Underparts immaculate white, sometimes with partial breastband. *Underwings dark gray to black,* may have a narrow white central stripe. The forward corner of the underwing has a white triangular patch. Wings are long and decidedly scimitar-shaped. Tail is long and wedge-shaped.
Flight behavior: Rapid flight with bounding arcs. Height of the arcs tends to be lower amplitude and quicker than other Gadfly Petrels. Tends to avoid boats.
May be confused with: Except for the critically endangered Zino's Petrel, no other northern Atlantic petrel combines white body and black underwings. Zino's is smaller, generally with proportionately small bill; Fea's bill is rather large. Some evidence suggests that compared with Fea's, Zino's is a little browner above, has a pale midwing panel instead of distinct M shape, and has proportionately shorter wings with rounded wingtips, but see comments under Zino's identification heading.
Range/distribution: Two populations worldwide—the nominate form breeds only on the Cape Verde Islands and apparently disperses southward into Equatorial waters; the other (*P. f. deserta*) breeds on Bugio Island near Madeira, possibly Great Salvage Island, and elsewhere in the northern Atlantic. Seen occasionally off England during summer and fall. In North America occurs regularly off Hatteras, North Carolina, most commonly during late spring and rarely north to Maritime Canada. Nominate form nearly

identical to *deserta* form but has barred flanks and slightly darker, more uniform upperparts.

11. **ZINO'S PETREL** (*Pterodroma madeira*)
(also Freira)
Plate 3.
Identification: L. 13 in (33 cm); W. 33 in (84 cm). Head grayish with dark eye-patch. Back brownish to gray. Rump distinctly pale gray to white with slightly darker tail. Underparts white, sometimes with partial breastband. Underwing pattern similar to Fea's. Compared with Fea's, upperwings tend to be browner with a pale midwing panel between darker secondaries and less distinct dark M-shaped pattern. Wings are proportionately shorter and broader, particularly in the "hand." This mark is the most obvious difference in the field.
Flight behavior: Similar to Fea's but probably more buoyant.
May be confused with: Fea's is most similar; see comparison above. Bermuda Petrel is larger, has a hooded appearance, and is uniformly darker above with pale gray restricted to the base of the rump only. The underwings are white with a black underwing bar, although the underwing pattern of some Zino's may approach that of Bermuda Petrel.
Range/distribution: Critically endangered. Breeds only on the high mountains of Madeira spring and summer (ca. 35 pairs). Distribution away from the breeding grounds is unknown.

12. **STEJNEGER'S PETREL** (*Pterodroma longirostris*)
Not illustrated
Identification: L. 10 in (26 cm); W. 25 in (66 cm). Small pterodroma with blackish cap contrasting with paler gray back. Upperwings show dark M-shaped pattern. Rump gray, same color as back. Tail darker. Underparts white. Majority of underwings white with narrow borders and limited dark diagonal bar.
Flight behavior: Rapid, erratic flight with jerky wingbeats.
May be confused with: Unlikely to occur in the northern Atlantic. From above, would most closely resemble small Fea's but with white underwings, not dark.
Range/distribution: Predominantly a bird of the southern Pacific with occasional records in the northern Pacific. There is a single record of a badly decomposed bird found dead on the Texas Gulf Coast. The circumstances of this bird's occurrence are uncertain.

Genus _Procellaria_ (Procellaria Petrels): Large, mostly all dark seabirds with heavy, light-colored bills. Four species worldwide, all from the southern oceans. One species has occurred as a vagrant in the northern Atlantic.

13. **WHITE-CHINNED PETREL** (_Procellaria aequinoctialis_)
Plate 4.
Identification: L. 22 in (56 cm); W. 56 in (142 cm). Large and somewhat albatross-like. Entirely blackish brown except for white on chin at base of bill (may not be visible in the field). Bill large, straw-yellow.
Flight behavior: Flight strong, alternating series of slow flaps with long glides.
May be confused with: Sooty Shearwater and dark morphs of Herald Petrel are much smaller and have black bills. Dark morph of Northern Fulmar is much smaller, with proportionately larger head and shorter wings.
Range/distribution: Very common in the southern oceans. Two records from the northern Atlantic: on the beach at Galveston, Texas, in April; and off Hatteras, North Carolina, in October. There is also an unconfirmed report from England in July.

Genus _Bulweria_ (Bulweria Petrels): Small, all-dark petrels with remarkably long wings and long, wedge-shaped tails. Two species worldwide, one of which breeds in the northern Atlantic.

14. **BULWER'S PETREL** (_Bulweria bulwerii_)
Plates 4, 7.
Identification: L. 10 in (25 cm); W. 26 in (66 cm). Small, uniformly dark brownish to black petrel, with contrastingly paler tan upperwing bar. The head is small and the wings and tail seem disproportionately long and slender. This combination gives the bird a T-shaped appearance in flight. Tail is wedge-shaped, but this may not be apparent except at close range.
Flight behavior: Flight close to the water with erratic twisting or rocking side to side, alternating flaps and glides; flapping flight is jerky, somewhat reminiscent of Leach's Storm-petrel. The wings may be held in a raked forward position, accentuating the T-shaped profile.
May be confused with: Sooty Shearwater, Herald Petrel, Northern Fulmar are much larger and have white in the wings, either above or below. Storm-petrels are a little smaller, with shorter wings and different flight. Except for Swinhoe's or a dark-rumped Leach's, all northern Atlantic storm-petrels have white rumps.
Range/distribution: Primarily Tropical to Subtropical worldwide. In the northern Atlantic, breeds on the Azores, Desertas, Great Salvage, and Ca-

nary Islands from May through September. Disperses southward and westward into offshore Tropical waters during winter. Possibly regular well offshore during summer from Portugal southward. Very rare or accidental in Caribbean and North America waters but possibly regular during summer.

LARGE SHEARWATERS Medium-size long-winged seabirds characterized by long slender bills and arcing flight on relatively stiff wings with intermittent flapping. Two genera, the most obvious difference being bill color. *Calonectris* have a mostly pale bill, *Puffinus* have a dark bill. Some species of the latter genus are all dark. Ten (possibly eleven) species worldwide, four or five from the northern Atlantic.

15. CORY'S SHEARWATER (*Calonectris diomedea*)
Plate 5.
Identification: L. 20 in. (54 cm); W. 44 in (112 cm). Large shearwater with proportionately broad wings. Head grayish and hooded. *Bill straw-yellow with black subterminal ring.* Nape and back grayish to grayish brown. Upperwings warm brown, with indistinct darker M-shaped pattern across back and upperwings. Rump brown with narrow white crescent separating rump from blackish tail. Sides of head grayish, or brownish, indistinctly grading into white chin and throat. Underparts and underwings pure white.
Flight behavior: Flies with slow, languid flaps, alternating with soaring on bowed wings. Gliding arcs are oriented rather parallel to water without the degree of vertical orientation typical of most shearwaters.
May be confused with: Greater Shearwater is darker, "colder" brown above, has white collar and dark belly smudge. Wings are proportionately narrower and held more stiffly. Fulmar has yellow bill but completely different shape, plumage, and flight. All other light-bellied petrels and shearwaters are much smaller.
Range/distribution: Breeds abundantly on offshore islands throughout the eastern Atlantic and Mediterranean. Migrates south into Equatorial and Tropical southern waters during October and November, returning from late January onward. The most abundant large shearwater in Temperate waters off North America, West Africa, and southern Europe late spring through early fall. Common in shallow to deep offshore waters.

16. CAPE VERDE SHEARWATER (*Calonectris edwardsii*)
(also Cape Verde Islands Shearwater)
Plate 5.
Identification: L. 17 in (43 cm); W. 38 in (97 cm). Small version of Cory's Shearwater. Plumage as Cory's except proportionately smaller, with duskier bill and darker back.

Flight behavior: Similar to Cory's.

May be confused with: Cory's is much larger; by comparison, Cory's is larger than Greater Shearwater, whereas Cape Verde Shearwater is smaller than Greater. Typical Cory's has paler, warmer brown back.

Range/distribution: Breeds on the Cape Verde Islands. Post-breeding dispersal is poorly known but likely south and west. Should be looked for in southern and eastern ranges of coverage area.

17. GREATER SHEARWATER[NA] **OR GREAT SHEARWATER**[E]
(*Puffinus gravis*)
Plates 2, 5.
Identification: L. 19 in (48 cm); W. 42 in (107 cm). Large, long-winged shearwater. Head distinctly capped with dark brown. The cap is separated from the back by a narrow white collar. Back and upperwings dark brown, fresh plumage with white scallops at feather ends (especially juvenile plumage). The rump is separated from the blackish tail by a white crescent. *Underparts mostly white with distinct brown oval patch in the midbelly.* Underwings white with narrow dark diagonal bar near body.

Flight behavior: Arcing flight on stiffly held, straight wings. In flight, often rotates to perpendicular orientation with ocean surface at top of arcs. Regularly approaches ships for close inspection.

May be confused with: Cory's Shearwater is larger and broader-winged, with more "horizontal" flight. Cory's is warmer brown, with yellow bill, not dark, and pure white underparts. Black-capped Petrel is smaller with blacker cap and back, usually much more extensive white rump, and pure white underparts.

Range/distribution: Breeds in South Atlantic. Migrates into colder waters of northern Atlantic May through October. Common to abundant in eastern Atlantic August to October. Most abundant in North America from Virginia north during summer. Typically found in shallow to deep offshore waters.

18. BULLER'S SHEARWATER (*Puffinus bulleri*)
Plate 5.
Identification: L. 18 in (46 cm); W. 38 in (97 cm). Crown, nape, and back gray. Wings with strong M-shaped pattern formed by dark brown to blackish median secondary coverts and pale gray greater secondary coverts. Rump pale gray, tail black. Face and underparts white.

Flight behavior: Glides easily close to the water, alternating with occasional slow flaps.

May be confused with: No other Atlantic shearwater has a strong M-shaped back pattern. Fea's Petrel has dark underwings and completely different flight.

Range/distribution: Breeds in New Zealand, disperses widely into the northern Pacific. Single Atlantic record off New Jersey.

19. SOOTY SHEARWATER (*Puffinus griseus*)
Plate 4.

Identification: L. 17 in (43 cm); W. 39 (99 cm). Slender-winged, entirely dark shearwater except for *frosty white underwing linings*.

Flight behavior: Stiff, arcing flight, particularly in moderate winds. Rotates to perpendicular orientation at the top of soaring arcs. Often flaps at the bottom of the arcs.

May be confused with: Dark-morph Herald Petrel is superficially very similar but has different distribution of white on the underwing, proportionately shorter head, and longer tail. Dark-morph Mediterranean Shearwater is smaller and shorter-winged, usually has paler belly than back, and lacks distinct white underwing linings.

Range/distribution: Abundant. Breeds in the southern oceans. Migrates northward in spring along the coast of the western Atlantic and southward in fall along the eastern Atlantic coastline. Frequents inshore waters.

SMALL "BLACK AND WHITE" SHEARWATERS

A distinct subgroup within the genus *Puffinus,* these species are all substantially smaller and proportionately shorter-winged than the larger shearwaters. With few exceptions, they are uniformly dark above and mostly white below. Flight tends to be more direct, closer to the water, and with considerably more flapping than that of the larger shearwaters. Ten species worldwide (taxonomy unsettled), four of which breed in the northern Atlantic.

20. MANX SHEARWATER (*Puffinus puffinus*)
Plate 6.

Identification: L. 14 in (36 cm); W. 33 (84 cm). Upperparts uniformly blackish brown, underparts brilliant white. Face (including cheek) dark, separated from broad, dark shoulder bar by narrow crescent of white. Undertail coverts white. Wings proportionately long, tail proportionately short.

Flight behavior: Rapid, direct flight with alternating periods of rapid flapping low and parallel to the water, then arcing in long, sweeping arcs, rotating to a nearly perpendicular orientation with the water. In flight, wings are often held in falcon-like aspect, so wingtips appear sharply pointed.

May be confused with: In the eastern Atlantic, Mediterranean Shearwater is slightly larger with proportionately broader wings, shorter tail, and feet that project beyond the end of the tail. Underparts of Mediterranean are seldom pure white, and undertail coverts are dark. In the western Atlantic, Audubon's Shearwater is smaller with proportionally shorter wings and a distinctly longer, wedge-shaped tail. The dark "hood" of Audubon's is broken by a white wedge partially separating the crown and side breast bar. See also flight comparisons with Audubon's. Little Shearwater is much smaller and paler-backed with a mostly white face, short rounded wings, and much more extensively white underwings. There is a general tendency for the larger species to have darker underwings: Mediterranean the darkest, Manx much more extensively white, Audubon's is slightly whiter than Manx, and Little the whitest of all.

Range/distribution: Breeds in cold northern waters from Canadian Maritimes to Iceland and England. Winters in the Southern Hemisphere. Often associated with shallow offshore waters.

21. MEDITERRANEAN SHEARWATER (*Puffinus mauretanicus*)
(also Balearic Shearwater, Levantine Shearwater, Yelkouan Shearwater)
Plates 4, 6.
Identification: L. 15 in (38 cm); W. 34 (86 cm). Dark and light morphs with near continuous variation between. Nominate ("Balearic") race more common in the eastern Atlantic, tends to be lighter and more Manx-like than the "Levantine" (or "Yelkouan") race of the Mediterranean. Some authorities treat the races as separate species, but identification differences are not yet conclusively described.

Light morph. Sooty brown above. Outermost primaries with white shafts at base. Chin and underbody off-white. Flanks sooty with spots and flecks. Underwing lining off-white with broad dark trailing edge. Undertail coverts dark.

Dark morph. Dark sooty brown above, variably pale brown to brown below. Many show paler midbelly than flanks or back, but may be nearly uniform in darkness. All morphs appear decidedly brown, not blackish. Feet project beyond the short tail.

Flight behavior: Similar to Manx but more fluttery or "loose." Outerwing ("hand") is more rounded or "fuller" than Manx.

May be confused with: Manx Shearwater is more cleanly black and white (but beware of sun-bleached or faded adults), has no observable foot projection beyond the tail, and has white undertail coverts. Sooty Shearwater is blacker and much larger, with proportionally longer, narrow wings. White of underwing is much brighter on Sooty.

Range/distribution: Breeds in Mediterranean. Many birds penetrate the northeastern Atlantic, mostly nominate form.

22. **LITTLE SHEARWATER** (*Puffinus assimilis*)
Plate 6.

Identification: L. 11 in (29 cm); W. 25 in (64 cm). Crown, back, upperwings slate blue-gray. Wings relatively short and distinctly rounded at the tips. Often shows frosty, pale midwing panel. Face and entire underparts white. Underwings almost entirely white with narrow gray margins. Tail short with bluish feet projecting beyond. Two subspecies in the northern Atlantic. Nominate (*assimilis*) is described above. Cape Verde Islands form (*boydi*) is browner-backed and has dark undertail coverts.

Flight behavior: Alcid-like, with rapid to whirring wingbeats alternating with short glides. In lighter winds, remains close and in parallel orientation to the water surface. In stronger winds, takes on more typical shearwater gliding and banking flight.

May be confused with: Little Shearwater is the palest-backed and proportionately shortest-winged member of the group. Manx and Audubon's are larger with longer bills and dark faces and do not have distinctly rounded wingtips. Underwings of Little Shearwater are much more extensively white than any of its cousins. Mediterranean Shearwater is larger and sootier overall.

Range/distribution: Three distinct races worldwide; two breed in the northern Atlantic. Cape Verde form possibly related to Audubon's Shearwater. Nominate form breeds in the Canary Islands, Madeira, and Azores. Tends to remain in adjacent waters near breeding grounds.

23. **AUDUBON'S SHEARWATER** (*Puffinus lherminieri*)
Plate 6.

Identification: L. 12 in (30 cm); W. 27 in (69 cm). Upperparts uniformly dark brown. Face and cheek are dark to just below the eye. Shoulder bar not always distinctly separated from dark of face and crown. Wings proportionately short. *Tail rather long and wedge-shaped.* Rump dark but may show white patches that wrap around the sides. Underparts are cleanly white, undertail coverts dark.

Flight behavior: Alternates rapid wingbeats with short, stiff-winged glides. In lighter winds, may arc but generally retains a more parallel than perpendicular orientation. Occasionally flies with fluttery rapid wingbeats. In high winds, may arc well above the water surface.

May be confused with: Manx Shearwater is longer-winged, shorter-tailed, and has white undertail coverts, not dark. Generally, flight profile of Manx has more sharply pointed wingtips; Audubon's wing is broader and slightly rounded. One seems to notice the tail of an Audubon's far more than that of Manx. Little Shearwater is smaller with shorter, rounded wings and short tail. Nominate form has white undertail coverts. Beware of Audubon's ability to duplicate Little Shearwater's "alcid-like" flight.

Range/distribution: Has several nonoverlapping populations worldwide. In the northern Atlantic, breeds in the Caribbean and disperses widely in the western Atlantic from Brazil to southern New England. Common in shallow to deep offshore waters.

Family OCEANITIDAE (Storm-petrels): Small, generally all dark seabirds, most having a white rump. About 20 species worldwide comprising eight genera. Most species are restricted to or breed in the Southern Hemisphere. Some undergo migrations of very long distances between southern breeding grounds and northern wintering grounds (Northern Hemisphere summer). Flight style is very important for identification. Six species occur in the northern Atlantic, of which four, possibly five, breed.

24. **WILSON'S STORM-PETREL** (*Oceanites oceanicus*)
    Plate 7.
    Identification: L. 7 in (18 cm); W. 16 in (41 cm). Entirely dark sooty brown swallow-like bird with prominent white oval-shaped rump. Upperwings have pale, crescent-shaped wingbar across greater secondary coverts. Tail square and relatively short, being nearly as long as the white of the rump. Feet project beyond the tail. At close range, distinctive yellow webs are visible.
    Flight behavior: Fluttery, somewhat erratic flight. Frequently foot patters ("walks" on the water) with wings held above the plane of the body. Also skips along on outstretched wings. Frequently follows ships, readily attracted to food bits or oil floating on the water.
    May be confused with: Leach's and Band-rumped Storm-petrels are larger and longer-winged with different flight style and somewhat different rump and tail patterns. Band-rumped is darker above, Leach's is paler and more brownish. European Storm-petrel is much smaller and darker above with a distinct white underwing-stripe. But beware of frosty underwing lining in some Wilson's.
    Range/distribution: Abundant breeding species in the Southern Hemisphere. Abundant transequatorial migrant to "winter" in Temperate to cold Northern Hemisphere waters. In the northern Atlantic, common to abundant; regularly found in nearshore waters off North America but remains offshore in waters off Europe.

25. **WHITE-FACED STORM-PETREL** (*Pelagodroma marina*)
    Plate 7.
    Identification: L. 8 in (20 cm); W. 17 in (42 cm). Dark grayish brown crown, separated from dark brown back by white collar. Secondary upperwing co-

verts same color as back and bordered with white. Flight feathers blackish. Rump white, tail blackish. Feet project well beyond end of tail. *Face and underparts white except for dark eye-patch and shoulder bar.* Underwings mostly white.

Flight behavior: Distinctive. Flies with wings parallel to water, swinging exceptionally long legs forward to plant feet on water surface and vault forward on legs. Otherwise flies with erratic banking and somewhat jerky wingbeats.

May be confused with: Resembles no other northern Atlantic storm-petrel. Autumn observers, particularly in North America, should be wary of Red Phalarope, which somewhat duplicates its plumage pattern. However, phalaropes and storm-petrels differ dramatically in bill structure and flight styles.

Range/distribution: Widespread but patchy breeding worldwide. In the northern Atlantic, breeds on the Cape Verde Islands and Madeira. Disperses westward, a few reaching waters of the North American continent mid-July through early October. Away from the breeding grounds, it is associated with deep offshore and canyon waters.

26.   EUROPEAN STORM-PETREL (*Hydrobates pelagicus*)
(also British Storm-petrel)
Plate 7.
Identification: L. 6 in (15 cm); W. 12 in (30 cm). Tiny blackish storm-petrel with white rump and *white underwing bar.* Upperwing bar barely evident. Tail short and square.

Flight behavior: Flight weak and fluttery, bat-like. Foot patters with wings raised, making short legs evident.

May be confused with: Wilson's is larger and browner with pale, prominent, crescent-shaped upperwing bar. Underwings may have a light area but are not bright white. Leach's and Band-rumped are much larger with proportionately longer wings and tails.

Range/distribution: Breeds in Iceland, Faeroes, United Kingdom, France, and Mediterranean. Disperses widely in the eastern Atlantic from Arctic Norway to South Africa.

27.   BAND-RUMPED STORM-PETREL (*Oceanodroma castro*)
(also Harcourt's Storm-petrel, Madeiran Storm-petrel)
Plate 7.
Identification: L. 8 in (21 cm); W. 18 (46 cm). Head, upperparts, upperwings uniformly dark blackish brown. Upperwings have narrow pale wingbar that is often indistinct. *Wings are long and rather falcon-like.* Rump-patch white and rectangular-shaped. Tail rather long, square or notched, and often ap-

pears to be roughly twice the length of white of rump. Underparts uniformly dark.

Flight behavior: Flight is direct and shearwater-like, with alternating flapping and glides, sometimes with arcing. Flapping flight may be somewhat jerky with a quicker "snap" to the upstroke, but the upstroke is rather shallow. Foot patters with wings held parallel to water.

May be confused with: Wilson's Storm-petrel is smaller and proportionately shorter-winged. Flight is more swallow-like. Feet of Wilson's project beyond tail. Leach's Storm-petrel is narrower-winged, tawnier brown. Flight is more erratic and with distinctly taller upstrokes. The tail of Leach's is deeply forked; Band-rumped's is slightly notched, although these differences are not always obvious. At close range, the white rump feathers of Band-rumped are black-tipped, but white-tipped in the other species.

Range/distribution: Breeds at scattered Tropical locations in Atlantic and Pacific. In the northern Atlantic, breeds on Cape Verde Islands, Canary Islands, and Madeira. Disperses widely offshore away from immediate breeding grounds, reaching as far west as the North American Gulf Stream and Gulf of Mexico. Generally restricted to deep offshore waters, particularly along the edge of the continental shelf.

28. **LEACH'S STORM-PETREL** (*Oceanodroma leucorhoa*)
Plate 7.

Identification: L. 8 in (21 cm); 18 in (46 cm). Head, back, and upperwings brown. Prominent pale upperwing bar continually expands toward leading edge of wing. Wings distinctly long and narrow. Rump variable, usually with oval- or wedge-shaped white patch divided by vertical dark bar. While eastern Pacific populations of Leach's regularly include birds with entirely dark rumps, this apparently is not the case with the Atlantic populations, although the possibility cannot be ruled out. Tail deeply forked. Underparts uniformly brown.

Flight behavior: Erratic and bounding. Wingbeats jerky, particularly on the upstroke. Flight somewhat erratic, producing a weaving zigzag course over the water. Capable of rapid, direct flight when chased or in strong wind.

May be confused with: Band-rumped is blacker overall and broader-winged with a proportionately smaller, square-shaped rump-patch. Wilson's and European are smaller, proportionately shorter-winged, and very different in flight styles. Swinhoe's is very similar to dark-rumped form of Leach's (see discussion below).

Range/distribution: Breeds widely in colder waters of northern Pacific and Atlantic. Disperses widely in late fall to southern Equatorial waters. In northern Atlantic, breeds commonly in northern New England, Maritime Canada, and to a lesser extent off Iceland, Scotland, and Norway. Disperses widely at sea and migrates south into warmer waters during winter. In migration, far more common in spring off North America and possibly more common in fall off Europe. Regularly seen from coastal to deep offshore waters, although seems to be more prevalent in the latter.

29. **SWINHOE'S STORM-PETREL** (*Oceanodroma monorhis*)
Plate 7.
Identification: L. 8 in (20 cm); W. 18 in (45 cm). Entirely dark blackish brown storm-petrel with *no white rump*. At close range, upperwing shows white shafts at base of primaries. Wings long, tail deeply forked.
Flight behavior: Erratic but tending more toward that of Band-rumped than Leach's.
May be confused with: Dark-rumped form of Leach's Storm-petrel (very rare in the northern Atlantic) is nearly identical in appearance. Leach's is browner and not as dark. Wings of Leach's have a narrower and more sharply pointed outerwing. At close range, Swinhoe's shows white primary shafts, but this is not infallible as some Leach's may also have them. Bulwer's is larger and proportionately longer-winged and tailed. Tail is wedge-shaped whereas Swinhoe's is forked.
Range/distribution: Primary breeding grounds in western Pacific, particularly Japan. But repeatedly observed during the early 1990s with European Storm-petrel colonies from Scotland to the Azores. In addition, there are one or two sight records off Hatteras, North Carolina, from the 1990s.

Order PELECANIFORMES: Diverse group of medium-size to very large seabirds, all possessing a fleshy throat patch (gular sac) and webbing between all four toes. Most species are Subtropical or Tropical in distribution and inhabit coastal or estuarine waters. Group consists of six families, comprising about 60 species. Because of their lack of pelagic habits in the northern Atlantic, cormorants and pelicans are not covered in this text.

Family PHAETHON (Tropicbirds): Medium-size, mostly white seabirds distinguished by long, streamer-like central tail feathers on adults. Flight somewhat pigeon-like. Rest buoyantly on the water with tails cocked upward. Three species worldwide, two of which occur in the northern Atlantic.

30. **RED-BILLED TROPICBIRD** (*Phaethon aethereus*)
Plate 20.
Identification: L. 40 in (102 cm), including 21 in (53 cm) tail streamers; W. 41 in (104 cm). In all plumages, head white with *comma-shaped black eye-*

stripe that wraps partially or completely around the back of the head. Back and upperwing secondary coverts finely barred. Rest of wing white with *black wedge on outermost primaries and greater primary coverts.* Wings distinctly narrow and sharply pointed.

Adult. Bill deep red. Barring on back and upperwing secondary coverts very fine, giving overall gray cast. Fully developed tail streamers over half the total length.

Immature. Bill yellow to orangey. Barring on upperparts darker and coarser than adult. *Tertials black.* Tips of tail feathers with black spots.

Flight behavior: Typically high-flying with strong, somewhat stiff wingbeats, mostly from the shoulder with little wrist flex. May soar hawk-like in upward spiral pattern.

May be confused with: White-tailed Tropicbird is smaller with straight eye-stripe, not comma-shaped, and broader, more rounded wings. Black primary bar does *not* include greater primary (upperwing) coverts. Adults have white back and two black upperwing bars. Superficially similar Royal Tern has solid pale gray back, upperwings, rump, and forked tail.

Range/distribution: Breeds in the Tropics, including southern Caribbean and Cape Verde Islands. Does not generally disperse widely away from breeding grounds, although occasional sightings are known from North America north to Massachusetts, generally associated with deep Gulf Stream water. Rare but regular off Hatteras, North Carolina, and in the Gulf of Mexico.

31. **WHITE-TAILED TROPICBIRD** (*Phaethon lepturus*)
Plate 20.

Identification: L. 30 in (76 cm), including 14 in (36 cm) tail streamers; W. 37 in (94 cm). In all plumages, straight, black eye-stripe, primary upperwing coverts white, outer primaries black, forming a black wedge on outerwing.

Adult. Bill yellow to orange. Head pure white except for black eye-stripe. Back and upperwings pure white except for two black bars—one on outermost primaries, the other a diagonal bar from midwing to tertials.

Immature. Bill straw-colored. Head white with dirty gray cast to crown. Restricted black eye-stripe. Back and upperwings coarsely barred with dark gray; single upperwing bar on outer primaries.

Flight behavior: Typically high-flying with rapid, pigeon-like, sometimes fluttery wingbeats with wing flex from the wrist and shoulder. Frequently investigates boats.

May be confused with: See Red-billed Tropicbird.

Range/distribution: Breeds in the Tropics worldwide, but often absent from same breeding locations as Red-billed. In northern Atlantic, restricted to the Caribbean and Bermuda. Typically does not disperse widely, but in

North America is by far the more common species. However, regular occurrence in the Gulf Stream off North Carolina may represent the limit of dispersal from Bermuda while rare but regular sightings from the Dry Tortugas, Florida, likely represent Caribbean birds. However, it is absent from the northern Gulf of Mexico. Away from its breeding grounds, most often seen along the continental shelf and beyond.

Family SULIDAE (Gannets and Boobies): Large seabirds with streamlined bills and heads, long narrow wings, and long wedge-shaped tails. Head and tail projections are equal. Plunge-dives arrow-like into the water for fish. Gannets are cold-water inhabitants, with three very closely related species worldwide, of which only one occurs in the northern Atlantic. Boobies are Tropical, with six species worldwide, of which four are known from the northern Atlantic.

32. NORTHERN GANNET (*Sula bassana*)
Plates 1, 8, 9.
Identification: L. 37 in (94 cm); W. 68 in (173 cm).
Adult. Head white with orangey yellowish wash. Bill horn-colored, separated from face by black border. Back and upperwings pure white with black "dipped-in-ink" primaries and primary coverts. Tail white. Underbody and underwings entirely white except for black primaries.
Immature. Upperparts entirely brown to brownish gray. Rump with off-white V-shaped pattern. Face, throat, and chin mottled brown to gray, grading to mottled white on belly and underwing linings. Young birds undergo many transition stages of progressive whitening to full adult plumage. Many of these mimic plumages of other species; most notably, subadults have nearly identical plumage to adult Masked Booby (see discussion below).
Flight behavior: Alternates graceful glides with bouts of steady wingbeats. Often occurs in large numbers with many birds flying in long strings, one following the other. Plunge-dives for food, sometimes in massive feeding flocks. In strong winds, dynamically soars shearwater-like.
May be confused with: The much smaller Cape Gannet (*S. capensis*) has been reported during winter in the Mediterranean. Adults have black secondaries and tail. Identification of nonadult plumages difficult, and not within the scope of this guide. Subadult Northern Gannet often mistaken for Masked Booby. The latter is smaller with bright yellow bill and broad black mask around bill. Gannet has horn-colored bill and narrow black surrounding eye and bill. Subadult Gannet usually shows black flecking on the upperwings; Booby is pure white. Immature gannets have been mistaken for small albatrosses of similar size, but the latter have longer wings, much

shorter tails, and distinctive underwing patterns. First-year Gannets are distinguished from immature Brown Booby by much larger size, grayer brown tones, and different underwing pattern.

Range/distribution: Breeds abundantly on coastal cliffs of northern Atlantic from St. Lawrence River mouth to Newfoundland, Labrador, Iceland, the United Kingdom, France, and Norway. Disperses widely along coastal and near offshore waters south to Florida and the Gulf of Mexico in the west and to Senegal and Cape Verde Islands in the east.

33. BLUE-FOOTED BOOBY (*Sula nebouxii*)
Plate 9.

Identification: L. 31 in (79 cm); W. 60 in (152 cm).

Adult. Head light brown streaked with white. *Nape with distinct white oval patch.* Back and upperwings brown with white patch on lower back and white crescent-shaped rump-patch. Tail dark. Chin and throat lightly streaked brown. Underbody white. *Underwing linings white with dark central band. Axillars white forming a white "box" at base of underwing. Feet bright powder blue.*

Immature. Similar to adult but duskier head and underwing.

Flight behavior: Flies with steady wingbeats or soars. Plunge-dives at acute angle, often into very shallow water.

May be confused with: Immature gannet is larger and lacks white oval on nape. Underwings without dark central band. Immature Masked Booby has dark head with white neck collar and different underwing. Brown Booby has dark brown head, solid dark brown back, and more evenly white underwing.

Range/distribution: Breeds in the Eastern Tropical Pacific from Mexico to Peru and Galapagos. Has occurred as a vagrant in Texas.

34. MASKED BOOBY (*Sula dactylatra*)
Plates 8, 9.

Identification: L. 34 in (86 cm); W. 60 in (152 cm). Largest, heaviest booby, approaching Northern Gannet in size.

Adult. Head white. *Bill bright yellow surrounded by broad black facial mask and throat.* Back and upperwings white with black wing ends and broad black trailing wing-stripe to body. Rump white, tail black. Underparts and underwing entirely white with black flight feathers and tail.

Immature. Head dark brown. Bill dusky yellow to yellow. Black of face outlined with white. Head separated from back by *white encircling neck collar.* Back, upperwings, rump, and tail uniformly dark brown. Underparts white, with sharply defined boundary to dark head. Underwings mostly white with dark carpal patches.

Flight behavior: Flight similar to that of Northern Gannet, including vertical plunge-dives.

May be confused with: Subadult gannet has a booby-like plumage but greater secondary upperwing coverts are white whereas Masked Booby has black. Immature gannet lacks the sharply defined boundary between head and body, lacks the white collar, and has a pale crescent on rump. Coloration of bill and face are different. White-morph Red-footed Booby is smaller, has blue bill with no black in the face. The tertials and tail are white, not black. Immature Masked Booby closely resembles adult Brown Booby, but the latter has a yellow facial area (around the eye), not black, and lacks the white collar. Subadult Brown Booby may show a gray base to the bill but is not black like Masked Booby.

Range/distribution: Widespread throughout the Tropics. In the northern Atlantic, breeds in the Caribbean and Dry Tortugas, Florida. Disperses into deeper Tropical waters but occasionally follows the Gulf Stream northward to at least the Carolinas.

35. RED-FOOTED BOOBY (*Sula sula*)
Plates 8, 9.

Identification: L. 28 in (71 cm); W. 58 in (147 cm). Proportionately longest-winged, biggest-eyed, and smallest member of the group. Highly variable plumage, particularly in darker-morph birds. Adults have *bright red legs and feet.*

Light-morph adult. Head white, *bill powder blue with red base.* Back and upperwings white with black wing ends and broad black trailing edge that does *not* include the tertials. Rump and tail white.

Dark-morph adult. Head may be either dark or white. Bill as light morph. Back, upperwings, and rump uniformly dark brown. Tail either white or brown. Underparts as upper. Underwings solidly brown.

Immature. Solidly dark brown. Bill ashy gray to pinkish gray. Head slightly darker than neck and belly. Nape may show blonde cast. Some have a dark neck collar. Underwings uniformly dark brown. Legs and feet yellowish gray.

Flight behavior: The only sulid with "grasping feet." Regularly attracted to ships, where it may perch crosswise on the rigging. Otherwise, flight as Masked Booby, although more "buoyant."

May be confused with: Light-morph birds similar to adult Masked Booby and subadult Northern Gannet, both of which have different bill colors. Masked Booby has black tertials and tail, as do most subadult gannets. However, gannet plumage with white tail and black secondaries possible. Size and bill differences should be evident. Dark-morph and immature birds differ from immature Brown and Masked Boobies by dark underwing linings. Masked Booby also has white collar and underbelly.

Range/distribution: Worldwide Tropical distribution similar to Masked Booby but less inclined to disperse widely away from breeding grounds. In the northern Atlantic, breeds in the Caribbean, with younger birds occurring rarely at Dry Tortugas, Florida.

36. **BROWN BOOBY** (*Sula leucogaster*)
    Plate 9.
    Identification: L. 27 in (69 cm); W. 56 in (141 cm).
    Adult. Head solid dark brown. *Bill and face bright yellow.* Remainder of upperparts uniformly dark brown, same color as head. Underparts bright white with *sharp transition* from dark of head. Underwings with white central area near body, otherwise dark. *Feet bright yellow.*
    Immature. Similar to adult but with dark gray to gray-green bill and dark brown belly, becoming mottled light with increasing age. Feet dull yellow.
    Flight behavior: Similar to Masked Booby, including vertical plunge dives.
    May be confused with: See immature Masked Booby and dark-morph Red-footed Booby.
    Range/distribution: Breeds widely throughout the Tropics, overlapping the range of other booby species. In the northern Atlantic, breeds in the Caribbean and Cape Verde Islands. In western half of range, disperses northward to southernmost Florida (Dry Tortugas) and Gulf of Mexico. Rare along the Atlantic Coast north to the Carolinas. In eastern half of range, the only likely booby species, but rarely occurs north of the Tropic of Cancer. Tends to remain in coastal to shallow offshore waters.

37. **MAGNIFICENT FRIGATEBIRD** (*Fregata magnificens*)
    Plate 10.
    Identification: L. 37 in (94 cm); W. 86 in (218 cm). This is the only regularly occurring species of frigatebird in the northern Atlantic. Unless obviously otherwise, *any* frigatebird in our region should be considered a Magnificent.
    Adult male. Solid black above and below. At very close range, tertials show deep purple sheen. Gular sac not evident except when inflated on breeding grounds.
    Subadult male. As adult but with white mottling on underparts.
    Adult female. Entire upperparts black. Head black, with V-shaped black projection onto white chest. Chest and upper belly white, forming an hourglass pattern.
    Subadult female. Similar to adult but with black of head restricted to crown

and face. Throat streaked or mottled blackish, white of chest and upper belly with black triangular projections from wings behind the shoulder and from lower belly.

Immature. Plumages progress through recognizable stages. Stage 1 is like subadult female but with all white head and more extensive black projections from the sides that may meet midchest. Stage 2 as Stage 1 but without black projections from the sides.

Flight behavior: Graceful and extremely buoyant, sometimes maintaining a stationary position in the air by "gliding" into a gentle headwind. When feeding, flight rapid, aggressive, and extremely agile, chasing after other birds in attacks that force them to disgorge a previous meal that the frigatebird then eats.

May be confused with: Slightly smaller Great Frigatebird (*F. minor*) is a Pacific species, unrecorded from the northern Atlantic, but the existence of an inland North American record raises the possibility, particularly for the Gulf of Mexico. Adult male differs from Magnificent by *pale upperwing bar* and, at very close range, scapulars with green sheen, not purple. Subadults have crescent-shaped belly patch instead of nondescript mottling in Magnificent. Female Great has *red eyering,* grayish throat, and box-shaped white chest. Immature has tan or russet brown head. See also Lesser Frigatebird.

Range/distribution: Restricted to the New World Tropics and Cape Verde Islands. In the northern Atlantic, common to abundant in the Caribbean and southernmost Florida. Cape Verde population critically endangered, if not extirpated. Most commonly seen in coastal and shallow offshore waters.

38. LESSER FRIGATEBIRD (*Fregata ariel*)
Plate 10.

Identification: L. 30 in (76 cm); W. 73 in (184 cm). World's smallest frigatebird. Different age and gender plumages.

Adult male. Solid black above and below except for white bar or patch in axillars, which may meet midbody on subadults.

Adult female. Upperwing with pale, diagonal midwing bars. Otherwise resembles diminutive Magnificent but has white axillar bar.

Immature. Head brown. Remainder of upperparts dark. Chest, upper belly, and flanks white. Central mid- and lower belly mottled black. White axillar bar.

Flight behavior: Similar to Magnificent.

May be confused with: Except for size, adult males closely resemble adult male Magnificent and Great. Best clue is prominent white axillar bar. Adult female nearly identical to adult female Magnificent. White axillar bar and body size are the keys. Immature is similar to immature Great but lacks black side wedges and has mottled midbelly.

Range/distribution: Breeds in the Tropical Indo-Pacific and on Trinidade Island off Brazil. In the northern Atlantic, known from single photographic record of subadult male from Maine.

Family PHALAROPODINAE (Phalaropes): Distinct group of shorebirds that swim and often may be seen spinning in circles on the surface of the water. Highly dimorphic, with different plumages for alternate (breeding), basic (nonbreeding) adults, and juveniles. Females are larger and *more* brightly colored than males. Three species worldwide, all of which occur in our region; only two have pelagic habits.

39. **RED PHALAROPE**[NA] **OR GREY PHALAROPE**[E] (*Phalaropus fulicarius*) **Plate 11.**
Identification: L. 8 in (20 cm.); W. 14 in (35 in). Largest phalarope with stoutest bill.
Adult alternate (breeding). Females much brighter-colored than males. Crown black, face white. Bill bright yellow with black tip. Back and upperwings dark gray with white wing-stripe. Rump bright cinnamon. Tail dark gray. Underbody entirely bright cinnamon red.
Basic (winter). Head white with small black eye-patch and black rear crown-patch. Bill black. Back and upperwings pale gray with white wing-stripe, remainder of wing darker gray. Underparts pure white.
Juvenile. Forehead white, crown and cheek brownish gray, separated by white eye-stripe. Remainder of upperparts brownish gray with white wing-stripe. Fresh plumage scalloped above by pale back and upperwing covert edges and with pale buff wash on neck. Transition plumages in fall create mixture of juvenile and basic characters, usually starting with pale gray back.
Flight behavior: Occurs in flocks or singly. Flight rapid and direct. On the water tends to be less animated than other phalaropes.
May be confused with: Juvenile and basic plumages very similar to Red-necked Phalarope. The latter is smaller, thinner-billed, and somewhat darker above. Juvenile Red-necked has white or tan V-shaped pattern on back. In all plumages the nonpelagic Wilson's Phalarope (*P. tricolor*) differs by long, needle-like bill and white rump. Transition-plumaged Reds have been mistaken in western coverage area for White-faced Storm-petrel. Although plumages are superficially similar, many other differences should facilitate identification. See White-faced Storm-petrel.
Range/distribution: Breeds in the Northern Hemisphere on Arctic tundra and taiga. Winters in southernmost South America and Africa. In the north-

ern Atlantic, breeds in Arctic Canada, Greenland, Iceland. Winters widely at sea, off western Africa and the southeastern United States.

40. **RED-NECKED PHALAROPE** (*Phalaropus lobatus*)
Plate 11.
Identification: L. 7 in (18 cm); W. 13 in (34 cm). Smallest phalarope. Short, needle-like bill.
Adult alternate (breeding). Females brighter, more colorful than males. Crown and face dark gray to black. Bill black. Sides of neck bright cinnamon red. Back dark gray with golden feather edges. Upperwings dark gray with white wing-stripe. Throat white, neck bright cinnamon red. Upper chest and flanks gray. Lower chest and belly white. Males duller with more brownish back.
Basic (winter). Forehead and face white with prominent black patch from eye to back of cheek. Nape and back gray, sometimes with pale V-shaped pattern. Upperwings gray with white wing-stripe. Rump and tail as back. Underparts white.
Juvenile. As basic plumage but darker grayish brown above with more prominent V-shaped pattern on back.
Flight behavior: Similar to Red Phalarope but more animated.
May be confused with: See Red Phalarope.
Range/distribution: Breeds worldwide in Subarctic and Arctic regions. Migrates south to southern South America and Africa. In the northern Atlantic, breeds in Arctic Canada, Greenland, Iceland, Norway. Common during migration along coasts and offshore but generally absent during winter. Has strong pelagic habits in western Atlantic but decidedly nonpelagic in Europe and the United Kingdom.

Family STERCORARIIDAE (Skuas, Jaegers): Predatory, gull-like seabirds that are notorious for chasing down and attacking other species until they disgorge their last meal. All species show considerable plumage variation, often with continuous variation from light to dark morphs. Many of these plumages are age-related, but that level of detail is beyond the scope of this guide. All have elongated central tail feathers in adult plumage, some distinctively so.

Genus *Catharacta* (Skuas): The European term "skua" also refers to the smaller members of the complex called "jaegers" (*Stercorarius*) in North America. This guide emphasizes the North American nomenclature. Skuas are similar to or smaller than Herring Gull in size but stockier. Mostly dark brown with a bright white wing-flash at the base of the primaries on both upper and lower surfaces. In flight, often appears "hunchbacked." Taxonomy very unsettled, but worldwide five species currently recognized. In the northern Atlantic, two species occur widely and a third has been reported on rare occasion.

Cautionary Note on the Skuas: This is a very confusing group. All are highly variable but are identifiable given a good view and the knowledge to tell them apart. The following points address some common misconceptions about skua identification:

1. Body size, bill length, and tarsal length may be useful identifiers with birds in hand but are *not* reliable *field identification* characters, except possibly when extremes are involved. Similarly, bill color and the presence of elongated central tail feathers may be useful only in the aging of skuas but provide no reliable species-specific clues.

2. Pale-bodied skuas are not automatically South Polar Skuas. All species have a light morph in which the body is washed with yellowish. However, only South Polar has a light morph in which the entire underbody is blonde or off-white, although this occurs rarely.

3. The presence of a yellowish or blonde neck collar is not automatically diagnostic for South Polar Skua. All species, particularly the lighter morphs, may have a pale hindneck. The extent of the collar, along with the presence or absence of streaks, spots, or mottling within the collar, is more important.

4. The presence of a dark cap and rusty plumage does not automatically indicate Great Skua but does eliminate South Polar. However, under some lighting conditions, a grayish plumage may appear rusty and vice versa.

5. Hybrid skuas are relatively rare and thus should not pose any serious identification problem, even when a vagrant species is potentially involved.

6. A summer skua in North America is not automatically South Polar. In Britain and Europe a summer skua, except on the breeding grounds, is not automatically Great. However, prudent observers should not assume otherwise until compelling field marks indicate a different species.

41. **GREAT SKUA** (*Catharacta skua*)
(also "Bonxie")
Plate 12.
Identification: L. 24 in (61 cm); W. 59 in (150 cm). Continuous variation between light and dark plumages. Some of the variation from age-related plumage. In general, younger birds are more uniformly dark brown, sometimes with diffuse cinnamon to yellowish streaks on the nape and upper back. With increasing age, the plumage becomes more strongly "spangled"

above and more cinnamon-colored below. Because a discussion of age-related plumages is beyond the scope of this text and because it could distract from the main point (which is species identification), the term "morph" is used generically. In all plumages, Great Skua is a robust dark brown to reddish brown bird with bright white upperwing- and underwing-flashes at the base of the primaries. The width of this wing-flash is greater below than above but perhaps somewhat more equal than in other skua species.

Light morph. Head brown to reddish brown with dark brown cap. Neck, back, upperwing secondary coverts, and rump dark brown to cinnamon brown with variable profusion of pale yellow vertical-shaft streaks. Outer-wing and secondaries contrastingly darker than secondary upperwing coverts except for broad white flash at base of primaries. Chin and neck warm brown, sometimes contrastingly darker than cinnamon brown belly. Under-wings dark. White-flash at base of primaries wider below than above.

Dark morph (including juveniles). Dark blackish brown to dark reddish brown. Lacks contrastingly dark cap of lighter-morph birds. Light yellow vertical-shaft streaking may be restricted to nape only. Young birds have minimal or no yellow coloration.

Flight behavior: Powerful and direct flight with steady flapping. Often flies well above the water surface. Aggressive and surprisingly agile when chasing other birds.

May be confused with: South Polar Skua is smaller and sleeker with proportionately narrower wings and longer tail. Lighter-morph Great shows rusty to cinnamon tones that are lacking in South Polar. Pale hindneck of South Polar is unstreaked. Brown to grayish brown back and upperwings are unstreaked. Darker-morph Great may resemble juvenile South Polar. The latter is distinctly grayish-bodied; Great is dark brown. Brown Skua is very similar but lacks strong rusty coloration and is not capped. Lighter-morph Brown has profusion of golden mottling on back and underparts. Yellow "spangling" of Great is more streaked and does not invade the chest and upper belly.

Range/distribution: Breeds in Iceland, Faeroes, Scotland. Disperses widely at sea in winter, south to Equatorial Africa and southwest to Virginia and North Carolina.

42. **BROWN SKUA** (*Catharacta lonnbergi*)
(also Subantarctic Skua)
Plate 12.
Identification: L. 26 in (61 cm); W. 61 in (155 cm). This Southern Hemisphere counterpart of Great Skua is slightly larger and lacks obvious rusty plumage. Continuous variation between lighter and darker birds.

Light morph. Head dark brown. Neck, back, and upperwings coarsely spangled or mottled with pale yellow. Remainder dark chocolate brown. Underparts dark brown, coarsely mottled with pale yellow. The extent of yellow mottling on upperparts generally coincides with that of the underparts.

Dark morph. Uniformly dark chocolate brown above and below. May show faint wash of golden head streaking that includes the nape and rear cheek area.

Flight behavior: As Great Skua.

May be confused with: Of all the skuas, Brown is the largest, with proportionately broader wings and shorter tail. Conversely, South Polar is the smallest skua (excluding jaegers) and has proportionately the narrowest wings and longest tail. Where young birds (lacking obvious back spangling) are concerned, differences in wing and tail proportion are likely among the most important criteria for separating Brown from South Polar. Great Skua is rustier and often has a dark cap, lacking in Brown. Some Greats show a darker chest than belly; this contrast is lacking in Brown. (A juvenile-plumaged large, uniformly dark, chocolate brown skua in spring or early summer would be a Brown.) Juvenile South Polar is gray, not chocolate brown, and has a back that is darker than the head and underbody. However, beware of apparent color shifts due to lighting conditions. These color differences may be subtle enough that they are not always reliable. Southern or Falkland Skua (*C. antarctica*) is unrecorded in the region. However, given its southern Atlantic breeding range and unknown dispersal, possible occurrence in northern Atlantic waters should not be dismissed. Southern Skua is smaller than Great or Brown, is variably spangled with bright yellow or blonde, and has a distinct dark cap. Great may be capped but has a rusty body, not mottled yellowish. Light-morph Brown lacks a distinct dark cap.

Range/distribution: Widespread breeder in the Southern Hemisphere. In Atlantic, breeds in the Antarctic Peninsula, South Georgia, South Orkneys, South Shetlands. In the northern Atlantic, known from fewer than a half-dozen sightings (May through August) off North America (North Carolina to Maryland), but may be more regular than current records indicate.

43. SOUTH POLAR SKUA (*Catharacta maccormicki*)
Plate 12.

Identification: L. 21 in (53 cm); W. 50 in (127 cm). Smallest skua (excluding jaegers) and by far the most common from late spring through early fall in most of North America. Highly variable plumages include some unique combinations within the genus. In all plumages, back and upperwings are evenly colored without streaking or spotting and are always darker than head and underbody.

Light morph. Head and neck pale yellow to tan, sometimes mottled with grayish brown. Back, rump, and tail uniformly grayish brown to brown. Upperwings dark grayish brown to brown with prominent white flash at base of primaries. Underparts from throat to undertail coverts pale yellow to off-white, often mottled with dark grayish brown. Underwings dark with white primary flash. On rare occasions, some individuals may be so pale as to be uniformly creamy white on the head, neck, and underbody.

Intermediate morph. Crown brown, grading into blonde neck. Back and upperwings dark brown with white wing-flash. Underparts mottled brown on yellow (lighter birds) or yellow on brown.

Dark morph. Head dark brown. Nape washed with pale yellow, often forming pronounced pale collar. Back and upperwings dark brown, somewhat darker than head. Underparts brown, same color as head.

Juvenile. Similar to dark morph but head and body grayish brown and lacking yellow wash on nape. Back and upperwings grayish brown but darker than head and body.

Flight behavior: Similar to Great Skua.

May be confused with: Great Skua usually has rusty tones in the plumage; many have dark cap and golden streaking on back and upperwings. Brown Skua is chocolate brown, with or without golden mottling. With Brown, the extent of yellow mottling on the underparts similar to upperparts. Any skua that has distinctly streaked or mottled back is not South Polar (see also discussion above). Subadult dark-morph Pomarine Jaeger may show considerable white flash in the underwing, but is smaller and has far less white on the upperwing compared with the lower. Skuas have nearly equal distribution of white on both upper and under surfaces.

Range/distribution: Breeds in Antarctica, migrates north into colder waters of the Northern Hemisphere. In the northern Atlantic, uncommon from eastern Caribbean to Maritime Canada April through October. Generally absent from Gulf of Mexico and eastern Atlantic.

Genus *Stercorarius* (Jaegers; Called "Skuas" in Europe/Africa): Medium to small members of the skua family, breeding adults have very long, distinctive central tail feathers. Highly variable in plumage. Identification is easy *only* during spring and summer when fully developed central tail feathers are evident. Popular opinion sometimes judges these birds to be much larger than in life, so errors may result if estimates of apparent size are relied upon for identification. Three species worldwide, all of which occur in the

northern Atlantic. Except with birds in full breeding plumage, few plumage characters appear to be unambiguous, and the majority of field marks apply to most but not all individuals. For that reason, some jaegers may not be reliably identified to species in the field. However, with experience, three species of jaeger are separable on the basis of wing and body proportions. Pomarine has the proportionately shortest and broadest wings and the shortest tail (excluding elongated central tail feathers). Parasitic has a slightly flattened crown, a more slender, somewhat falcon-like wing, and a longer tail. Long-tailed has the shortest, most rounded head, the longest, most slender wing, and a longish tail. Size differences exist but with overlap. Pomarine is the largest, followed by Parasitic, and then Long-tailed. Pomarine and Long-tailed never overlap in size, but the same is not true with other pairings. Plumage differences are often useful, but none are infallible. Generally speaking, a Pomarine Jaeger generally shows 8−10 bright white upper primary-shaft streaks, Parasitic shows 4−6, and Long-tailed usually shows 2.

44. POMARINE JAEGER[NA] **OR POMARINE SKUA**[E] (*Stercorarius pomarinus*)
Plates 12, 13, 14.

Identification: L. 20 in (51 cm), plus 8 in (20 cm) center tail feathers; W. 49 in (125 cm). Excluding central tail feathers, size of a Ring-billed Gull but stockier. Much plumage variation within light- and dark-morph adults as well as different season- and age-related plumages. In all plumages, upperwing usually shows white primary shafts on 8−10 primaries. Underwing often with white "double" wing-flash from white bases and dark tips to greater primary coverts. Underwing-flash often extends well over halfway to wingtip.

Adult alternate (breeding). Crown black. Neck white, washed with yellow. Back, upperwings, rump, and tail dark brown. *Elongated central tail feathers are spoon-shaped and twisted 90° at ends.* In profile at distance, fully developed tail appears very elongate. Chest band dark brown of variable width and often mottled with white. Lower chest to upper belly pure white. Lower belly and undertail coverts brown. Underwings dark with broad white primary flash and often second or "double" flash.

Adult basic (fall/winter). Similar to immature plumage except underwing coverts solid brown and not spotted or mottled. Central tail feathers may appear as short, blunt projections (molt). Chest band more mottled than alternate plumage and often grades continuously with the mottled flanks.

Dark-morph adult. Solid blackish brown above and below except for white wing-flash.

Immature. Head and neck grayish brown and generally unstreaked. Upperparts same color as head with white crescents on back and wing coverts in fresh juvenile plumage. Uppertail coverts barred with white. Underparts evenly brown to grayish brown in juveniles, becoming coarsely barred with white by winter and spring. The underwings often show a second pale crescent at the base of the primary coverts—the precursor to the "double" wing-flash of adults. Undertail coverts coarsely barred with white. Central tail feathers barely extend past the trailing edge as short, blunt projections. **Flight behavior:** Flight steady and direct, often well above the water. Flies with strong, even wingbeats. Agile and aggressive when pursuing other birds.

May be confused with: Skuas are larger and have proportionately broader wings and shorter tails. The white wing-flash of a skua includes both upper- and underwings; the upper surface flash of a jaeger is generally limited to the primary shafts. The underwing primary coverts of an adult Parasitic are generally grayish brown whereas these coverts of a Pomarine often have white bases, giving a "double" wing-flash. However, a few Parasitics show this flash pattern. Alternate-plumaged adult Parasitic has sharply pointed central tail feathers, not blunt or twisted, and otherwise has a more uniformly colored and often paler chest band, which in some birds may be incomplete. At all times of the year, adult Parasitic typically shows a pale or whitish spot above the bill, which Pomarine lacks. Juvenile-plumaged Parasitic often has a distinctly rusty plumage and sometimes dark streaks on a paler nape. Pomarine is usually grayer and more evenly colored on the nape, although this is not entirely safe. In fresh plumage, the primary tips of Parasitic show obvious white crescents; all are dark in Pomarine. Long-tailed is much smaller and rather tern-like; alternate-plumaged adult is distinctly grayish-backed.

Range/distribution: Breeds in the circumpolar Arctic zones May through August; disperses widely to the southern Tropics and beyond. In the northern Atlantic, breeds in Arctic Canada and Greenland. During migration, is generally the most common jaeger offshore. Winters primarily in the Southern Hemisphere but with some individuals remaining as far north as the middle Atlantic states and northern Africa.

45. PARASITIC JAEGER[NA] OR ARCTIC SKUA[E] (*Stercorarius parasiticus*)
Plate 13, 14.

Identification: L. 17 in (43 cm), plus 5 in (13 cm) center tail feathers; W. 42 in (106 cm). Much plumage variation within light- and dark-morph adults as well as different season- and age-related plumages. In all plumages, obvious white upperwing primary shafts are usually limited to the outermost 4–6 primaries, but this is not always obvious under field conditions. Underwing with single white wing-flash at base of primaries, generally extending about halfway to wingtip.

Adult alternate (breeding). Capped in brown with pale spot above base of bill. Face and neck white. Back, upperwings, rump, and tail dark brown. *Elongated central tail feathers sharply pointed at ends.* In profile at distance, Parasitic is the proportionately shortest-tailed jaeger. Chin and throat white. Chest band medium brown and sharply defined trailing edge where it meets chest. Some birds have an incomplete chest band or, rarely, lack one. Lower chest to upper belly, including flanks, pure white. Undertail coverts medium brown. Underwings grayish brown with single broad white primary flash. *Adult basic (fall /winter).* Cap and chest band darker, more clearly defined, and often mottled with white. Undertail coverts barred. Upperparts and remainder of underparts as alternate plumaged adult. Central tail feathers appear as short, needle-like points.

Dark-morph adult. Solidly blackish brown except for pale spot above base of bill and characteristic white primary shafts.

Immature. Head brown to reddish brown. Nape often paler with dark streaks. Upperparts brown to reddish brown with white crescents on back and wing coverts in juvenile plumage. Uppertail coverts coarsely barred with white. Older birds may show uniformly colored upperparts. In fresh juvenile plumage, outermost primaries have distinct pale, crescent-shaped tips. Underparts, including undertail coverts, brown to reddish brown and densely barred, sometimes at a distance, appearing solidly dark below. Central tail feathers pointed but often barely visible.

Flight behavior: Similar to Pomarine but more agile with quicker wingbeat; differences are not sufficient to be reliable for identification.

May be confused with: Pomarine Jaeger averages 15 percent larger, with some overlap occurring. In fact, a large Parasitic could be larger than a small Pomarine, so size estimates should be taken cautiously. Adult Parasitic sometimes distinguished from Pomarine by a paler, more streaked nape, a paler, evenly colored chest band, and the number of white upper primary shafts. On full adult birds, the central tail feathers are diagnostic. Parasitic also shows a distinctive pale spot at the base of the bill; this region is dark and continuous with the cap on both Pomarine and Long-tailed. See comments under Pomarine and generic jaeger descriptions. Long-tailed has slimmer body and proportionately longer, narrower wings, and, with most birds, only 2 outermost white primary shafts. Alternate-plumaged adult Long-tailed has lighter gray mantle, which contrasts with darker secondaries and outerwing; Parasitic is uniformly dark above. Adult Long-tailed lacks the white underwing-flash at the base of the primaries, has a sharply defined black cap, and lacks a chest band. Juvenile and basic-plumaged birds are more difficult to separate, but Long-tailed is grayer, never rusty, and tends to have coarser white scalloping on the back, uppertail, and undertail coverts. With few exceptions, the number of white primary shafts is a reliable indicator.

Range/distribution: Breeding range overlaps that of Pomarine but is more widespread. Disperses in winter to southernmost extent of continental land masses, preferring coastal or nearshore waters. In the northern Atlantic, breeds in Arctic Canada, Greenland, Iceland, Scotland, Norway. Winters primarily in the Southern Hemisphere but with some individuals remaining as far north as the middle Atlantic states and northern Africa through December.

46. LONG-TAILED JAEGER[NA] OR LONG-TAILED SKUA[E]
(*Stercorarius longicaudus*)
Plates 10, 13, 14.

Identification: L. 11 in (28 cm), plus 10 in (25 cm) center tail feathers; W. 31 in (80 cm). Excluding long central tail feathers, about the size of Bonaparte's Gull but stockier. Much variation among age and seasonal plumages. In all plumages, *upperwing with white primary shafts on outermost 2 primaries only* (rarely 1–4). Underwing lacks white flash at base of primaries.

Adult alternate (breeding). *Black cap, extending to below level of the eye, contrasts sharply with white head.* Nape washed with yellow. Back and upperwing coverts gray; *distinctly lighter than outerwing and secondaries. Fully developed central tail feathers extremely long, flexible, and streamer-like.* In profile at a distance, tail appears longer than head and body. Underparts pure white without chest band. *Underwings dark without white flash.* Lower belly and undertail coverts grayish brown.

Adult basic (fall/winter). As immature-plumaged, with dark brown upperparts and variable underparts, possibly including distinct chest band. At times, the head and chest appear uniformly dark. Uppertail and undertail coverts are coarsely barred with white. It is a misconception that the contrastingly paler back is a good mark for Long-taileds in all plumages. True basic (winter) plumage includes a solidly gray-brown head, chest, and upperparts with a clean white belly and uniformly dark gray underwings. However, this plumage is acquired long after birds have departed our region and is generally lost prior to their return. Thus, it is unlikely to be observed in the coverage area.

"Dark-morph" adult. No true dark morph is known, but the extent of the dark underparts varies. In the darkest of individuals, only the throat and upper chest are white, with the remainder of the underparts uniformly brownish gray. Otherwise as alternate-plumaged adult.

Immature. Head brown to grayish brown, often with contrasting pale hindneck in juvenile plumage. In some juvenile-plumaged birds, the head, neck, and underparts may appear creamy white while others are rather uniformly dark. Upperparts brownish gray with broad white crescent-shaped tips to the coverts of fresh juvenile plumage, becoming uniformly gray to grayish brown by winter. Uppertail coverts barred dark gray and white. Tail blackish. Underparts variably barred brownish gray and white, the barring becoming much coarser on the undertail coverts. Central tail feathers project slightly and are blunt or rounded in juvenile and first basic birds but become pointed thereafter.

Flight behavior: Somewhat tern-like with buoyant flight and light, slightly fluttery wingbeats. Remarkably agile and fast when pursuing other birds.

May be confused with: Pomarine Jaeger is twice the size and "barrel-chested." Alternate-plumaged Pomarine and Parasitic jaegers have dark backs without contrast to the primaries and secondaries. They have chest bands and prominent white underwing-flashes, which alternate-plumaged Long-tailed lacks. However, some alternate-plumaged Parasitics may lack the breastband and have completely white underparts. Note that basic-plumaged Long-taileds may have a dark breastband and uniformly dark upperparts. Most juvenile-plumaged Parasitics differ from Long-tailed by rusty brown plumage, which is always lacking in Long-tailed. Parasitics typically show 4–6 white primary shafts whereas Long-tailed shows 2. On occasion, the primaries of a juvenile Long-tailed may have pale tips, but generally they are not as bold those of *fresh-plumaged* juvenile Parasitics. Several subtle differences may aid identification but should not be used as the sole criteria: (1) while both juvenile Parasitic and Long-tailed jaegers may have a pale napes, Parasitic often has dark streaks, which Long-tailed lacks; (2) the base of Parasitic's bill is grayish while Long-tailed's is pinkish; (3) the barring of the uppertail and undertail coverts on Long-tailed is generally coarser than on Parasitic. In all plumages, wing-shape differences are also important, Long-tailed being rather tern-like while Parasitic is falcon-like. See comments under generic jaeger description.

Range/distribution: Breeding range overlaps that of the other species but extends farther north. Winters in the Southern Hemisphere. In the northern Atlantic, breeds in Arctic Canada, Greenland, Norway. Typically the most highly pelagic jaeger species, being far more common in deeper offshore waters than nearshore.

Family L A R I D A E (Gulls, Terns, Noddies): Large, diverse group of several distinct subgroups. All are aquatic, but many have little or no affiliation with the ocean. Some are semipelagic, some are truly pelagic.

Subfamily L A R I N A E (Gulls): Primarily Northern Hemisphere species popularly known as "seagulls." That name not withstanding, the vast majority of its members are *not* truly pelagic and are generally far more common on shore or inland. However, a few are truly pelagic and several other species regularly venture into near offshore waters, particularly during winter. Gull identification and taxonomy are highly complicated, made worse by a propensity for hybridization, particularly among the larger species. About 45 to 50 species worldwide, half of which are recorded from the northern Atlantic coast and waterways. However, only those with semipelagic or pelagic habits are included here. Additionally, descriptions of the semipelagic species are limited to adult and first basic (first winter) plumages, the latter called "immature" plumage for simplicity.

47. **RING-BILLED GULL** (*Larus delawarensis*)
    Plate 15.
    Identification: L. 19 in (49 cm); W. 49 in (124 cm).
    Adult. Head and neck white, streaked with brown in winter. Bill bright yellow with bold black subterminal ring. Back and upperwings pearly gray with black triangular wedge on outer primaries. Remainder of plumage white. Legs greenish yellow.
    Immature. Head and neck white, streaked with brown. Bill pink with black tip. Back gray. Upperwings brown, outer primaries blackish brown. Rump white with fine brown bars. Tail with dark terminal band and often multiple subterminal banding. Legs pink.
    Flight behavior: Buoyant and graceful. Follows boats in coastal waters, particularly when food may be available.
    May be confused with: Common Gull is slightly smaller and more "dove-headed." Adults have a darker mantle, a bill ring that is less distinct or lacking, and large "mirrors" on tips of outermost two primaries. Eye is yellow in adult Ring-billed, dark in Common. Immatures are darker above, particularly the upperwing coverts, which lack the white mottling of Ring-billed. Tail-band solid black with white sides and no subterminal banding.
    Range/distribution: Common or abundant on North American coast, particularly fall through spring, but *rarely* ventures offshore. Very rare in Britain and Europe during winter.

48. **COMMON GULL** (*Larus canus*)
    Plate 15.
    Identification: L. 17 in (43 cm); W. 47 in (120 cm).
    Adult. Head and neck white, streaked brown in winter. Bill yellow, generally unmarked in summer, but often with dark gray subterminal band in

winter. Back and upperwings gray with black triangular wedge on outer primaries. Tips of outermost two primaries with large white oval "mirrors." Remainder of plumage white. Legs yellow.

Immature. Head and neck white, streaked with brown. Bill light pink to greenish with black tip. Back gray. Upperwings grayish brown with dark brown outer primaries. Rump and tail boldly white with solid black terminal band that is flanked by white outer tail feathers.

Flight behavior: As Ring-billed.

May be confused with: See Ring-billed Gull. The Mew Gull (*L. c. brachyrhynchus*) of western North America is likely a different species. Superficially similar to Common Gull, immatures have dark rumps and solid brown tailbands; adults have far more white, with less black in the outer primaries. Mew is a Pacific bird and even less likely in eastern North America than Common Gull.

Range/distribution: Breeds throughout Europe. Winters along coasts south to northern Africa, but unlike North American cousin, regularly ventures into offshore waters. Very rare in northeastern North America during winter.

49. HERRING GULL (*Larus argentatus*)
Plates 12, 18.

Identification: L. 25 in (63 cm); W. 56 in (142 cm). The quintessential "seagull."

Adult. Head and neck white, variably streaked or mottled brown in winter. Bill bright yellow with red spot on lower mandible. Back and upperwings pearl gray with black wedge on outer primaries, the tips of which have small white "mirrors." Remainder of plumage white. Legs pink.

Immature. Head, neck, upperwings, and body uniformly brown in first winter, becoming progressively lighter with age. Outer primaries darker, inner primaries paler than mantle. Tail brown with white base. Progresses through several stages of acquiring gray back and white underparts. Bill starts black, becoming pink with black tip, then pink replaced by yellow. Legs dusky pink.

Flight behavior: Graceful and soaring or direct with steady flapping. Fond of following boats, particularly when food may be available. During winter, regularly ventures well offshore during the day but generally returns to shore before dusk.

May be confused with: Adult Ring-billed and Common Gulls are smaller with different bill and leg colors and, with immature birds, different tail-band patterns. All large, light mantled gulls should be compared against Herring Gull. Recently separated Yellow-legged Gull (taxonomy still unsettled) has darker back, proportionately longer wings, and bright, mustard yellow legs. However, extreme caution should be exercised with this identification, particularly in North America where hybridization of Herring with Lesser Black-backed has resulted in nearly identical-looking individuals.

Range/distribution: Breeds throughout Northern Hemisphere in more northerly latitudes. Winters widely throughout region. Most common in coastal and nearshore waters but sometimes follows fishing boats well offshore.

50. YELLOW-LEGGED GULL (*Larus cachinnans*)
Plate 18.

Identification: L. 23 in (58 cm); W. 53 in (135 cm).

Adult. Head and neck white in summer and most of the winter. During autumn, Azores population may show a bit more neck streaking, which persists longer than in Mediterranean population. Bill and feet bright lemon yellow, comparatively less orange-toned than other species. Back and upperwings medium gray with black wingtips and one or two large white spots on outer primaries. Wings proportionately long.

Immature. Head mostly white with dark brown streaking. Back and upperwings contrastingly darker. Outer primaries darker and inner primaries paler than mantle. Rump mostly white, tail black. Underbody slightly darker than head.

Flight behavior: Similar to Herring Gull but more buoyant.

May be confused with: Adult Herring has pink feet and paler back. Young Herring is uniformly darker with less contrast between head and back. Adult Lesser Black-backed is darker-backed, bill and legs more orangey. Immature Lesser is blacker on the back and lacks the pale inner primary panel. Immature Great Black-backed is similar in plumage but much larger.

Range/distribution: Recently separated from Herring Gull. Taxonomy and subspecific points of identification presently unsettled. Nominate race from Black Sea eastward and Asiatic races not within the range of this guide. Race *michahellis* in Mediterranean Basin winters regularly (and increasing) along the Atlantic coast from England through northern Africa. Race *atlantis* breeds in the Azores. Occasional reports of Yellow-legged Gulls from North America may refer to either *michahellis* or *atlantis* or possibly misidentified hybrids of other species.

51. THAYER'S GULL (*Larus thayeri*)
Plate 18.

Identification: L. 24 in (61 cm); W. 55 in (140 cm).

Adult. Head and neck white, streaked or mottled brown in winter. Bill yellow with red spot. Back and upperwings gray with dark gray and white incomplete wedge on outermost primaries. At close range, outermost primaries show large white "mirrors" *behind* subterminal dark gray bars. Remainder of body white. *Underwings completely white, including wingtips.* Legs pink.

Immature. Entire bird uniformly tan to light brown except for outermost primaries, which are darker tan (but not black) above and pure white below with a narrow grayish border. The tail is dark tan, contrastingly darker than the back. Bill solid black during first winter, progressing as Herring Gull to adulthood.

Flight behavior: As Herring Gull.

May be confused with: Adult Herring Gull has more extensive black outerwing wedge that shows through as dark gray below. Thayer's underwing is pure white. At very close range, adult Thayer's has dark eye; Herring has pale yellow. Kumlien's race of Iceland Gull is very similar, but the dark of the outer primaries is restricted to narrow dark gray subterminal bands. Immature Iceland usually much whiter, with white outer primaries, not dark tan, and a pale tan tail that does not contrast strongly with upper back.

Range/distribution: Breeds in Arctic Canada. Winters primarily along west coast of North America. In northern Atlantic, very rare during winter from Maritime Canada through middle Atlantic states. Unrecorded from the eastern Atlantic.

52. ICELAND GULL (*Larus glaucoides*)
Plate 19.

Identification: L. 24 in (61 cm); W. 55 in (140 cm).

Adult. Head and neck white. Bill pale yellow with red spot. Back and upperwings very pale gray. Flight feathers, including outermost primaries, pure white. Race *kumlieni* (breeding in Canada) has gray bars near tips of outermost primaries, otherwise pure white wingtips.

Immature. Entire bird pale tan-white. Outerwings pure white. First basic birds have solid dark bill, becoming pink at base, then eventually yellow as birds age.

Flight behavior: Typical large gull.

May be confused with: In all plumages, Thayer's is darker and has dark wingtips. Immature Thayer's has a contrastingly dark tail; Iceland's is pale tan without obvious contrast. Glaucous is much larger with a proportionately smaller head, larger bill, and slenderer wings. First winter Glaucous has pink bill with distinct black tip; bill is entirely or mostly dark in Iceland.

Range/distribution: Breeds in eastern Arctic Canada and Greenland. Winters along coasts to middle Atlantic states in North America and to Britain and Scandinavia. Regularly ventures offshore with flocks of Herring Gulls.

53. **GLAUCOUS GULL** (*Larus hyperboreus*)
Plate 19.
Identification: L. 28 in (71 cm); W. 54 in (137 cm).
Adult. Head and neck white. Bill large and pale yellow with red spot. Back and upperwings very pale gray. Flight feathers, including outermost primaries, pure white. Remainder of plumage pure white.
Immature. Entirely white with pale tan mottling on body as well as upperwing and undertail coverts. Bill bright pink with black "dipped-in-ink" tip.
Flight behavior: Typical large gull.
May be confused with: See Iceland Gull.
Range/distribution: Breeds in high Arctic Russia, Siberia, Alaska, Canada, Greenland. In northern Atlantic, winters from pack ice south along coasts through middle Atlantic states of North America and to England and southern France. Rarely ventures offshore.

54. **LESSER BLACK-BACKED GULL** (*Larus fuscus*)
Plate 18.
Identification: L. 22 in (56 cm); W. 49 in (125 cm). Taxonomy somewhat unsettled. Three races, considered by some to be different species, although this distinction is unlikely.
Adult. Head and neck white, streaked with brown in winter. Bill yellow with red spot. Back and upperwings dark gray (*L. f. graellsii*) to blackish gray (*L. f. intermedius*) to coal black (*L. f. fuscus*). Outer primaries black with small white "mirrors" at tips. Remainder of plumage white. Legs yellow.
Immature. Head and neck mostly white, lightly streaked with dark brown, often with darker area around the eye. Bill completely dark, progressively lightening with age to pink, then yellow. Back and upperwings dark brown with white feather edgings. Primaries and secondaries blackish brown. Tail blackish brown with mottled white rump.
Flight behavior: Typical large gull.
May be confused with: Great Black-backed Gull is nearly twice as large. Adults have solid black backs, flat heads, large heavy bills, and pink legs. Gray-backed races of Lesser are distinctly paler-backed and have yellow legs. Blackest-backed races of Lesser have dove-like heads, small bills, and yellow legs. Immature Great Black-backed has more contrast in the rump and tail pattern. See also comments about hybridization with Herring Gull under that entry.
Range/distribution: Breeds primarily in Iceland, Britain, and Scandinavia but also in likely Canada and Greenland. Winters coastally and occasionally in shallow offshore waters throughout range in northern Atlantic.

55. GREAT BLACK-BACKED GULL^{NA} **OR GREATER BLACK-BACKED GULL**^E (*Larus marinus*)

Plates 1, 18.

Identification: L. 30 in (76 cm); W. 63 in (160 cm). World's largest gull, approaching the size of a small albatross, although with proportionately much shorter wings.

Adult. Head and neck white, sometimes with faint dusky streaks in winter. Bill heavy and yellow with red spot. Back and upperwings black with white tips of flight feathers. Remainder of plumage white.

Immature. Head and neck white, lightly streaked with brown. Bill completely dark except for white tip. Starting the second year, bill lightens with age, becoming pink at base, then mostly yellow. Back and upperwings dark, checkered or spotted white and dark brown. Primaries blackish. Rump white. Lightly mottled with brown. Tail with dark terminal band.

Flight behavior: As other large gulls but decidedly heavy and strong.

May be confused with: See Lesser Black-backed Gull. On the water, adult resembles small adult Black-browed Albatross. The latter has a proportionately much larger bill and black dash through eye.

Range/distribution: Breeds in the northern Atlantic from North American middle Atlantic States to Greenland, Iceland, Scandinavia, Britain. Winters coastally from breeding range south to Florida in the west and to Africa and Canary Islands in the east.

56. LAUGHING GULL (*Larus atricilla*)

Plate 16.

Identification: L. 16 in (41 cm); W. 41 in (104 cm).

Adult alternate (summer). Head black, bill red. Neck white. Back and upperwings medium gray with black outer primaries. Rump and tail white. Underparts pure white with dark gray underwings. Legs reddish.

Adult basic (winter). Head white with dark ear smudge. Bill and feet blackish.

Immature. Head and neck grayish. Bill black. Back and upperwings brown, becoming gray by first winter. Primaries and secondaries black. Rump white, tail black. Underbody white.

Flight behavior: Lightweight and buoyant, with lighter wingbeat than larger gulls.

May be confused with: Franklin's Gull of western North America occurs rarely on eastern coast. Accidental in Britain. Winter adults are smaller and paler-backed than Laughing, with dark nape and distinct black wingtips separated from gray by line of white. Wings are distinctly rounded; wings of Laughing are proportionately longer and more pointed. Immatures have partial dark hood with broad, rounded eye arcs, rounded wings, and black tail-band encircled by white border.

Range/distribution: Breeds on eastern coast of North America from northeastern United States south through northernmost South America. Winters in coastal and nearshore waters of western Atlantic. Absent from northern half of range during winter.

57. **FRANKLIN'S GULL** (*Larus pipixcan*)
   Plate 16.
   Identification: L. 14 in (36 cm); W. 36 in (90 cm).
   Adult. Head black (alternate plumage) or white with dark hood above and behind the eyes (basic plumage). Bill red (alternate) to black (basic). Back and upperwings gray. Wings somewhat rounded with black primary tips, the black separated from the gray by a distinct bar of white. Tail and underparts white.
   Immature. Head and back rather like basic adult. Back gray but upperwings brownish. Tail white with distinct black band.
   Flight behavior: Similar to Laughing but somewhat more "fluttery."
   May be confused with: See Laughing Gull.
   Range/distribution: Breeds in interior and western North America. Rare along the eastern coast of North America, mostly during fall. Extremely rare offshore, although there are records from at sea and from the United Kingdom.

58. **MEDITERRANEAN GULL** (*Larus melanocephalus*)
   Plates 15, 19.
   Identification: L. 16 in (40 cm); W. in 36 (91 cm).
   Adult alternate (summer). Head black, bill bright red. Remainder of plumage pale gray to white. Outermost primary with narrow black line on outer edge.
   Adult basic (winter). As alternate adult, except head mostly white with dark ear-patch that may wrap around nape.
   Immature. Younger birds with dusky hood on white head, gray back, and dark brown upperwings with pale gray midwing panel. Bill blackish, gradually becoming reddish with age. Tail white with distinct narrow black subterminal band. Older birds resemble basic-plumaged adults except for the presence of black subterminal bars on the outer primaries.
   Flight behavior: Flight heavier compared with that of other small gulls (e.g., Black-headed) but not so heavy as medium-size gulls (e.g., Common).
   May be confused with: Adult is the only "white-winged" gull with head pattern of small gull (e.g., Laughing, Black-headed, etc.). First-year birds resemble Common Gull but differ in head and bill coloration.

Range/distribution: Breeds in Mediterranean, occasionally on both coasts of the English Channel. Most remain in the Mediterranean during winter but occur regularly from Spain and northwestern Africa north through Britain. Numbers in the northern Atlantic may be increasing. Typically found in coastal to shallow offshore waters.

59. **BLACK-HEADED GULL** (*Larus ridibundus*)
(also Common Black-headed Gull)
Plates 16, 17.
Identification: L. 16 in (41 cm); W. 36 in (91 cm).
Adult alternate (summer). Head dark brown. Bill bright red. Neck white. Back and upperwings gray with white triangular wedge on outer primaries, the tips of which are black. Remainder of plumage white. Underwings gray with dark primaries except for outermost two, which are white.
Adult basic (winter). As alternate plumage except for white head with black earspot.
Immature. Head white with dark earspot. Bill yellowish with black tip. Neck white. Back and upperwings gray with brown bar across median secondary coverts. Outer primaries mostly white, forming an indistinct white wedge. Trailing edge of wing black. Tail white with black terminal band. Underwings dark gray on outer third, becoming paler toward body. Outermost primary mostly white.
Flight behavior: Typical of smaller gulls (e.g., Laughing).
May be confused with: Adult Bonaparte's Gull also has white upperwing wedge but is smaller, has a black bill, and has an all white underwing. Young Bonaparte's has different upperwing and underwing patterns and a black bill. Young Ring-billed is larger and more robust with mostly black outer primaries, not white.
Range/distribution: Most abundant gull in Britain and Europe. Occurs regularly in small numbers in North America. During winter, abundant inland and coastally. Tends to remain close to shore.

60. **BONAPARTE'S GULL** (*Larus philadelphia*)
Plates 16, 17.
Identification: L. 14 in (35 cm); W. 33 in (83 cm).
Adult alternate (summer). Head and bill black. Neck white. Back and upperwings gray. Outer primaries white, forming white triangular wedge. Remainder of plumage white. Underwings white.
Adult basic (winter). As alternate plumage except for white head with black earspot.

Immature. Head white with black earspot. Bill black. Back gray. Upper-wings gray with brown diagonal bar on secondary coverts. Primaries black with white centers, secondaries black. Tail white with dark terminal band. Remainder of plumage white.

Flight behavior: Buoyant and fluttery. Often occurs in large flocks.

May be confused with: Black-headed Gull is larger and does not have a black bill (red in adults, yellowish with black tip in immatures). Primaries of adults have dark underside. Little Gull has shorter, distinctly rounded wing-tips. Adults lack the white upperwing wedge and have blackish underwings. Immatures have dark M-shaped pattern on back and upperwings.

Range/distribution: Breeds in northern North America. Winters south to northern South America. Common in winter in coastal and near offshore waters north to southern Maritime Canada.

61. **LITTLE GULL** (*Larus minutus*)
   Plates 16, 17.
   Identification: L. 11 in (28 cm); W. 25 in (64 cm). World's smallest gull. Has distinctly rounded wingtips.
   Adult alternate (summer). Head and bill black, neck white. Back and upper-wings uniformly pale gray with white trailing edge to entire wing. Rump and tail white. Body white, contrasting with blackish underwings with narrow white trailing border.
   Adult basic (winter). As alternate plumage except for white head with black-ish cap and earspot.
   Immature. Head white with blackish cap and earspot. Back and upperwings light gray with bold blackish M-shaped pattern. Rump and tail white with black terminal tail-band.
   Flight behavior: Hovers buoyantly, somewhat like Black Tern. Direct flight with deep wingbeats.
   May be confused with: Plumage very similar to Ross's Gull. In all plumages, Ross's is larger and has pointed wingtips and a longer, distinctly wedge-shaped tail; Little has slightly notched tail. See also discussion under Ross's Gull. Adult Bonaparte's has white underwings, not black, and a white up-perwing wedge that Little lacks. Immature Bonaparte's has different upper-wing pattern that does not include dark, well-defined M shape. Adult Black-headed is much larger and has less extensively dark underwings.
   Range/distribution: Breeds inland from northeastern Europe to Siberia. Winters on open water from southern Scandinavia to northwestern Africa. Rare in North America, a migrant or winter visitor from Maritime Canada

to North Carolina. Mostly remains in coastal waters, but some regularly venture into deeper offshore waters.

62. BLACK-LEGGED KITTIWAKE (*Rissa tridactyla*)
Plates 15, 17.

Identification: L. 17 in (43 cm); W. 36 in (91 cm). One the few gull species that is truly pelagic and by far the most commonly encountered in the northern Atlantic away from coastal waters.

Adult alternate (summer). Head and neck white, bill yellow. Eye dark. Back and upperwings gray with black "dipped-in-ink" wingtips. Remainder of plumage white. Legs and feet coal black.

Adult basic (winter). As alternate plumage but with dusky crescent-shaped neck collar and dark earspot. Subadult plumages resemble adult basic, except wingtips may show irregular patterning of black and white. Tail may have narrow tail-band.

Immature. Head and neck white with blackish neck collar and earspot. Bill dark in first winter, becoming yellow by first summer. Back and upperwings gray with bold, black M-shaped pattern. Tail white with black V-shaped tail-band. Remainder of plumage white.

Flight behavior: Flight buoyant, with a bit more "snap" to the upstroke compared with other gulls. Alternate bouts of flapping with buoyant glides that seem to be suddenly interrupted by instability, causing the bird to jerk or rock sideways.

May be confused with: Ring-billed and Common Gulls have black wingtips that are more extensive along leading edge whereas Kittiwake's black wingtip is more extensive along trailing edge. Immature Little Gull is much smaller with more rounded wings and a dark cap, not a neck collar.

Range/distribution: Breeds on Arctic coastal cliffs. Winters at sea, often well offshore. In the northern Atlantic, breeds in Arctic Canada, Greenland, Iceland, England, Scandinavia. Winters south to the Carolinas in the west and northern Africa in the east.

63. SABINE'S GULL (*Larus sabini*)
Plates 16, 17.

Identification: L. 14 in (35 cm); W. 35 in (89 cm). Distinctly pelagic gull, generally occurring well offshore.

Adult alternate (summer). Head dark gray with narrow black border. Bill black with bright yellow tip. Neck white, back gray. *Upperwings with distinctive pattern of three colored wedges:* gray median and lesser secondary coverts, black outer primaries and primary coverts, white inner primaries, secondaries, and greater secondary coverts. Tail white and remainder of plumage white.

Adult basic (winter). As alternate plumage but with white head and dark neck collar.

Immature. Head, nape, back, and upperwings brown, often with white feather margins giving scaly appearance. Remainder of upperwing pattern otherwise like adult. Tail with black terminal band.

Flight behavior: Buoyant and tern-like, with full wingstrokes.

May be confused with: Immature kittiwake has a dark M-shaped back pattern but nothing like the tricolored pattern of Sabine's in any plumage. Although distinctly larger, subadult Common and Ring-billed may show a superficially similar upperwing pattern but lack the broad and distinct wedge of white that occupies the distal third of the wing on a Sabine's in any plumage.

Range/distribution: Breeds in high Arctic North America, Greenland, Siberia. Winters at sea off southwestern Africa and western South America. Rare but somewhat regular in migration from eastern North America, with most records from fall off Maritime Canada and New England. Migration poorly known but likely remains in deep offshore waters.

64. **ROSS'S GULL** (*Rhodostethia rosea*)
Plates 16, 17.
Identification: L. 12 in (31 cm); W. 33 in (84 cm).

Adult alternate (summer). Head white with black encircling neck collar. Bill short and black. Back and upperwings uniformly pale gray with narrow black leading edge of outermost primary. Tail white and distinctly wedge-shaped. Underbody white with variable wash of pink, at times quite strong. Underwings dark gray with white trailing border.

Adult basic (winter). As alternate plumage but with dark ear-patch instead of neck collar and underbody usually without pink tones.

Immature. Head white with dusky ear-patch. First alternate birds may show neck collar. Back and upperwings gray with dark M-shaped pattern. Tail with dark terminal wedge-shaped band.

Flight behavior: Variably tern-like or pigeon-like. May be seen to "patter" reminiscent of a storm-petrel.

May be confused with: Little Gull is superficially similar in all nonbreeding plumages. It is smaller with proportionately shorter and rounded wings and a squared tail. Adults have dark cap and generally darker underwings. In all plumages, tail shape is a good mark for separating the two.

Range/distribution: Breeds in the high Arctic, mostly western Siberia. Winters in the Arctic, where its large eyes are adapted to nocturnal feeding. Extremely rare anywhere in northern Atlantic south of the Arctic Circle.

65. **IVORY GULL** (*Pagophila eburnea*)
Plate 19.
Identification: L. 17 in (43 cm); W. 44 in (111 cm).
Adult. Plumage entirely pure white. Bill horn gray with yellow tip. Large, black eye contrasts like "lump of coal" against white of head. Legs and feet black.
Immature. Head white with dark mottling or smudging on face, particularly between bill and eye. Bill pale gray with yellow tip. Eye dark. Back and upperwings white, flecked, or checkered with black. Primaries, outer secondaries, and tail feathers white with small black tips. Remainder of plumage pure white. Legs and feet black.
Flight behavior: Rather pigeon-like in appearance, owing partly to stocky body and rather broad wings, particularly near body. Otherwise graceful in flight.
May be confused with: Second-year Iceland Gull may appear nearly pure white with black bill, but on close inspection it is larger and has a pale gray mantle. Beware of albino gulls that have pure white plumage. Differences in bill color, head and body shape, and other marks should help distinguish Ivory Gull.
Range/distribution: Breeds in high Arctic. Winters south to limit of pack ice with occasional stragglers wandering south to the Delmarva Peninsula.

Subfamily STERNINAE (Terns and Noddies): Generally smaller than gulls, with more sharply pointed bills, thinner wings, and longer, generally forked tails. Like gulls, the group includes many nonpelagic species but also a number of highly pelagic species.

66. **BLACK TERN** (*Chlidonias niger*)
Plate 22.
Identification: L. 9 in (23 cm); W. 26 in (66 cm).
Adult alternate (summer). Head, back, and upperwings black. Rump and uppertail gray. Underbody black. Underwings pale gray with darker flight feathers. Undertail coverts white.
Adult basic (winter). Face white, head with black cap that extends behind the eye to the lower cheek. Neck white. Back, upperwings, rump, and uppertail gray. Underparts white with dark shoulder bar extending onto sides of breast.
Juvenile. Resembles basic plumage adult but with more brown on back and upperwing.

Flight behavior: Flies with somewhat jerky wingbeats. Flight may be erratic, close to the water when feeding; at other times, direct and well above the water.

May be confused with: Closely related Whiskered Tern (*C. hybridus*) and White-winged Tern (*C. leucopterus*) are coastal and marshland species of Europe that may occasionally drift offshore. Alternate-plumaged Whiskered has red bill, black cap, white cheek, and dark gray underbody and looks superficially like sooty version of Arctic Tern. Adult basic and juvenile plumages similar to Black Tern, but bill is longer, upperparts are paler, wings and tail are proportionately longer (more like *Sterna* terns), and overall size is slightly larger. White-winged Tern in all plumages has a white rump, not gray like Black Tern. Most plumages of White-winged Tern have frosty gray upperwings that are contrastingly paler than back. Upperwing of Black Tern is the same color as or darker than the back. The undersurface of the flight feathers of White-winged are white, often contrasting with *darker* underwing linings. Black Tern has gray flight feathers, often contrasting with *paler* underwing linings.

Range/distribution: Breeds in inland marshes of North America and Europe. Regularly occurs well offshore during migration. Winters in the Tropics.

"CAPPED TERNS" (Genus *Sterna*)

Predominantly white-bodied birds with dark crowns and gray backs. Many are associated with Temperate to Arctic breeding habitats. In the northern Atlantic, there are three pelagic to semipelagic species, but several others may venture offshore, presenting identification challenges. The latter group is covered under a single header.

67. **COMMON TERN** (*Sterna hirundo*)
Plate 21.

Identification: L. 14 in (36 cm); W. 31 in (80 cm).

Adult alternate (summer). Head white with black cap that extends through eye. Bill red, usually with black tip. Back and upperwings gray with darker gray "wedge" in middle primaries. Rump and tail white. Tail deeply forked. At close range, outer edges of tail have dark border. Underparts pale gray to white. Underwings pearly white with broad, dark gray trailing edge to primaries.

Adult basic (winter). As alternate plumage but with black bill, white forehead, and broad dark carpal bar. Secondaries darker than upperwing coverts. Tail shorter and less deeply forked.

Juvenile. Similar to adult basic but with duskier crown and brownish crescents on back and upperwing feathers. Bill may show dusky orange base to lower mandible.

Behavior: Flight steady with rowing wingbeats. Hovers with rapid wingbeats. Plunge-dives when feeding.

May be confused with: Arctic Tern has a shorter bill, more rounded head, and distinctly shorter neck. Upperparts are uniformly frosty gray above, although secondaries of Arctic are paler than those of Common. Dark underwing border of Arctic Tern is narrower and more sharply defined. Both Arctic and Common terns have pale gray underparts, but Arctic tends to be a bit darker. Roseate Tern is distinctly paler overall, with mostly blackish bill, proportionately shorter wings, and much longer tail.

Range/distribution: Breeds widely throughout Northern Hemisphere. Disperses widely from coastal waters to well offshore, particularly during migration. Winters from northern Tropics to southern Temperate waters. In the northern Atlantic, breeds from southern Canada to the Carolinas and from southern Scandinavia to the Madeiras. Winters in the Caribbean, southern Florida, and northwestern Africa. Although technically more semipelagic than truly pelagic, it is the most widely distributed tern found offshore.

68. ARCTIC TERN (*Sterna paradisaea*)
Plate 21.

Identification: L. 14 in (35 cm); W. 31 in (79 cm).

Adult alternate (summer). Head with prominent black cap that extends through eye. Cheek white, throat gray. Bill bright red. Back and upperwings uniformly pearl gray. Rump and tail white. Tail long and very deeply forked, often held closed as long streamer. Underbody light gray, sometimes contrasting with white cheek. Underwings white with dark gray, sharply defined, narrow border to primaries.

Adult basic (winter). As alternate plumage but with black bill and white forehead. Upperwing with narrow grayish carpal bar. Secondaries and tail white. Tail shorter and less deeply forked. (Given Arctic Tern's pole-to-pole migration, observing this plumage in the northern Atlantic is highly unlikely.)

Juvenile. Similar to adult basic but with dusky crown and slightly darker upperparts.

Flight behavior: Similar to Common Tern, but wingbeats are faster and more "fluttery."

May be confused with: Common Tern has a longer head and bill profile, dark wedge in middle primaries, and shorter tail. Beware that the popularly touted field mark of Arctic Tern's solid red bill does not apply after midsummer, when many Common Terns lose the black-tip coloration to their bills. Basic-plumaged adults differ from Common Tern by secondaries that are lighter than upperwing coverts, not darker. Juvenile-plumaged Arctic Tern has brownish gray edges on the back and wing covert feathers whereas those of Common Tern are warmer brown. Roseate Tern has a much longer, mostly dark bill, is paler above, and has shorter wings with dark leading edge to primaries, not trailing. Juvenile-plumaged Roseate is much browner-backed than Arctic.

Range/distribution: Breeds throughout the Arctic and subarctic regions of the Northern Hemisphere. Winters in the Antarctic and Subantarctic. In the northern Atlantic, breeds in northern New England, Canada, Greenland, Iceland, Britain, Scandinavia. Migratory pattern is circular: predominantly in the western Atlantic during spring, eastern Atlantic during fall. During migration, most commonly seen in shallow to deep offshore waters.

69. **ROSEATE TERN** (*Sterna dougallii*)
Plates 20, 21.
Identification: L. 15 in. (39 cm); W. 31 in (78 cm).
Adult alternate (summer). Head with black cap that extends through eye. Bill long and reddish black to black. Back and upperwings silvery gray with narrow dark leading edge to outer primaries. Tail long, streamer-like, and deeply forked. Underparts white with rose blush in some at height of breeding season.
Adult basic (winter). As alternate plumage but with white forehead and crown, the black of the rear crown forming a bridge between the otherwise black eye-patches.
Immature. Forehead grayish, rear crown and rest of cap area black. Back and upperwings gray with dark brown V-shaped feather edges. Dark leading edge of inner wing forms carpal bar in folded wing.
Flight behavior: Flies with rapid, shallow wingbeats. Compared with other terns, wings seem rather short.
May be confused with: Common and Arctic Terns have darker gray upperparts and dark trailing edges to the underside of the primaries. Comparatively, the head and bill are longest on Roseate, shortest on Arctic; wing is proportionately shorter on Roseate than either Common or Arctic, and the tail is longest on Roseate, shortest on Common. During summer, Roseate is the only tern of the group whose adults have a dark bill. In winter, adults of all three species have dark bills, but Common and Arctic have carpal bars, which Roseate lacks. Immature Roseate is very similar to young Common but browner-backed and with pale secondaries.
Range/distribution: Breeding primarily in Tropics and Subtropics but with isolated populations at various Cold Temperate locations. Threatened and

declining throughout much of its range. In the northern Atlantic, disjunct breeding populations occur from New England to Maritime Canada, southernmost Florida through the Caribbean, and in England. Most remain in coastal to shallow offshore waters. Winters in South America and Africa.

70. OTHER "CAPPED" TERNS
Plates 20, 21.

Four other species of "capped" tern are covered briefly here. These species are not typically found offshore, but they are included for comparative purposes because they may occasionally drift to sea and may be confused with other species.

70A. SANDWICH TERN (*Sterna sandvicensis*)
Plate 20.

Identification: Large, pale tern with long bill grading into slender head and neck. At close range the black bill has a yellow tip. Nape black; crown black in summer, white in winter. Underwings with broad blackish border. Not normally pelagic but may occasionally be found in shallow offshore waters perched on buoys or light towers.

70B. GULL-BILLED TERN (*Sterna nilotica*)
Plate 20.

Identification: Distinctly larger than Common Tern with stout black bill, pale gray to white upperparts, and short tail. In the northern Atlantic, Gull-billed Tern does not normally exhibit pelagic habits except where bodies of water are flanked by land, such as the English Channel.

70C. ROYAL TERN (*Sterna maxima*)
Plate 20.

Identification: Large, frosty gray and white tern with heavy orange bill. Breeding birds with black cap. In winter birds, the black is restricted to an eye-stripe that wraps around the back of the head, reminiscent of that shown by the Red-billed Tropicbird. Given the large size of this tern, confusion with tropicbird is as likely as with the smaller pelagic "capped" terns.

70D. FORSTER'S TERN (*Sterna forsteri*)
Plate 21.

Identification: Adults resemble Common Tern but bill has orange rather than red base, back is paler, and center of tail is slightly grayish. Winter birds are very pale gray to white; black patch is restricted to eye and ear (not crossing the back of the nape) and carpal bar is lacking. Forster's Tern is a marsh and coastal bird and rarely ventures offshore. However, it winters much farther north than Common, Arctic, or Roseate and would be the most likely candidate during winter for most of the northern Atlantic.

70E. LEAST TERN[NA] **OR LITTLE TERN**[E] (*Sterna albifrons*)
Not illustrated
Identification: Very small tern with black cap and white eye-stripe. Bill is yellow with black tip. Upperparts pale gray, remainder frosty white. Rarely occurs offshore, even where common coastally, but noted here for completeness.

TROPICAL TERNS (Genus *Sterna*)

Dark-backed terns with black caps as adults and deeply forked tails. Restricted to the Tropics. All are pelagic.

71. BRIDLED TERN (*Sterna anaethetus*)
Plate 22.
Identification: L. 15 in (37 cm); W. 30 in (76 cm).
Adult. Black crown and eyeline separated by white stripe that *extends to behind the eye.* Nape white. Back and upperwings dark grayish brown. Long, deeply forked tail, same color as back with broadly white outer edges. Underwings white with narrow dark trailing edge.
Immature. Head mostly white with variable brown on crown. Narrow brownish eyeline. Back and upperwings brown. Tail light brown with white sides; deeply forked but not quite as long as that of adult. Underparts and underwing linings white.
Flight behavior: Flies with easy wingbeats. Often flies well above water surface. Frequently perches on debris, boards, or logs floating on the water.
May be confused with: Sooty Tern has an eye-stripe that *does not* extend past the eye whereas white eye-stripe of adult Bridled extends past the eye. On adult Sooty, the black of the crown crosses the nape and touches the back, which is also black. With Bridled, the black of the crown is separated from the back by a white nape and the back is paler than the crown. Underwings of Sooty have a broader dark trailing edge that broadens toward the outerwing. Tail of Bridled has broad white sides; adult Sooty has narrow white edges.
Range/distribution: Breeds throughout the Tropics excluding the eastern Atlantic. Winters at sea in vicinity of breeding grounds. In the northern Atlantic, breeds in the Caribbean. Nonbreeding birds drift with the Gulf Stream north to North Carolina and occasionally beyond, associated with shallow to deep offshore waters. Particularly fond of perching on floating debris.

72. SOOTY TERN (*Sterna fuscata*)
Plate 22.
Identification: L. 17 in (43 cm); W. 36 in (90 cm).
Adult. Black of crown and eyeline separated by white stripe that *does not extend past the eye.* Black of cap touches the back but "pinched" on the sides of nape by white. Back and upperwings black. Tail long and deeply forked, same color as the back with narrow white outer edges. Underwing linings white. Dark gray secondaries and primaries form a broad dark trailing edge that widens toward the outerwing.
Immature. Uniformly blackish above, with profusion of white flecks on back and upperwings at close range. Tail deeply forked but not as long as adult. Underparts black from chin to midbelly. Lower belly and vent white. Underwing duskier but otherwise as adult.
Flight behavior: Flight rather strong and determined with somewhat rowing wingbeat.
May be confused with: See Bridled Tern. Black Tern is much smaller than Sooty and black of underparts includes lower belly. Noddies have a light crown and uniformly dark underparts, including vent and undertail. Noddy tail is wedge-shaped, not forked.
Range/distribution: Widespread throughout the Tropics excluding the eastern Atlantic. In northern Atlantic, breeds in the Caribbean and southern Florida with isolated breeding attempts as far north as Hatteras, North Carolina. Nonbreeding birds commonly follow the Gulf Stream to the Carolinas and are occasionally blown by hurricanes as far north as Maritime Canada. The majority of young birds congregate in the Gulf of Mexico and drift southeast to winter in Tropical waters off southwest Africa.

NODDY TERNS (Genus *Anous*)

Uniformly dark terns with a pale cap and wedge-shaped tail. Tropical and pelagic.

73. BROWN NODDY (*Anous stolidus*)
Plate 22.
Identification: L. 17 in (43 cm); W. 33 in (84 cm). Crown grayish white. At close range, white crown is separated from bill by dark line. Entire remaining plumage medium to dark brown. Tail long and wedge-shaped. Young birds show a rather indistinct pale crown.
Flight behavior: Flight strong and direct with steady wingbeats.
May be confused with: Rarer Black Noddy is smaller with proportionately thinner bill and more boldly contrasting white cap. However, nonadult

Black Noddies in worn plumage may appear notably paler brown. Immature Sooty Tern is dark on crown and has white lower belly.

Range/distribution: Widespread throughout the Tropics. In the northern Atlantic, usually restricted to the Caribbean, Gulf Stream off Florida, and Dry Tortugas west of Florida Keys.

74. **BLACK NODDY** (*Anous minutus*)
(also White-capped Noddy)
Plate 22.
Identification: L. 13 in (34 cm); W. 30 in (76 cm). Crown white, extending to bill. In fresh plumage, entire remaining plumage uniformly brownish black. In worn or faded plumage, birds may appear distinctly paler brown to grayish brown. Tail long and wedge-shaped.
Flight behavior: More buoyant and fluttery than Brown Noddy.
May be confused with: Brown Noddy is larger-bodied and thicker-billed. Bill lengths of the two species are similar, but skinnier bill of Black Noddy may *appear* a bit longer. Pale crown of Brown Noddy is less sharply defined, duller, and separated from the bill by a dark line visible at close range. Brown Noddy is slightly browner and paler, but plumage coloration should not serve as the sole identification criteria.
Range/distribution: Breeds in the Tropical Atlantic and Pacific. In the northern Atlantic, known only from handful of nonbreeding birds that appear annually with the Brown Noddy colonies at the Dry Tortugas west of Florida Keys.

Family ALCIDAE (Alcids): Small to medium-size chunky seabirds that superficially resemble penguins, except all living alcid species can fly. (The common opinion that alcids are ecological counterparts of penguins is incorrect. Their true Southern Hemisphere counterparts are the diving petrels.) Most have sharply pointed bills, but a few, particularly the puffins, have broad, ornately colored bills during the breeding season and molt the outer sheath afterward, thereby reducing the size and intensity of color for the fall and winter. Restricted to the Northern Hemisphere, there are 23 species worldwide (plus a recently extinct one), of which 6 breed in the northern Atlantic and 2 more have occurred as vagrants.

75. **DOVEKIE**[NA] **OR LITTLE AUK**[E] (*Alle alle*)
Plate 23.
Identification: L. 9 in (22 cm); W. 13 in (32 cm).
Alternate (summer). Head and upperparts blackish. Underparts white with

sharp demarcation between black throat and white chest. Overall shape of a small, chunky bird with imperceptible bill.

Basic (winter). Crown black. Cheek and throat white, extending upward on the sides of the neck to create a partial capped appearance. Upperparts dark, underparts pure white. Younger birds are dingier than basic-plumaged adults.

Flight behavior: Rapid whirring of wings that seem undersized for the bird.

May be confused with: Razorbill and murres are larger with obvious bills and "slower," more duck-like wingbeats.

Range/distribution: Breeds in the high Arctic, mostly Greenland and Iceland. Winters at sea in shallow to deep offshore waters south through the middle Atlantic states in the west and southern England in the east.

76. **RAZORBILL** (*Alca torda*)
   Plate 24.
   Identification: L. 17 in (42 cm); W. 25 in (64 cm).

   Adult alternate (summer). Head black. Bill broad, squarish, and black with distinct vertical white subterminal line and horizontal white line from top of bill to eye. Upperparts uniformly black. Throat black, contrasting sharply with white underparts. Underwings linings bright white.

   Adult basic (winter). Crown black, separated from back by white partial neck collar. Bill duller than alternate-plumaged adult but otherwise with recognizable white line to eye. Black back may be tinged with brown. Chin, face, underparts, and underwing linings white.

   Juvenile. Similar to adult basic but with a more slender bill and duller upperparts.

   Flight behavior: Flight low and direct on rapid, almost duck-like wingbeats.

   May be confused with: Murres have a longer, less "bull-necked" head and neck profile. Of the two murres, Thick-billed is more like Razorbill, with black plumage and white line on side of bill. In summer, Thick-billed has a dagger-like bill that is quite different from the bill of Razorbill. In winter, Thick-billed has a more extensively dark neck and dusky underwings; Razorbill has white underwings. When swimming, the longer tail of Razorbill is carried higher out of the water than that of murres, but given a lone bird, this is subjective.

   Range/distribution: Breeds in the northern Atlantic from Maritime Canada and northern New England to southern Greenland, Iceland, Britain, Scandinavia. Winters at sea south to the middle Atlantic states and northwestern Africa, most commonly in nearshore waters.

77. **THICK-BILLED MURRE**[NA] **OR BRUNNICH'S GUILLEMOT**[E]
(*Uria lomvia*)
Plate 24.
Identification: L. 18 in (46 cm); W. 30 in (76 cm).
Alternate (summer). Head and neck black. Bill stout, sharply pointed, and black with white stripe between base of bill and eye. Upperparts black, continuous with neck. Chest and underparts gleaming white with sharp line of demarcation. Underwing linings grayish.
Basic (winter). As alternate plumage except for chin, throat, and underside of neck white. Bill as summer but with less distinct white bill stripe.
Flight behavior: Direct flight on rapid wingbeats.
May be confused with: Common Murre is more slender-necked whereas Thick-billed is more "bull-necked." Alternate-plumaged Common is distinctly browner and paler on head and neck. In winter, Common has far more white behind the eye, with a distinct black line bisecting white area behind the eye. Razorbill has broader bill shape, is even more "bull-necked," and has bright white underwing linings.
Range/distribution: Widespread breeding throughout coastal Palearctic. Winters at sea, generally in shallow to deep offshore waters. In the northern Atlantic, breeds in Canada, Greenland, Iceland, northern Norway. Winters south to the middle Atlantic states and southern Norway.

78. **COMMON MURRE**[NA] **OR GUILLEMOT**[E] (*Uria aalge*)
Plate 24.
Identification: L. 17 in (43 cm); W. 28 in (71 cm).
Alternate (summer). Head and neck blackish brown. Bill black and sharply pointed. Some birds, particularly in more northern populations, have bold white eyering with white line bisecting area behind eye. Upperparts dark brown, generally a little browner than the head and neck. Chest and underparts gleaming white with sharp line of demarcation. Underwing linings white.
Basic (winter). Differs from alternate plumage by broad area of white from chin to behind eye. A dark comma-shaped line extends from eye to side of neck, bisecting the white cheek.
Flight behavior: Flight direct with rapid wingbeats.
May be confused with: Alternate-plumaged Thick-billed Murre is blacker-backed and more "bull-necked." At close range, the white bill stripe is diagnostic. In winter, Thick-billed has less white on sides of head and neck and lacks dark bisecting line. Razorbill is larger and stockier, blacker overall, and broader-billed.

Range/distribution: Widespread breeding throughout coastal Palearctic. Winters at sea. In the northern Atlantic, breeds in Canada, Greenland, Iceland, northern Norway. Winters south to New England and Portugal. Compared with Thick-billed Murre, southernmost limit of Common Murre's winter range is more northerly in North America and more southerly in Europe.

79. BLACK GUILLEMOT (*Cepphus grylle*)
Plate 23.
Identification: L. 13 in (33 cm); W. 23 in (58 cm).
Alternate (summer). Plumage entirely black except for large white oval patches on upperwings and white underwing linings. Bright red legs and feet.
Basic (winter). Drastically different from alternate plumage. Head and neck pale, mottled gray and white. Upperparts darker, barred gray and white. Adults are whiter-bodied than immatures and retain characteristic white oval wing patch; juvenile-plumaged birds have less distinct wing patch with dark barring. Underparts white.
Flight behavior: Rapid direct flight. When landing, flares bright red legs and feet at last minute before touching water.
May be confused with: Alternate plumage is unmistakable. Molting birds may have blackish back and white underparts, creating possible confusion with murres. However, the latter are clean; molting guillemots are heavily mottled and would always show the characteristic white wing patch.
Range/distribution: Breeds mostly in the northern Atlantic from Maine and Canada to Greenland, Iceland, Britain, Scandinavia. Winters at sea in vicinity of breeding grounds south to Massachusetts and southern Britain.

80. ANCIENT MURRELET (*Synthliboramphus antiquus*)
Plate 23.
Identification: L. 10 in (25 cm); W. ?
Basic (winter). Crown and face black. Bill stubby and pale. Sides of neck white. Back gray, contrasting with blackish nape and dark upperwings. Chin dark, underwings and body white.
Flight behavior: Typical small alcid.
May be confused with: Basic-plumaged Dovekie has black bill and back. Ancient Murrelet is thus far the only small alcid recorded in the northern Atlantic with white underwings.
Range/distribution: A Pacific species that very rarely occurs along Atlantic coast of North America and Britain, but with fewer than a half-dozen records collectively.

81. **LONG-BILLED MURRELET** (*Brachyramphus perdix*)
Plate 23.
Identification: L. 11 in (28 cm); W. ?
Alternate (summer). Crown dark grayish brown. Bill elongated and sharply pointed. Upperparts same color as head with pale scapular bar. Throat mottled grayish brown and white. Underparts ashy grayish brown with pale scalloping along flanks.
Basic (winter). Crown and nape blackish, contrasting sharply with white of throat and sides of neck. The transition is uniform, lacking a white collar. Upperparts blackish with bold white scapular bar. Underwings dark, underbody white.
Flight behavior: Rapid, direct flight on whirring wings.
May be confused with: Dovekie has a stubby bill and partial white collar and lacks the white scapular bar. Thick-billed Murre is much larger. Closely related to Marbled Murrelet (*B. marmoratus*) of North American Pacific Coast, but that species is unrecorded from the Atlantic.
Range/distribution: Breeds in northern Japan and coastal Siberia. Extremely rare vagrant to North America with a half-dozen records from Newfoundland to Gulf Coast of Florida. Most but not all birds were in winter plumage.

82. **ATLANTIC PUFFIN** (*Fratercula arctica*)
Plate 23.
Identification: L. 11 in (29 cm); W. 22 in (56 cm).
Adult alternate (summer). Unmistakable. Crown, neck, and throat black, surrounding large, spade-shaped, pale gray face. Bill broad and triangular-shaped, brightly colored with concentric areas of red, then yellow, then blue-gray, then yellow. Upperparts black, underparts white.
Adult basic (winter). As adult alternate but with bill greatly reduced in size and color. Face slightly duskier.
Juvenile. Similar to basic adult but with somewhat smaller, mostly dark bill and even duskier face.
Flight behavior: Rapid direct flight typical of large alcids.
May be confused with: Juvenile- and basic-plumaged puffins. Razorbill has white cheek and foreneck outlined by dark crown and hindneck. Puffin has a gray cheek and throat completely surrounded by dark crown, hindneck, and foreneck collar. Common Murre and Thick-billed Murre have much slimmer heads, necks, and bills.
Range/distribution: Breeds in Maine, Maritime Canada, Greenland, Iceland, Britain, Norway, and farther north into the Barents Sea. Winters at sea south to the middle Atlantic states and northernmost Africa. During winter, seemingly prefers deeper offshore waters.

CETACEANS (Whales and Dolphins)

Unique group of marine mammals that epitomize the pelagic life. Sometimes mistaken as relatives of sharks and fish, they are not. Cetaceans are highly intelligent air-breathing mammals that give live birth and suckle their young on milk. Some species grow to gargantuan size; the Blue Whale is the largest animal to have ever lived on earth. Other species are rather small. Regardless of size, all cetaceans uniquely share a nostril, or blowhole, on the top of the head. It is through this breathing orifice that forceful exhalations create the "blow," which may resemble a sudden blast of steam. Many species, particularly the larger ones, may be identified by the angle and shape of the blow. Most species have a single dorsal fin; a few have none. The presence, shape, and relative placement of the dorsal fin is often the key to identification. All have paired pectoral fins used for steering and a horizontally oriented tail fin (flukes) used for propulsion. The tail fins of sharks and fish are vertically, not horizontally, oriented.

TOPOGRAPHY OF A WHALE

1. Rostrum	**10.** Blowhole	**Dorsal Fin Shapes**
2. Rostral Ridges	**11.** Head	
3. Back	**12.** Callosite	**19.** Pointed
4. Dorsal Fin	**13.** Upper Jaw	**20.** Rounded
5. Tail Stock	**14.** Baleen	**21.** Dorsal Hump
6. Flukes	**15.** Lower Jaw	**22.** Erect
7. Pectoral Fin	**16.** Melon	**23.** Triangular
8. Throat Pleats	**17.** Beak	**24.** Falcate
9. Eye	**18.** Jaw Line	**25.** Hooked

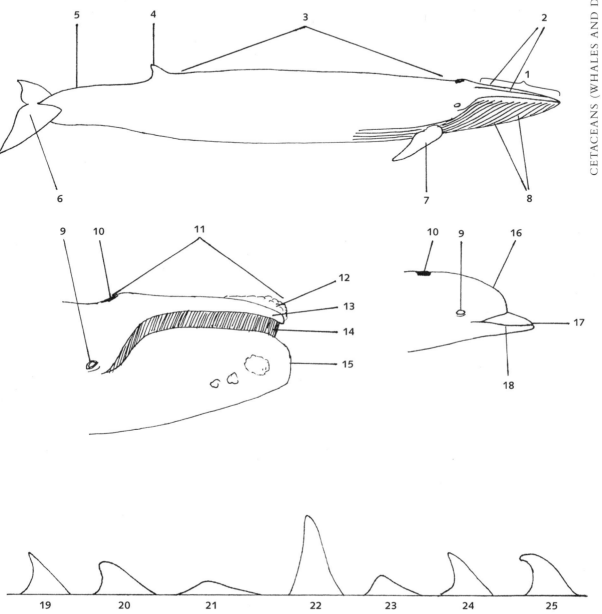

Suborder MYSTICETI (Baleen Whales): Medium to extremely large whales with paired blowholes and baleen plates suspended from the upper jaw. These plates, made of fingernail-like material, strain food from the water as the animals eat. Feeding behavior at the surface is distinctive and may help with identification.

Family BALAENOPTERIDAE (Rorqual Whales): Medium to extremely large, sleek whales with a prominent dorsal fin set well behind the midback. The family is defined by the presence of multiple elongated pleats in the skin from the tip of the lower jaw to the belly. These pleats allow the throat to expand greatly when the animals feed. Blows are vertical, usually quite prominent and columnar to bushy. Some species raise their flukes preceding deep dives.

83. **BLUE WHALE** (*Balaenoptera musculus*)
    Plates 25, 26.
    Identification: L. 70–90 ft (22–28 m); Wt. 90–120 tons. Massive but streamlined blue-gray whale with broad, U-shaped head when viewed from above. The small dorsal fin is set well behind the center of the back. The body is marked with a profusion of off-white "freckles."
    Surfacing behavior: Blow/roll sequence begins with the head plowing the water ahead of it, followed by a columnar blow about 30 feet (10 m) tall. The paired blowholes, when open, are flanked by prominent ridges that merge anteriorly into a prominent central ridge that extends to the tip of the rostrum. After the blow, the head is thrust down and the back rolls forward for a considerable time before the dorsal fin becomes visible. The tail stock is often arched prior to diving, particularly on deep dives when the massive tail flukes may be raised high out of the water. The flukes are triangular-shaped with a nearly straight trailing edge. Blue Whales feed by lunge-feeding. They begin by swimming rapidly on their sides, rising to the surface, open-mouthed until the sides of their jaws rise well above water surface. They then close their mouths, expel the water, right themselves, submerge, then resurface to blow and roll.
    May be confused with: Fin Whale, the only species to approach an adult Blue in size, is brownish black and has a much taller dorsal fin. The asymmetrical head pattern of Fin is diagnostic. Sei and Bryde's Whales are smaller, with proportionately taller dorsal fins, and are dark gray without any freckling. Although their blow does proceed the emergence of the dorsal fin, there is minimal time lag between the two events. Sperm and Humpback have very different blows, are dark brown to black, and have fleshy dorsal humps rather than distinct fins. Right and Bowhead are black and lack a dorsal fin.

Range/distribution: Worldwide Cold Temperate to Subarctic waters. In the northern Atlantic, most common in continental shelf waters from Greenland and the North Sea to southern Canada, particularly the Gulf of St. Lawrence, Quebec, where their "inland" penetration may be considerable. They are rare in waters south of New England as well as western Europe and Africa.

84.   FIN WHALE (*Balaenoptera physalus*)
Plates 25, 26.
Identification: L. 55−75 ft (17−23 m); Wt. 45−75 tons. Large to extremely large, streamlined brownish black whale. *The asymmetrically colored lower jaw—black on the left side, white on the right—is diagnostic.* The head, when viewed from above, is a slightly rounded V shape. The neck and upper back regions are usually marked by alternating dark and light chevrons. The prominent dorsal fin is placed well behind the center of the back.
Surfacing behavior: The rostrum barely breaks the water surface before the blow, which is tall and columnar. The paired blowholes are flanked by prominent ridges that merge into a central ridge that does not reach the end of the rostrum. The dorsal fin appears after the blow but may show before the blowholes submerge. The roll is often rather low to the water. Fin Whales do not raise their flukes before diving. They lunge-feed similarly to Blue Whales.
May be confused with: The white right-side lower jaw is unique. Otherwise, Blue Whale is larger and blue-gray colored with off-white freckles. Sei and Bryde's roll differently, are paler-bodied, and have head ridges that reach the tip of the rostrum. In addition, Bryde's has three head ridges rather than one. Humpback and Sperm have dorsal humps rather than sharply defined dorsal fins. Right and Bowhead lack dorsal fins.
Range/distribution: Worldwide distribution from Subarctic to Warm Temperate waters. In the northern Atlantic, Fin Whales are relatively common in coastal and shelf waters from the middle Atlantic states to Greenland and in the North Sea. They are uncommon to rare off western Europe.

85.   SEI WHALE (*Balaenoptera borealis*)
Plates 25, 26.
Identification: L. 40−50 ft (12.5−15.5 m); Wt. 20−25 tons. Large, dark gray, streamlined whale. When viewed from above, the head is narrow and V-shaped with a single median ridge extending from the blow to the tip of the rostrum. In addition, the rostrum, viewed from the side, is noticeably curved downward from blowhole to tip. The back is mottled, giving a somewhat silvery or galvanized appearance. The dorsal fin is tall, falcate, and placed well behind the center of the back.

Surfacing behavior: The blow precedes the appearance of the dorsal fin, but the blowholes remain above the surface as the dorsal fin becomes visible. The blow is tall and expands upward in an inverted cone shape. Following the blow, the head is thrust down at a steep angle and the back arches well out of the water. The result is an asymmetrical roll profile. Flukes do not show. Sei Whales lunge-feed (see Blue Whale description).

May be confused with: Bryde's and Sei Whales are nearly identical in size, coloration, and behavior. Four features best distinguish them:

1. Head ridges. Sei has a single ridge, Bryde's usually (but not always) shows three.

2. Preferred water temperature. Sei tends to inhabit Cold Temperate and Subarctic waters while Bryde's inhabits Tropical to Subtropical waters.

3. Blow pattern. The blow of a Sei is a bushy column whereas Bryde's has two "branches" that emanate laterally from the sides of and flank the main blow.

4. Dorsal fins. Sei tends to have a slightly taller and rather erect dorsal fin whereas Bryde's has a falcate to hooked dorsal.

Experienced observers will also note the slightly paler back of Sei. Fin Whale is larger, blacker overall, and has a distinctive white right-side lower jaw. Sperm and Humpback are similar in size but have very different back and dorsal fin profiles and lack ridges on the top of the head.

Range/distribution: Uncommon in offshore waters in Subarctic waters from Newfoundland to Greenland and the North Sea. Rare in Cold Temperate and near offshore waters.

86. BRYDE'S WHALE (*Balaenoptera edeni*)
Plates 25, 26.
Identification: L. 35–45 ft (10–14 m); Wt. 18–23 tons. Pronounced "BREW-as." Virtually identical to Sei Whale except for the presence of typically three (rather than one) prominent ridges on the top of the head. By direct comparison, or with experience, Bryde's is a little sleeker and darker and has shorter, more falcate dorsal fin than Sei. Bryde's prefers warmer waters than Sei, so location may serve as a guide to identification. The blow of a Bryde's may be diagnostic if seen well. Rather than a single bushy column, the blow is flanked laterally by two side "bushes."
Surfacing behavior: See Sei Whale.
May be confused with: See discussion under Sei Whale.
Range/distribution: Uncommon in Subtropical and Tropical waters world-wide. In northern Atlantic, most common south of 30°. The most common large whale in the Gulf of Mexico.

87. **MINKE WHALE** (*Balaenoptera acutorostrata*)
Plates 25, 28.
Identification: L. 20−30 ft (6−9 m); Wt. 8−10 tons. A small, sleek whale that resembles a miniature Fin Whale. When viewed from above, the head is a sharply pointed V shape. An indistinct central ridge runs from the paired blowholes to the tip of the rostrum, but due to the narrowness of the head, it results in a somewhat diamond-shaped cross section. If visible, the *pectoral fins have bold white patches* or bands—a definitive mark. The back and sides are dark olive black with a pale gray blaze extending upward from behind the pectoral fin. The dorsal fin is tall, falcate, and placed well back.
Surfacing behavior: Blow/roll sequence begins with the tip of the rostrum emerging from the water at a sharp angle. Immediately following is the blow and appearance of the dorsal fin. The blow is short, bushy, and sometimes rather indistinct. As soon as the blow is complete, the head is thrust downward and the back rolls low to the water. Flukes are not shown. Feeds by upright lunge-feeding, which may include porpoising.
May be confused with: Pilot Whales and their relatives are similar in size but stockier and their dorsal fins are broadly rounded and longer (front to back). Young Fin, Sei, Blue, Bryde's, and Humpback Whales may look deceptively similar, but they lack the distinctly pointed head, and the blow/roll sequence will more closely resemble that of the adults.
Range/distribution: Worldwide but with three distinct populations, likely different species—one from the Northern Hemisphere, one from Antarctic and Subantarctic waters, and one from Australian waters. In the northern Atlantic, fairly common from Newfoundland, Greenland, and the North Sea south to New England and Britain, regularly in nearshore waters, but not limited there. Uncommon to rare in Warm Temperate to Tropical waters.

88. **HUMPBACK WHALE** (*Megaptera novaeangliae*)
Plates 25, 26, 27, 28.
Identification: L. 38−48 ft (12−15 m); Wt. 25−30 tons. Robust blackish whale with head uniquely covered by rows of raised tubercles. The wing-like flippers, a third of the body length, are largely white. Flukes are distinctive with an irregular trailing edge and the underside so uniquely patterned white and black as to allow researchers to identify individuals.
Surfacing behavior: Blow/roll sequence begins with the head emerging from the water about the same time as the blow. The head is broad and rounded but is generally kept close to the water. The blow is bushy, sometimes taking on a V shape. Following the blow, the head is thrust downward and the back rises high out of the water, becoming progressively arched as the dorsal fin appears. The dorsal fin is variable in shape but typically appears as an

irregular triangular hump. On shallow dives where the flukes are not raised, the dorsal fin is the last part to sink below the water. On deep dives, Humpbacks usually raise their flukes. Most, if not all, species of whales breach (leap out of the water), but Humpbacks are famous for this behavior. These spectacular displays involve the animal bursting forth, often fully clearing the water to the flukes, rotating a quarter-turn in the air, and falling back with a thunderous splash that displaces water equivalent to their full weight. When feeding, Humpbacks often blow circular or oval patterns of bubbles, then surface open-mouthed in the center of the pattern, then remain motionless with the upper jaw above the water. After straining the water, they roll forward, blow, and submerge.

May be confused with: Fin, Sei, and Bryde's Whales are more streamlined with taller, distinctly falcate dorsal fins; they do not arch their backs high out of the water or show flukes. Sperm Whale has a blow that angles sharply to the left, is brown instead of black, and has very different fluke shape and coloration. Young Humpbacks are distinguished from Minke and the larger-beaked whales by their more prominent blow, the knobs on the head, and the irregular, hump-like dorsal fin.

Range/distribution: Highly migratory with worldwide distribution. In the northern Atlantic, summers in cold coastal and shelf waters from New England to Greenland and the North Sea in five distinct areas: Gulf of Maine, Gulf of St. Lawrence, Newfoundland-Labrador, southwestern Greenland, and the Denmark Strait off Iceland. In winter these populations migrate south with distinct segregation. Adults congregating in the western Tropics to breed and calve from January through March. Immature males congregate in coastal waters of the middle Atlantic states. The species is uncommon elsewhere, although in Bermuda and the eastern Atlantic, is most likely seen during migration. It is virtually unknown from the Gulf of Mexico.

Family BALAENIDAE (Right Whales): Extremely robust black whales lacking both dorsal fin and throat pleats. The lower jaw is strongly arched and substantially larger than the upper jaw. Blows are distinctively V-shaped.

89. **NORTHERN RIGHT WHALE** (*Eubalaena glacialis*)
   Plates 25, 27.
   Identification: L. 35–50 ft (11–15.5 m); Wt. 40–50 tons. Large, thickset, brownish black whale with *prominent tan to cream white encrustations (callosites)* on the end of the jaws and top of the head. The back is completely smooth with no dorsal fin, although some animals may show crenellations ("knuckles") on the tail stock. The flukes are elongated and symmetrically triangular with a smooth trailing edge.

Surfacing behavior: Blow/roll sequence begins with the upper jaw emerging from the water, followed by a bushy blow that splits into a distinctive V shape. After the blow, the head is thrust downward with the broad back rolling well out of the water. Flukes may be raised high out of the water preceding deep dives. When feeding, swims slowly with mouth open and with only the tip of the rostrum and callosites showing, then, closing the lower jaw upward, brings the head out of the water to strain the water and food.

May be confused with: Bowhead is very similar but lacks the callosites, has a white chin and nonoverlapping range. Fin and Sei are sleeker, have columnar blows and prominent dorsal fins. Humpback may show a slightly V-shaped blow but dorsal fin is prominent and flukes have an irregular trailing edge. Sperm Whale prefers much deeper waters, has a blow that projects sharply to the left, and has a fleshy hump on the back.

Range/distribution: Formerly worldwide, now quite rare. In the northern Atlantic, rare to locally uncommon in coastal and shelf waters of North America; extremely rare in eastern Atlantic. Most commonly seen in Gulf of Maine during summer and occasionally in migration or winter along the coast, south to Florida and the southern Gulf of Mexico. Most frequently observed in coastal and nearshore waters.

90. **BOWHEAD WHALE** (*Balaena mysticetus*)
    Plate 27.
    Identification: L. 45−65 ft (14−20 m); Wt. 45−60 tons. Large thickset black whale with massive dome-shaped head that peaks at position of blowhole, then drops noticeably to the back, which is smooth and lacks a dorsal fin. The chin is largely white.
    Surfacing behavior: Similar to Northern Right Whale.
    May be confused with: Northern Right Whale is slightly smaller and has callosites, which Bowhead lacks. For other comparisons, see Northern Right Whale.
    Range/distribution: Formerly far more common than now. Largest extant populations are from Alaska and western Arctic Canada. In the northern Atlantic, uncommon to rare from northern Labrador, Greenland, and the waters north of Iceland, including Spitzbergen.

Suborder ODONTOCETI (Toothed Whales): Small to large whales with teeth in the lower jaw or both upper and lower jaws. Single blowhole and rounded melon on the head.

Family PHYSETERIDAE (Sperm Whales): Small to large whales with squared heads and teeth restricted to the lower jaw.

91. **SPERM WHALE** (*Physeter macrocephalus*)
Plates 25, 27.
Identification: L. 35–60 ft (11–18.5 m); Wt. 20–50 tons. Males are substantially larger than females. Dark brown to grayish with massive squared head and narrow underslung jaw. Head may include nearly a third of the body length. Back is distinctly wrinkled. Dorsal fin is reduced to a rounded, fleshy hump. Larger animals, particularly adult males, have a distinct flat indentation behind the head.
Surfacing behavior: Blow/roll sequence begins with the head surfacing, followed by the blow. The short bushy blow projecting at an acute angle to the left is diagnostic. By the time the blow is complete, the entire back, including the dorsal hump, may be above the surface. Sperm Whales often remain surfaced for several blows without submerging again. Deep dives may be preceded by raised flukes. The flukes are broad and distinctly rounded along the trailing edge.
May be confused with: No other large whale has a left-projecting blow. Some Humpbacks have a dorsal hump similar to Sperm Whale's but lack the wrinkled skin. All other large whales either have a prominent dorsal fin or lack one altogether.
Range/distribution: Widespread, worldwide distribution from Tropical to Subarctic waters. Tends to occur in deep offshore waters along the outer edge of the continental shelf. In the northern Atlantic, uncommon throughout range.

92. **PYGMY SPERM WHALE** (*Kogia breviceps*)
Plates 31, 33.
Identification: L. 9–12 ft (3–4 m); Wt. to 900 lbs (400 kg). Small but stocky, slow-moving whale. Head square with small underslung jaw. Upperparts brownish black. Pale crescent between eye and pectoral fin looks very much like a gill slit. Dorsal fin small and generally hooked.
Surfacing behavior: Rises slowly to the surface to blow. Blow very indistinct and directed slightly to the left. Following blow, sometimes remains on the surface, swimming slowly, resembling a floating log. When startled, may defecate before diving. Also rolls porpoise-like.
May be confused with: Nearly identical Dwarf Sperm Whale is smaller with much larger dorsal fin (about twice as large). Harbor Porpoise is smaller without a distinct dorsal fin.
Range/distribution: Worldwide but rarely seen. In the northern Atlantic,

most common off southeastern United States and Gulf of Mexico, fewer records north to Maritime Canada. In eastern range, has occurred from southern England to Senegal.

93. **DWARF SPERM WHALE** (*Kogia simus*)
Plates 31, 33.
Identification: L. 7–9 ft (2–3 m); Wt. 300–600 lbs. (400 kg). Small but stocky, slow-moving whale. Head square with small underslung jaw. Upperparts brownish black. Pale crescent between eye and pectoral fin looks very much like a gill slit. Dorsal fin tall and broad-based.
Surfacing behavior: As Pygmy Sperm Whale.
May be confused with: See Pygmy Sperm Whale.
Range/distribution: Worldwide but rarely seen. Most common off Southern Africa. In the northern Atlantic, known range restricted to Tropical and Warm Temperate waters of North America.

Family ZIPHIIDAE (Beaked and Bottlenosed Whales): Small to medium-size whales with distinctive dolphin-like beak and head. Most are extremely rare and very poorly known. Males usually show profuse scarring, particularly around the head and back. Usually seen singly or in small family groups. Superficially dolphin-like in appearance but not in behavior.

94. **CUVIER'S OR BEAKED WHALE** (*Ziphius cavirostris*)
(also Goose-beaked Whale)
Plates 28, 29, 30.
Identification: L. 18–23 ft (5.5–7 m); Wt. 3–5 tons. Distinctly brownish-colored whale with torpedo-shaped head and robust body with small pointed beak and rounded forehead. When seen in profile, the head shape is diagnostic. Broad, falcate to nearly triangular dorsal fin placed far behind the center of the back. Exhibits strong sexual dimorphism.
Adult male. Head and upper back cream white to white with profusion of scarring. Lower jaw with two teeth that erupt from the tip of the jaw. From midback to tail, gray-brown to brown. Generally much larger than females and sometimes a far more active swimmer.
Female and immature. Uniformly brownish gray to dark grayish brown, with paler grayish head, occasionally marked with white spots and blotches. Many animals show a pale collar behind the blowhole.
Surfacing behavior: The point of the beak is the first to emerge, followed by the broadly rounded head. The blow is low, bushy, and often indistinct. It occurs after the head is clear of the water, but long before the dorsal fin is visible. The head is then thrust down and the back rolls rather rounded,

bringing the dorsal fin into view. The dorsal fin then rolls forward and is the last to disappear. Flukes are not shown. Dives may last 20 to 30 minutes.

May be confused with: Bottlenose Whale is larger with distinctly gray coloration, not brown. The forehead is more squared and the sharply defined beak is not lifted above the water surface.

Range/distribution: This is the most widespread and commonly seen ziphiid from Tropical to Cold Temperate waters. In the northern Atlantic, occurs from the North Sea and southernmost Canada south throughout the range. Most likely to be seen in deep water along the edge of the continental shelf or over canyons.

95. NORTHERN BOTTLENOSE WHALE (*Hyperoodon ampullatus*) **Plates 28, 29.**

Identification: L. 26–32 ft (8–9.8 m); Wt. ? Head square, forming sharp demarcation with small, slightly upturned beak. Males more blocky-headed than females. Medium gray to buff color, becoming generally paler with age. Head often demarcated from body by a pale collar that passes through the blowhole. Dorsal fin tall, falcate, and placed far behind the center of the back. Often occurs in small pods that may approach and investigate boats.

Surfacing behavior: Forehead emerges from the water to level of beak, which is generally *not* raised. As soon as the top of the head emerges, the blow occurs. It is bushy, projects slightly forward, and may be indistinct. After the blow, the head and back continue to rise from the water until the dorsal fin is exposed. The head is then turned downward, bringing the dorsal fin forward. On deep dives, flukes may be raised. They are smooth across the trailing edge with no central notch.

May be confused with: Sperm Whale has a square forehead but is much larger, with a wrinkled back and a very different blow. Cuvier's is smaller and browner, with a rounded forehead. Minke is similar in size but does not show a blunt forehead on surfacing and the blowhole is surrounded by a ridge rather than an indentation.

Range/distribution: Restricted to deep cold waters of the northern Atlantic from northern New England and northern Spain north to above the Arctic Circle, including the English Channel. Fairly common all year from "the Gully," near Sable Island, Nova Scotia. Also in the Labrador Sea, Davis Straits, around Iceland, and the Denmark Strait. In western range, occasionally wanders south to New England. In eastern range, migrates to southern Europe, reaching the Faeroes by early March, Iceland during late April through early June; then returns in late July, past the Faeroes in August and September, Britain and Europe in September and October.

Genus *Mesoplodon:* This is the world's rarest and poorest-known group of whales (if not mammals) and requires the utmost caution for identification. Indeed, world authorities cannot always identify them, even with photos. Although some helpful coloration differences may exist, accurate species identification should require that the head and beak profile are clearly seen. Fortunately, with a little patience, one may have an opportunity to observe them repeatedly. Although they are deep divers, they tend to swim slowly and generally stay submerged for only about 15 minutes. By drifting along their last surface path and waiting, one may be able to predict their next appearance.

96. **TRUE'S BEAKED WHALE** (*Mesoplodon mirus*)
Plates 29, 30.
Identification: L. 15–16 ft (5 m); Wt. 1.5 tons. Light brownish gray whale with distinct dolphin-like head and beak. The melon is very rounded. Head length from indentation at blowhole to base of rostrum is longer than length of rostrum. The jawline is relatively straight and may be highlighted with black jaw line. Adult males have one pair of teeth at the tip of the rostrum. At close range, there is a rounded black eye-patch and a slightly darker collar located just behind the blowhole. The back may show a contrastingly dark dorsal blaze from blowhole to dorsal fin. Small, falcate, triangular fin is set well behind midback and usually is *contrastingly dark* with the much lighter back.
Surfacing behavior: Before the blow, rostrum and top of melon emerge from water at acute angle, followed by much of the head. Blow is very indistinct. The head is then rolled forward and downward, disappearing as the dorsal fin emerges from the water. Dorsal fin is the last part to submerge. Flukes are not shown.
May be confused with: Sowerby's has a much longer beak and proportionately smaller melon. Gervais' has a slightly smaller melon and proportionately narrower beak but is generally a rather darkly colored species, lacking the contrastingly dark eye and dorsal fin of True's. Blainville's has a strongly arched lower jaw, which is particularly evident in males. Gervais', Sowerby's, and Blainville's males have tooth placement on the sides of the jaw; True's has teeth at the tip.
Range/distribution: Considered extraordinarily rare. First documented live sighting was by the author in May 1993 off Cape Hatteras, North Carolina, near the location of its discovery in 1912. Subsequently known from a handful of sightings and fewer than three dozen beached animals worldwide. However, as with all Mesoplodonts, their apparent rarity may be

more an artifact of inadequate observation than actual scarcity. Most likely to be encountered in very deep Temperate waters of the northern Atlantic.

97. GERVAIS' BEAKED WHALE (*Mesoplodon europaeus*)
(also Gulf Stream Beaked Whale)
Plates 29, 30.

Identification: L. 15−17 ft (4−5.5 m); Wt. 2−2.5 tons. Proportionately small-headed and robust-bodied whale with generally dark grayish brown back and sides and lighter belly. Animals may appear uniformly dark or with a lower jaw that is noticeably paler than the upper. Back and dorsal fin are dark brownish gray to blackish without strong contrast.

Surfacing behavior: Head and entire rostrum emerge from the water, followed by the blow. Afterward the head is thrust downward, bringing the back and dorsal fin into view. Fin is the last to submerge. Flukes are not raised.

May be confused with: True's is lighter-colored on the head with a distinct, rounded, black eye-patch. However, *most* mesoplodonts can have a dark eye-patch as young animals, but the shape and presence in adults may be significant. When present, the eye-patch of Gervais' is elongated and somewhat continuous with the jawline. True's has a prominent, rounded eye-patch that is not continuous with the jawline. Sowerby's has a very long rostrum with a smaller melon and is paler overall. Blainville's has a strong arched jaw, is browner, and females may be heavily blotched with white.

Range/distribution: Very rare throughout most of range. Known only from the Atlantic. Although the first known specimen was found floating in the English Channel, the main distribution is likely Tropical. Center of distribution may be around the Bahamas where it is seen occasionally in deep water.

98. SOWERBY'S BEAKED WHALE (*Mesoplodon bidens*)
(also North Sea Beaked Whale)
Plates 29, 30.

Identification: L. 13−15 ft (4−5 m); Wt. ca. 1 ton. Slender brownish gray whale with small melon and very long, sometimes pencil-like rostrum. Jawline is slightly arched only at the rear of the jaw. The dorsal fin is slightly darker than the upper back. Some animals show a paler area behind the blowhole.

Surfacing behavior: Long, slender beak emerges at steep angle, followed by the melon, then the blow. After the blow, the head rolls forward to parallel with the water, then downward, bringing the dorsal fin into view. Fin is the last to submerge. Flukes are not raised.

May be confused with: True's and Gervais' have larger melons and darker backs or dorsal fins or both. Blainville's has a stronger arch to the jaw, and females tend to show a profusion of white blotches that are lacking in Sowerby's.

Range/distribution: Range appears limited to the Cold Temperate to subarctic waters of the Atlantic. The center of distribution has been reported to be the North Sea, but recent research suggests the possibility of moderate numbers in the deep offshore waters off New England.

99. BLAINVILLE'S BEAKED WHALE OR DENSE-BEAKED WHALE
(*Mesoplodon densirostris*)
Plates 29, 30.
Identification: L. 13.5−15 ft (4−5 m); Wt. 2−2.5 tons.
Adult male. Head small, rostrum narrow, with distinctive steep arch on off-white lower jaw that rises above the top of the rostrum. The top of each arch is adorned with a broad triangular tooth that is somewhat forward-facing. Teeth may be barnacle-encrusted. Body otherwise evenly brownish gray, sometimes darker on the back and dorsal fin.
Female and immature. Brownish to grayish brown above, paler below with off-white lower jaw. Arch of lower jaw prominent but does not reach top of rostrum. Melon small with prominent notch at blowhole. Head and rostrum seem to be "caved in." Often shows a pale collar located just behind the blowhole. Adult female may be marked with a profusion of white blotches. Body otherwise as adult male.

Surfacing behavior: Beak and melon emerge rapidly from the water at a moderately steep angle, sometimes followed by a downward slap of the chin. The blow occurs during this motion. As soon as the head returns to the water, it is plunged downward to start the roll. The back rolls high, bringing the dorsal fin into view. Fin is the last to show. Flukes are not raised.

May be confused with: No other Atlantic Mesoplodont (yet recorded) has the high arching jawline with big triangular teeth. Females differ from others by the arched jaw, white blotches, and lack of prominent dark eye-patch. Although unconfirmed, the chin-slap behavior may be diagnostic.

Range/distribution: Worldwide, most widespread mesoplodont, but distribution mainly Tropical to Warm Temperate. Best known from Hawaii and the Caribbean. In the northern Atlantic, most common in the Gulf of Mexico, Caribbean, and Bahamas. Possibly regular in deep offshore waters to middle Atlantic states. Has occurred to northern Canada. Rare or unknown from most of eastern Atlantic. Except in the Bahamas, where they are regularly seen in nearshore waters, most at-sea sightings are well offshore, associated with rather deep water.

Family DELPHINIDAE (Killer and Pilot Whales, Oceanic Dolphins): This is the most familiar family of cetaceans and includes a diverse array of members ranging from the tiny 4-foot-long Commerson's Dolphin to the 30-foot-long Killer Whale, whose dorsal fin may be 6 feet tall. All share the presence of conical teeth in both upper and lower jaws. Most are quite active at the water surface, frequently leaping from the water. Many are attracted to boats and may frolic along their sides or "surf" the wake off the bow or stern.

100. KILLER WHALE (*Orcinus orca*)
Plates 28, 31, 32.
Identification: L. 25–30 ft (8–9 m); Wt. 4–9 tons. Utterly distinctive. Top of head and back glossy coal black with bold white oval patch behind eye. Underparts white with broad white crescent-shaped blaze interrupting black along flanks below and posterior to position of dorsal fin. Wispy grayish white blaze immediately behind dorsal.
Adult male. Much larger than females, with astoundingly tall, erect dorsal fin that may be as much as 6 feet (2 m) high. Pectoral fins are large paddles. Flukes are held in a downward bowed arch.
Female and juvenile. Much smaller than adult males, with proportionately smaller (yet very tall) falcate dorsal fin. Pectorals paddle-shaped but smaller than males; flukes held flat.
Surfacing behavior: Travels in large groups (pods). Head breaks water at acute angle, rising out of water to level of white spot or beyond. Blow is short and bushy. With adult males, the dorsal fin emerges well before anything else, looking like a giant knife blade. With females and immatures, the dorsal fin appears at the same time as the head. As they roll forward and submerge, the dorsal fin is the last to disappear. Surface behavior may be rather acrobatic, including breaches and spyhopping (raising the head and forebody vertically out of the water to look around).
May be confused with: Pilot Whales have broad rather than tall dorsal fins and are uniformly black. False Killer Whales are smaller, uniformly black, and have much smaller dorsal fins.
Range/distribution: Worldwide distribution but patchy because several distinct populations (herds) exist. In the northern Atlantic, these populations occur from southern New England to Arctic Labrador and Greenland, from

Iceland and Norway, and from the Gulf of Mexico to the Caribbean. Widely distributed, they occur from coastal to deep offshore waters.

101. FALSE KILLER WHALE (*Pseudorca crassidens*)
Plates 31, 32.
Identification: L. 16–20 ft (5–6 m); Wt. 1–2 tons. Black torpedo-shaped whale with bluntly rounded head. Pectoral fins are small and have a distinct "kink." Dorsal fin is prominent and placed midbody.
Surfacing behavior: Travels in large groups. Fast swimmer, often porpoises clear of the water. Head emerges completely from the water, followed immediately by dorsal fin. May leap clear of the water.
May be confused with: Pilot Whales are more robust and generally far less animated. Pygmy Killer and Melon-headed Whales are half the size and have white lips; False Killer Whale has black lips.
Range/distribution: Worldwide Temperate to Tropical waters, particularly deeper waters well offshore. In the northern Atlantic, most common in warmer offshore waters of the Gulf of Mexico and Caribbean. Less common north to New England and northern United Kingdom, reaching as far north as southern Norway.

102. MELON-HEADED WHALE (*Peponocephala electra*)
Plates 31, 33.
Identification: L. 8–9 ft (2.4–2.7 m); Wt. 350–450 lb (150–200 kg). Sleek black whale with narrow white lips. The head and rostrum form a bluntly pointed oval or "football" shape. Dorsal fin, centered on back, is broad, distinctly falcate, and rounded at the tip. Pectoral fins are pointed at the tips.
Surfacing behavior: Typically occurs in large pods. Slower swimming behavior is dolphin-like, with head rising to blow, followed by roll forward, bringing the dorsal fin out of the water. When stressed or excited, highly animated with rapid swimming and porpoising with considerable splash, often in "chorus line" synchrony.
May be confused with: Pygmy Killer Whale is nearly identical but has a blunter snout, with upper jaw overhanging lower, and rounded pectoral fins. False Killer and Pilot Whales are much larger and have black lips.
Range/distribution: Worldwide but restricted to deep offshore Tropical and Subtropical waters. In the northern Atlantic, from the Gulf of Mexico and southern Florida to west central Africa.

103. PYGMY KILLER WHALE (*Feresa attenuata*)
Plates 31, 33.
Identification: L. 7–8 ft (2.1–2.4 m); Wt. 300–400 lb (140–180 kg). Sleek

black whale with narrow white lips. Head and rostrum are rounded, upper jaw overhangs lower. Falcate dorsal fin is centered on back and tall and pointed. Pectoral fins are rounded at the tips.

Surfacing behavior: Same as Melon-headed Whale.

May be confused with: See Melon-headed Whale.

Range/distribution: Worldwide in Tropical to Warm Temperate waters, generally well offshore in deep water. In the northern Atlantic, mostly from the Gulf of Mexico and northern Florida to the mouth of the Mediterranean and south.

104. LONG-FINNED PILOT WHALE (*Globicephala melas*)
Plates 31, 32.

Identification: L. 16–20 ft (5–6 m); Wt. 3–3.5 tons. Medium-size, glossy black whale with squared head and large, rather broad dorsal fin placed forward on the back. Pectoral fins have a distinct "kink" at the elbow, and the trailing portion is *at least three times* as long as the distance from the elbow to the body. Adult males are much larger than females and have a broad dorsal fin that is rounded on the leading edge and falcate to strongly hooked on the trailing edge.

Surfacing behavior: Slow moving, often in large pods. Surfaces with rounded top of head emerging from the water, followed by the blow. As the back emerges, the elongated dorsal fin (particularly in adult males) seems to unfold like a jackknife from the water. May swim on the surface for extended period after blowing.

May be confused with: Nearly identical Short-finned Pilot Whale may be distinguished with certainty only by pectoral fin proportions (visible if viewed from above at close range). Many Long-finned Pilot Whales show a pale streak behind the eye, which Short-finned lacks. Long-finned is also larger, with a longer dorsal fin, but these differences, without direct comparison, are marginal for field identification. False Killer Whale is more torpedo-shaped and has a much smaller dorsal fin placed more centrally on the back. Pygmy Killer Whale and Melon-headed Whale are half the size, and their swimming behavior is completely different.

Range/distribution: Cold Temperate to Arctic waters. In the northern Atlantic, from southern New England and southern Spain north to Greenland and the North Sea. Most common from Newfoundland to Greenland to northern United Kingdom, particularly Shetland, Orkney, and Faeroe Islands, where regularly seen in coastal waters. Southern limits of range more offshore extend farther during winter. See also discussion under Short-finned Pilot Whale.

105. SHORT-FINNED PILOT WHALE (*Globicephala macrorhynchus*)
Plates 31, 32.
Identification: L. 13–19 ft (4–5.8 m); Wt. 2.5–3.3 tons. Medium-size, glossy black whale with squared head and large, rather broad dorsal fin placed forward on the back. Pectoral fins have a distinct "kink" at the elbow, and the trailing portion is *less than two times* as long as the distance from the elbow to the body. Adult males are much larger than females and have a broad, rounded dorsal fin. Dorsal fins of females are more distinctly falcate.
Surfacing behavior: See Long-finned Pilot Whale.
May be confused with: See Long-finned Pilot Whale.
Range/distribution: Warm Temperate to Tropical. This is the warm-water counterpart of Long-finned Pilot Whale. In the northern Atlantic, occurs from middle Atlantic states and southern Europe south. Retreats from northern extent of range during winter when Long-finned Pilot Whales extend theirs south. Thus in regions of range adjoinment, summer animals would most likely be Short-finned and winter animals Long-finned. However, in spring and fall, both species may occur in the waters east of Chesapeake Bay.

106. RISSO'S DOLPHIN (*Grampus griseus*)
(also Grampus)
Plates 31, 34.
Identification: L. 9–11 ft (2.8–3.3 m); Wt. 1,100–1,500 lb (500–680 kg). Large, stocky dolphin with blunt head; a crease divides the forehead into right and left halves. The dorsal fin is tall and rather straight on the leading edge. Younger animals and females are dark gray. Older animals, particularly males, develop extensive amounts of white on the head, some becoming nearly pure white in front of the dorsal fin. Adults of both sexes, but especially males, may show considerable scarring.
Surfacing behavior: Surfaces with head emerging partially or completely from the water, followed by an indistinct blow. The back rolls forward, exposing the rather tall dorsal fin. May engage in porpoising.
May be confused with: Other dolphins have a distinctly elongated narrow beak. Female Killer Whale is larger and blacker, although the dorsal fin of a large Risso's may appear as prominent as that of a female Killer. Pilot Whale is blacker and has more elongated dorsal fins.
Range/distribution: Worldwide in Tropical to Cold Temperate waters. In the northern Atlantic, occurs from the Gulf of Mexico, Caribbean, and western Africa north to Newfoundland and southern Scandinavia. Most common in warmer waters of range.

107. ROUGH-TOOTHED DOLPHIN (*Steno bredanensis*)
Plates 34, 35.
Identification: L. 8 ft (2.4 m); Wt. 330 lb (150 kg). Robust dolphin with *forehead that grades smoothly into the beak with no discernible break.* Upperparts are dark grayish brown with a *pale "suspenders" stripe down the length of the back.* Upper lip and lower jaw pinkish white, grading into dark with profusion of dark freckles on white at point of change. Dorsal fin is tall, falcate, and positioned ahead of the midback. Belly pale pink to white.
Surfacing behavior: Beak first breaks the water, followed by the top of head and the blow. Roll exposes tall dorsal fin. May sometimes swim just below the surface with dorsal fin exposed. Rarely rides bow wave of boats.
May be confused with: Bottlenose Dolphin has a distinct crease separating forehead from beak, and both upper and lower jaws are gray. Spinner Dolphin is more slender with narrow beak that is distinctly separated from forehead.
Range/distribution: Uncommon. Occurs in deep warm waters along the continental shelves and beyond. In the northern Atlantic, occurs from the southeastern United States and Caribbean to West Africa.

108. BOTTLENOSE DOLPHIN (*Tursiops truncatus*)
Plates 31, 34, 35.
Identification: The quintessential "dolphin." Recent research suggests that two distinct populations, largely segregating by habitat, may represent different species. They differ in size and some skeletal attributes but are otherwise identical in appearance. Head with rounded melon separated from short, rounded beak by a crease. Color uniformly medium to dark gray, becoming paler on the belly. The tall, falcate dorsal fin is centrally placed.

108A. OFFSHORE BOTTLENOSE DOLPHIN: L. 10–13 ft (3–4 m); Wt. 800–1,400 lb (350–650 kg). Averages 50 percent larger than Coastal Bottlenose. Typically found in deeper offshore waters, particularly associated with the Gulf Stream. However, Offshore Bottlenose may venture into nearshore waters where it overlaps with Coastal Bottlenose. For identification purposes, Bottlenose Dolphins seen in harbors and from the beach may be considered Coastal while those found well offshore in deep water are Offshore.

108B. COASTAL BOTTLENOSE DOLPHIN: L. 6–8 ft (1.8–2.4 m); Wt. 200–300 lb (90–130 kg). Smaller form typically seen in shallow coastal and nearshore waters, including bays, harbors, and inland waterways.
Surfacing behavior (both forms): Typical porpoising behavior with leaps and acrobatics. Otherwise surfaces with forehead breaking the surface, followed

by indistinct blow and roll that exposes the dorsal fin. Most of the time, the fin is the last to disappear below the water. Often travels in pods and is fond of boats, wave-riding from either the bow wave or in the stern wake.

May be confused with: No other predominantly gray dolphin occurs along the coasts. Offshore, Rough-toothed lacks the demarcation of forehead and beak. Atlantic Spinner is smaller and has a much longer, more slender snout. At a distance, several other dolphins may appear similar, but look for distinctive patterning on back or sides to distinguish these.

Range/distribution (both forms): Widespread from Tropical to Temperate waters. In the northern Atlantic, common to abundant from the Gulf of Mexico and Caribbean to middle Atlantic states in the west and from western Africa to Portugal and southern France in the east. Uncommon to rare farther north to southern Canada and the North Sea.

109. ATLANTIC SPINNER DOLPHIN (*Stenella longirostris*)
Plates 34, 35.

Identification: L. 5−6 ft (1.5−2 m); Wt. 100−125 lb (45−55 kg). Slender, lightweight dolphin. Forehead low but with distinct separation from long, slender beak. Coloration uniformly gray, with darker line between eye and beak. Lips may be black. Tall, falcate dorsal fin is centrally placed. (Some Spinner populations have dorsal fins that are strongly raked forward, but this does not seem to occur in the northern Atlantic populations.)

Surfacing behavior: Similar to others in the group. However, Spinners are highly acrobatic species, frequently leaping from the water and sometimes making several revolutions about their long axis (like a figure skater) before falling back into the water.

May be confused with: Bottlenose Dolphin is stockier with a shorter snout. Offshore Bottlenose is nearly twice the size. Clymene has a shorter beak and a three-tone pattern on its flanks.

Range/distribution: There are several distinct populations worldwide and taxonomy is unsettled. The northern Atlantic population is called the Long-snouted Spinner Dolphin. It occurs from the warm waters of the Gulf of Mexico, Caribbean, and Equatorial West Africa south as well as in the Indian Ocean.

110. CLYMENE DOLPHIN (*Stenella clymene*)
(also Short-snouted Spinner Dolphin)
Plates 34, 36.

Identification: L. 6−7 ft (1.8−2 m); Wt. 200 lb (90 kg). Small but rather stout dolphin with rounded forehead and short, slender beak. Tip of beak and lips are black. Forehead and upper third of body dark gray to black. Middle portion—including rostrum, area through eye, and tail stock—medium gray and hourglass-shaped. Tall dorsal fin is triangular to falcate and centrally placed. Underside, including lower jaw, white.

Surfacing behavior: Fairly acrobatic with porpoising leaps well above the water surface.

May be confused with: Atlantic Spinner Dolphin has a much longer beak. Common Dolphin has a stronger contrasting pattern on the forward portion than the rear portion of the body. It also tends to have an amber cast. Clymene is more uniformly tricolored with three distinct bands of color— darkest above, intermediate in the middle, and palest below.

Range/distribution: Uncommon to rare. Restricted to Tropical and Equatorial Atlantic. In our region, known from the Caribbean and western Atlantic, but apparently most common in the Gulf of Mexico. Associates with deep offshore water.

111. PANTROPICAL SPOTTED DOLPHIN (*Stenella attenuata*)
Plates 34, 35.

Identification: L. 6–7 ft (1.8–2 m); Wt. 225–250 lb (105–115 kg). Slender dolphin with elongated, narrow beak that may be white-tipped. Forehead and beak dark gray, which extends along the upper back to include the dorsal fin. The eye is surrounded by dark gray, often with a dark line extending from below the eye to the front of the flipper. Side of head and flanks pale gray, the color sweeping upward toward a point that meets behind the dorsal fin. Young animals are unspotted. Adults are spotted, the profusion generally increasing with age, although generally the spotting is limited to the ventral area. The spots are small, white on the dark areas and darker gray on the pale. The dorsal fin is tall, falcate, and centrally placed.

Surfacing behavior: Animated and acrobatic, often porpoising clear of the water. Readily surfs the bow wave of a ship.

May be confused with: Atlantic Spotted Dolphin is more robust and has a pale streak (spinal blaze) from the forehead, across the blowhole and extending toward the dorsal fin. Bottlenose Dolphin is larger and more robust, particularly offshore where Pantropical Spotted Dolphins are likely to be encountered. Young spotteds, more likely to be confused with Bottlenose, have a stronger pattern to the flanks, including the dark line from eye to flipper. Young, unspotted animals are unlikely to be seen alone, without the presence of older, spotted adults.

Range/distribution: Worldwide Tropical waters. In the northern Atlantic, occurs primarily in deep offshore waters from the southeastern United States and Gulf of Mexico, Caribbean, and west central Africa.

112. ATLANTIC SPOTTED DOLPHIN (*Stenella frontalis*)
Plates 34, 35.
Identification: L. 7−8 ft (2−2.4 m); Wt. 250−300 lb (115−140 kg). Medium-size, robust dolphin with short, narrow beak. Forehead and back dark gray with distinct stripe across the top of the forehead and reaching toward the dorsal fin. Young animals are unspotted, becoming moderately to heavily spotted as they age. The spots range from fine to coarse. Dorsal fin is falcate and centrally placed.
Surfacing behavior: Head and back emerge from the water, but lower body tends to remain submerged or in contact with the water surface.
May be confused with: See Pantropical Spotted Dolphin. Bottlenose Dolphin is similar in shape but lacks spots and the white head stripe.
Range/distribution: Restricted to the Atlantic, preferring warmer, shallow water to deep offshore waters. In the northern Atlantic, most common from the Gulf of Mexico, Caribbean, and southeastern United States.

113. STRIPED DOLPHIN (*Stenella coeruleoalba*)
Plates 34, 36.
Identification: L. 7−8 ft (2.2−2.5 m); Wt. 300−330 lb (135−150 kg). Robust dolphin with a short beak. Top of head and back are dark gray. Sides of body and belly are pale gray. *Black line bisects the body from the eye to the anus.* A distinct *pale stripe* sweeps from the area behind the eye into the dark back and reaches nearly to the base of the dorsal fin. The dorsal fin is erect and triangular to slightly falcate.
Surfacing behavior: Frequently forms large herds. Individuals travel by leaping high out of the water. Large pods create a frothy region of whitewater as they move along.
May be confused with: Spotted Dolphins have the dark upperparts and pale flanks but lack the distinctive lateral stripe. Clymene is smaller and has a broad, medium gray central band. Fraser's lacks a well-defined beak and has a broad black stripe.
Range/distribution: Worldwide oceanic distribution from Tropical to Cold Temperate waters. In the northern Atlantic, occurs from Nova Scotia and the United Kingdom southward, generally in deep offshore waters.

114. COMMON DOLPHIN (*Delphinus delphis*)
(also Short-snouted Common Dolphin)
Plates 34, 36.
Identification: L. 7−8 ft (2.1−2.4 m); Wt. 200−300 lb (90−135 kg). Robust dolphin with rounded melon separated from elongated beak by distinct crease. Head and back are dark brownish gray. Flanks have distinct *two-toned*

hourglass pattern: tan-buff to straw-colored in front and gray behind; the two halves seemingly crisscross at their intersection. Tall, distinctly falcate dorsal fin is centrally placed on the back.

Surfacing behavior: Porpoising often brings the entire animal clear of the water, but leaps tend to remain close to the water.

May be confused with: Coastal Bottlenose Dolphin is similar in shape and size. Some may show a paler flank area but never so pronounced or shaped as that of Common Dolphin. See also Clymene Dolphin.

Range/distribution: Worldwide in Tropical to Temperate waters, generally well offshore. May refer to two species, Short-snouted and Long-snouted Common Dolphins. To date, only the former is known from northern Atlantic waters, occurring from Newfoundland and the North Sea southward. In North America, it is most common in non–Gulf Stream waters from Virginia to George's Bank. In the eastern range, it is most common from southern United Kingdom, Portugal, and France southward.

115. FRASER'S DOLPHIN (*Lagenodelphis hosei*)
Plates 34, 36.

Identification: L. 7–8 ft (2.1–2.4 m); Wt. 140–180 lb (64–82 kg). Slender dolphin with short, rather indistinct beak. Most striking is the broad black band that extends from the beak through the eye and continues to the anus. Otherwise, body is gray above and white below. The dorsal fin is small and triangular.

Surfacing behavior: Travels in large herds; very active at the surface, with porpoising close to the surface of the water. Otherwise apparently not as playful as other dolphins.

May be confused with: Striped Dolphin has a distinct beak and more robust body, and the flank stripe is narrow, not broad.

Range/distribution: Rare Tropical species most commonly observed in the Asian Pacific. In the northern Atlantic, known only from the Caribbean.

116. WHITE-BEAKED DOLPHIN (*Lagenorhynchus albirostris*)
Plates 34, 36.

Identification: L. 10 ft (3 m); Wt. 500–600 lb (225–275 kg). Large, robust dolphin with very short beak. Head dark gray, beak and chin white. Sides of body patterned with ill-defined regions of light and dark, generally with black, teardrop-shaped midbody patch. The dorsal fin is slender, tall, pointed, and sharply falcate. *Fin and adjacent back area are black, contrasting with pale gray to white below and behind.*

Surfacing behavior: Typically travels in small groups. May be highly acrobatic with leaps and breaches. Otherwise, surfaces with only the beak, then melon and upper back exposed above the water surface.

May be confused with: No other northern Atlantic dolphin has a broad area of white on the back behind the dorsal fin. Fraser's Dolphin has a similar beak profile but is much smaller and has a bold black flank stripe. Atlantic White-sided has a white midbody patch, not black, and a dark back. In addition, Fraser's and White-beaked have completely different ranges.

Range/distribution: Restricted to colder, deeper waters of the northern Atlantic from New England to Greenland, the United Kingdom, and the North Sea. Most common around Newfoundland, the United Kingdom, and the North Sea.

117. ATLANTIC WHITE-SIDED DOLPHIN (*Lagenorhynchus acutus*)
Plates 34, 36.

Identification: L. 8−10 ft (2.4−3 m); Wt. 400−550 lb (180−250 kg). Robust dolphin lacking a distinct beak. Head and forebody banded with three colors: dark gray on top, medium gray in the middle, off-white below. The eye is positioned at the intersection of the medium gray and the white. There is a *bold white rectangular patch midbody* that borders the dark gray band, with a *straw-colored band above and behind*. The dorsal fin is tall and sharply falcate.

Surfacing behavior: Occurs in small to large groups, often porpoising clear of the water. Otherwise, similar to White-beaked.

May be confused with: Common Dolphin is the only other delphinid with a straw-colored patch. On that species it appears as an oval patch on the side ahead of the dorsal fin. On Atlantic White-sided, it is narrower and behind. White-beaked is similar in shape but has a black midbody patch, not white, and the area behind the dorsal fin is frosty gray, not dark. Clymene has three bands of coloration but is smaller, has a distinct beak, and lacks the white and straw-colored body patches.

Range/distribution: Occurs exclusively in the northern Atlantic. Common from New England to Newfoundland, particularly in the Gulf of Maine. Also common from southern Greenland to southern Scandinavia and the United Kingdom. Typically found in shallow nearshore to shelf-edge waters. Most common in waters from New England to Newfoundland.

Family MONODONTIDAE (Beluga, Narwhal): Unique group of medium-size whales without a dorsal fin. Both species exhibit a peculiar feature of the flukes: at least some individuals have a straight leading edge and strongly rounded trailing edge, giving the impression the flukes were "attached" backwards.

118. BELUGA (*Delphinapterus leucas*)
Plate 27.
Identification: L. 10–16 ft (3–5 m); Wt. 0.5–1.5 tons. Utterly distinctive, pure white whale. Head supports a bulbous melon and tiny rounded beak. There is no dorsal fin.
Surfacing behavior: Head and upper back emerge from the water prior to the blow. Although low and indistinct, the blow can be heard at considerable distance, especially on a calm day.
May be confused with: No other species of whale is pure white (Moby Dick of Herman Melville's classic novel was an albino Sperm Whale). Older Narwhals are pale gray to white, but generally show dark spots on the head and forebody.
Range/distribution: Inhabitant of the high Arctic. In the northern Atlantic, occurs from western Greenland to Gulf of St. Lawrence, commonly penetrating the St. Lawrence River. During winter, a few also follow the cold-water currents into the Gulf of Maine.

119. NARWHAL (*Monodon monocerus*)
Plate 27.
Identification: L. 13–16 ft (4–5 m); Wt. 1–2 tons. Unique. Robust whale with bulbous forehead. Males support an extraordinarily long, spiral tusk that may be 7–10 feet (2–3 m) long. They are pale gray with a profusion of darker streaks and spots. The dark spotting is dense in younger animals, resulting in a rather dark gray appearance that pales with age. Adults are mostly pale gray to white with dark spotting, particularly around the head. Although they lack a dorsal fin, there is a distinct dorsal ridge that extends from midback to the flukes. Flukes may be quite rounded on their trailing edge, giving some the appearance of being "attached" backwards.
Surfacing behavior: Usually travel in small groups. In open water, surfacing brings the rounded head out of the water; males expose the tusk. In the vicinity of pack ice, they will rise gently into ice holes to breathe.
May be confused with: Beluga lacks the spotting and of course the tusk.
Range/distribution: High Arctic, generally in association with or near pack ice. In the northern Atlantic, known from western Greenland to Labrador, although not common.

Family PHOCOENIDAE (Porpoises): Group of small cetaceans distinguished from dolphins by spade-shaped rather than conical teeth. Often confused with dolphins, the vast majority of small coastal cetaceans that are often called porpoises are, in fact, not. Six species worldwide, one in the northern Atlantic.

120. HARBOR PORPOISE (*Phocoena phocoena*)
Plates 31, 33.
Identification: L. 4.5–5.5 ft (1.4–1.7 m); Wt. 90–130 lb (40–60 kg). Smallest cetacean in the northern Atlantic. Head torpedo-shaped with no beak. Upperparts dark grayish brown, grading to light grayish brown below. Dorsal fin is rounded, broadly triangular, and centrally placed on the back.
Surfacing behavior: Rather slow and unanimated. Top of head emerges first, followed by short, rounded roll exposing the dorsal fin. Due to size and minimal surface exposure, they are easy to overlook.
May be confused with: Dolphins (e.g., Coastal Bottlenose) are much larger with tall, generally falcate dorsal fins. Several species of shark may superficially resemble a Harbor Porpoise, but they generally do not show their back above the water, do not surface in a roll sequence, and of course have a completely different tail shape.
Range/distribution: Murky coastal waters of the Northern Hemisphere. In the northern Atlantic, occurs from middle Atlantic states to northern Newfoundland, southern Greenland, Iceland, coastal Europe, the United Kingdom, and western Africa. Avoids warmer waters, which generally have greater clarity than colder waters.

PINNEPEDS (Seals)

Unique group of marine mammals characterized by paddle-like limbs. In some species, these appendages, particularly the forelimbs, are capable of supporting the body weight while on dry land. In others, notably the phocids or true seals, they cannot. All members of the group possess long, coarse whiskers called vibrissae. For the most part, the group occurs coastally or in association with pack ice and is very rarely seen far from land.

TOPOGRAPHY OF A SEAL

1. Muzzle
2. Head
3. Neck
4. Back
5. Hind-flippers
6. Fore-flippers
7. Face
8. Eye
9. Ear
10. Nostrils
11. Jaw Line
12. Vibrissae (Whiskers)

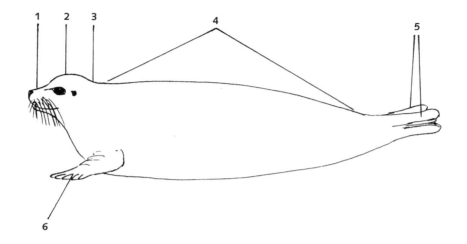

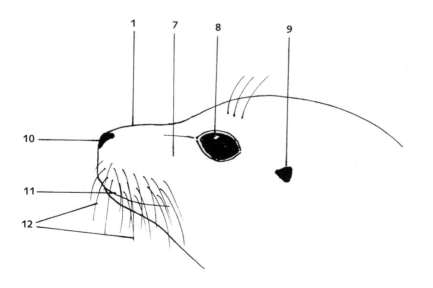

Family ODOBENIDAE (Walrus): Two populations of one species worldwide distinguished by elongated tusks, large size, and rather wrinkled hide.

121. WALRUS (*Odobenus rosmarus*)
Plate 37.
Identification: L. 8−10 ft (2.5−3 m); Wt. 1−1.5 tons. Unique. Massive blocky head with large paired ivory white tusks. Entire body covered with thick, warty, wrinkled reddish skin. Flippers may be turned to partially support body weight. Males are considerably larger than females. Frequently occurs in huge herds, most commonly seen hauled out on icebergs and ice floes.
May be confused with: No other pinneped in the northern Atlantic approaches the size of a walrus or has the distinctive wrinkled reddish skin. No other marine animal in the world has paired tusks.
Range/distribution: High Arctic. In the northern Atlantic, far more common and widespread historically than now. At present, the only population within the scope of this text is restricted to the Davis Strait off western Greenland, a few reaching as far south as northern Labrador.

Family OTARIIDAE (Fur Seals, Sea Lions): Includes two groups commonly known as eared seals. Members are most readily distinguished by external ear flaps and the ability to rotate their hind-flippers beneath the body. Approximately 14 species worldwide. In the northern Atlantic, none occur natively but one—the California Sea Lion, a popular feature of zoos and marine parks—has occurred as an escapee from captivity.

122. CALIFORNIA SEA LION (*Zalophus californianus*)
Plate 37.
Identification: L. 5−7 ft (1.5−2 m); Wt. 200−400 lb (90−180 kg). Head small, muzzle elongated and slender. External ear flaps slender and pointed. Fore-flippers long and distinctly triangular. Body color variable from medium brown to blackish brown. Most captive animals are females, which are considerably smaller than males.
May be confused with: In the northern Atlantic, only Gray and Bearded Seals are uniformly dark brown. Both differ in head profile, flipper size, and inability to gather their flippers underneath the body. In western Tropical waters, the West Indian Manatee is a possible source of confusion. Manatees have a very different head and body shape, cannot haul themselves from the water, and are rarely seen in coastal waters.
Range/distribution: Pacific coast with many populations from northern North America to southern South America. In the northern Atlantic, has

occurred as an escapee from captivity, so most often seen near larger population centers where zoos, circuses, and aquariums are located.

Family PHOCIDAE (True Seals): Largest and most diverse group of pinnepeds. All members are recognizable by their lack of external ears, short, squared fore-flippers that *cannot* be used to raise the body, and hind-flippers that cannot be rotated beneath the body. Most species live in colder waters, frequently associated with pack ice. Worldwide, 19 species are generally recognized, of which 9 have occurred in the northern Atlantic.

123. HARBOR SEAL (*Phoca vitulina*)
(also Common Seal)
Plate 38.
Identification: L. 4–6 ft (1.2–1.8 m); Wt. 175–300 lb (80–140 kg). Head rounded, muzzle short and squarish, eyes large. Overall appearance is rather cocker spaniel–like. When viewed head on, the nostril openings form a V-shaped pattern. Coloration highly variable, but generally a mixture of dark gray with light tan spotting and blotching above and tan below with sparse dark spots.
May be confused with: Ringed Seal is grayer with distinct ring-shaped spots rather than randomly shaped spots and blotching. Female Gray Seal is larger and has a flat forehead that ill defines the muzzle and a W-shaped nostril pattern.
Range/distribution: Widespread in colder waters of the Northern Hemisphere but not generally associated with sea ice. In the northern Atlantic, common from New England to Greenland, Iceland, Scandinavia, Scotland. During winter, some migrate south, rarely reaching the Caribbean and northern Africa. Most commonly seen along the coasts. Sea sightings are most likely in nearshore and shelf waters.

124. RINGED SEAL (*Phoca hispida*)
Plate 38.
Identification: L. 4–5 ft (1.2–1.5 m); Wt. 100–200 lb (50–80 kg). Smallest seal. Head and muzzle silver gray to dark brownish gray. Body plump, but weight varies considerably with season and geographic location. Back generally dark gray with paler circular spots evident on adults.
May be confused with: Harbor Seal is larger and more mottled, lacking the ring-shaped spots. Female Gray Seal is much larger with different head profile and mottled back.
Range/distribution: Restricted to pack ice and adjacent Arctic waters. Occurs singly, generally around holes in the ice that the seals claw open. In the

northern Atlantic, occurs from Labrador and Newfoundland to Greenland and, to a lesser extent, east to Norway. During winter, may wander far south of its normal range.

125. HARP SEAL (*Phoca groenlandica*)
Plate 38.
Identification: L. 4.5–5.5 ft (1.4–1.7 m); Wt. 220–285 lb (100–130 kg). Predominately white seal, variably marked with black. The distribution of black is age-dependent. Pups are born with a pure white coat. These are the seals that aroused public outrage when they were slaughtered en masse for their pelts. After about one year, they begin to develop a profusion of dark gray to black spots and blotches. Over the next several years, they develop a black face. Commonly, these subadults have a grayish, eggplant-toned cast on the head and back. Finally, they develop the broad, black, U-shaped pattern on the back that is characteristic of an adult.
May be confused with: Female Hooded Seal has a black face and spots but the spotting is coarser. The muzzle of a Hooded Seal is more rounded; Harp Seal tends to have a pointed muzzle. On close inspection, Hooded has dark flippers; Harp's are white. Female Gray Seal is darkly spotted on pale coat, but the background color is gray, not white, and the head profile is quite different.
Range/distribution: Principally in the waters of Greenland and eastern Arctic Canada from Labrador and Newfoundland to the Gulf of St. Lawrence. Dispersal after breeding is widespread, with animals occasionally reaching south to at least Virginia and east to Scandinavia.

126. BEARDED SEAL (*Erignathus barbatus*)
Plate 37.
Identification: L. 7–9 ft (2.1–2.8 m); Wt. 450–900 lb (200–400 kg). Head small in proportion to rather long body. Muzzle short and squared with prominent white whiskers. Coloration rather uniformly brown, slightly darker on back, often with darker blotches on body.
May be confused with: The only other northern Atlantic seals that are large and brown are Gray Seal and California Sea Lion. The former has a rather flat "horsehead" and is darker gray. Sea Lion has more slender head with external ear flaps and long, pointed fore-flippers, not short, squared fore-flippers like Bearded Seal. Range is also a key: Sea Lion escapees are unlikely to occur in Arctic waters, the home of Bearded Seal.
Range/distribution: Arctic distribution from Siberia, North America, and Arctic Sea to Greenland. In northern Atlantic, from northeastern New-

foundland to Greenland east to Norway. Occasionally wanders south to Gulf of St. Lawrence and Portugal.

127. HOODED SEAL (*Cystophora cristata*)
Plates 37, 38.

Identification: L. 7–8.5 ft (2.1–2.6 m); Wt. 500–800 lb (225–365 kg). Large seal with rounded head and short, rounded muzzle. Face black. Adult males have a unique distensible pouch from the forehead to the end of the muzzle. During breeding season, it is inflated in a "double bubble." One is an inflation of black skin from the top of the nose; the other is a reddish balloon that extrudes out of the nostrils. Outside the breeding season, these inflatable tissues appear as a flaccid mass of skin. Body is pale grayish white with irregular black patches and spots. Young Hooded Seals, called "blue-backs," are dark, blue-gray above and cream white below. The head and face above the nostril and eye are black, white below. The eyes are very large and laterally displaced.

May be confused with: Subadult Harp Seals may have a black face and dark-spotted, white coats, but the head shape is different and flippers are white. Hooded Seals are black. "Blue-backs" can possibly be confused with Monk Seals. The latter are brownish above, not blue-gray, and have tan faces, not black.

Range/distribution: Breeding range is from central Arctic Canada to Greenland, generally in association with outer edges of pack ice over deep water. Winter distribution is poorly known, but dispersal may be considerable. Hooded Seals are known as far south as Florida and Portugal.

128. GRAY SEAL[NA] OR GREY SEAL[E] (*Halichoerus grypus*)
Plate 37.

Identification: L. 6.5–7.5 ft (2–2.3 m); Wt. 450–770 lb (200–350 kg). Large seal with rather flat-topped, horsehead-shaped head. Males may be considerably larger than females, and western Atlantic animals grow to about 20 percent larger than those in the eastern Atlantic. Coloration is quite variable, ranging from frosty gray with dark spots and blotches to dark gray with white blotches to nearly solid black. Males are generally dark with white patches while females are white with dark patches, but coloration is not a reliable means of determining sex.

May be confused with: Harbor Seal is smaller with a distinct forehead and dark spotting that is finer. Subadult Harp Seal has a different head profile and is generally whiter than the palest Gray Seal. Bearded Seal is brown, not black, and has a very different head profile.

Range/distribution: Restricted to the northern Atlantic. In the western part of the range, most common in Maritime Canada and southern Maine, particularly off Mount Desert and Swans Islands and lower Penobscot Bay. In the eastern range, most common from southwestern Norway and Great Britain. Sightings are known farther south to southern New England and Portugal.

129. MEDITERRANEAN MONK SEAL (*Monachus monachus*)
Plate 37.

Identification: L. 7.5−9 ft (2.3−2.8 m); Wt. 525−770 lb (240−350 kg). Head small and rounded. Body elongate with small, distinctly "bent" elbows of the fore-flippers. Coloration variable but generally darker brown above, grading to pale below, sometimes with white midbelly patch.

May be confused with: No other entirely brown seal is likely to occur in similar range. Gray Seal has a different head shape and is much darker. California Sea Lion is darker, has much longer flippers, and shows a very different head profile. See Caribbean Monk Seal.

Range/distribution: Formerly common in Mediterranean and eastern Atlantic from Spain to Senegal. Most populations were decimated during World War II. Now rare in the northern Atlantic, although a small population lives at Deserta Island, Madeira.

129A. CARIBBEAN MONK SEAL (*Monachus tropicalis*)
Not illustrated

Identification: Very likely extinct. Close relative of Mediterranean Monk Seal but generally smaller and paler-colored. Historically, ranges of the two did not overlap, so range should eliminate possible confusion.

Range/distribution: Formerly from the Bahamas, Caribbean, and Gulf of Mexico south. No verified sightings since early 1950s.

Family TRICHECHIDAE (Manatees or "Sea Cows"): Large plump-bodied aquatic animals with short forearms and broad, rounded, paddle-shaped tails. They are slow-moving, rather docile animals of coastal marine and inland freshwater waterways. Although rarely encountered at sea, they occur nonetheless in marine waters and may be mistaken for small whales.

130. WEST INDIAN MANATEE (*Trichechus manatus*)
(also Caribbean Manatee)
Plates 27, 37.

Identification: L. 10−16 ft (3−5 m); Wt. 1,100−3,300 lb (500−1,500 kg). Head small with large, flat, "cow-like" snout, the end of which is covered with short, stiff hairs. Coloration ranges from gray to brown. Several discrete populations exist, but presently all are united under one species.

May be confused with: With a good view, unlikely to be mistaken for anything. At a distance or under poor viewing conditions, might resemble a small whale with no dorsal fin. However, location, color, and size should eliminate any finless whale that occurs in the northern Atlantic.

Range/distribution: Rare in marine waters off coastal Florida, the Caribbean, and the Gulf of Mexico. Has wandered as far north as Chesapeake Bay.

SEA TURTLES

Medium to very large turtles that live entirely at sea except when females drag themselves onto the beach to lay eggs. Most encounters at sea result in views of the head only; the large body (carapace) remains just beneath the surface. Most common in Tropical to Warm Temperate waters, they do range into the Cold Temperate Zone and even occasionally into Subarctic waters.

TOPOGRAPHY OF A SEA TURTLE

1. Beak
2. Eye
3. Prefrontal
4. Head
5. Nuchal
6. Vertebral Scutes
7. Carapace
8. Tail
9. Fore-flipper
10. Costal Scutes
11. Hind-flipper

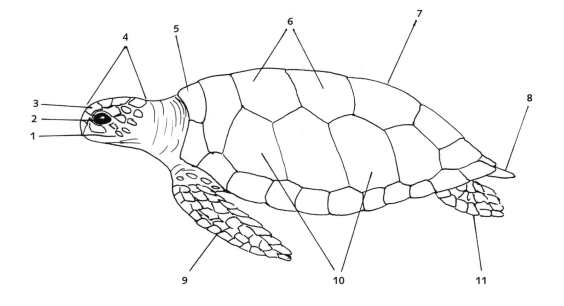

Family CHELONIDAE (Scaled Sea Turtles): Turtles with heart-shaped carapaces made of large, interlocking plates (scutes) and large scales on the head and flippers. The arrangement and color of these scutes and scales are keys to identification. Seven species worldwide, five in northern Atlantic.

131. LOGGERHEAD TURTLE (*Craetta caretta*)
Plate 39.
Identification: L. 31–48 in (79–122 cm); Wt. 170–500 lb (43–127 kg). Scales of head and carapace reddish orange with yellowish skin. There are two pairs of prefrontal scales between the eyes. Carapace with five or more pairs of costal scutes, the first always touching the nuchal. In males, the tail extends visibly beyond the shell.
May be confused with: Green Turtle has whiter skin and a more rounded head with one pair of prefrontal scales between the eyes; the first costal scute never touches the nuchal. Hawksbill is smaller and not as reddish, with distinct keel on back and overlapping scutes; the first costal does not touch the nuchal. Ridley turtles are smaller and distinctly olive-colored and have two pairs of prefrontals between the eyes.
Range/distribution: Common in Subtropical and Temperate shelf and estuary waters. Most common in North America from Chesapeake Bay to the Caribbean. Has occurred as far north as Newfoundland and England.

132. GREEN TURTLE (*Chelonia mydas*)
Plate 39.
Identification: L. 28–60 in (71–153 cm); Wt. 200–650 lb (91–295 kg). Scales of head and carapace olive brown to dark reddish brown, skin cream-colored. The smallish, rounded head has only one pair of prefrontals between the eyes. The carapace has four costal scutes, the first never touching the nuchal.
May be confused with: Loggerhead is more reddish with yellow skin; the first costal touches the nuchal, and there are two pairs of prefrontals between the eyes. Hawksbill is smaller with yellowish skin and two pairs of prefrontals between the eyes; the head has a hooked, hawk-like beak. Ridley turtles are smaller and distinctly olive-colored and have two pairs of prefrontals between the eyes.
Range/distribution: Tropical inshore to offshore waters but prefers shallower water. Ranges north into the Warm Temperate Zone.

133. HAWKSBILL TURTLE (*Eretmochelys imbricata*)
Plate 39.
Identification: L. 30–36 in (76–90 cm); Wt. 95–280 lb (43–127 kg). Scales of head and carapace greenish brown to reddish brown. Skin yellowish. The

head has a distinct hawk-like beak with two pair of prefrontal scales between the eyes. Carapace is shield-like with central keel, overlapping scutes, and distinct radiating tortoiseshell pattern, particularly evident in smaller animals. First costal does not touch the nuchal. Edge of carapace sometimes sawtooth-like.

May be confused with: Atlantic and Olive Ridley Turtles are a lighter olive color without patterning on the carapace. Loggerhead and Green are larger without overlapping scales or a tortoiseshell pattern. Combination of prefrontal scales and first costal differ (see descriptions).

Range/distribution: Inhabits rock and reef habitats of clear, shallow Tropical and Subtropical waters worldwide. In the northern Atlantic, most common from southwestern Gulf of Mexico, Caribbean, Florida Keys, and Bahamas.

134. ATLANTIC RIDLEY TURTLE (*Lepidochelys kempi*)
(also Kemp's Ridley Turtle)
Plate 39.

Identification: L. 23−29 in (58−74 cm); Wt. 80−110 lb (36−50 kg). Small sea turtle. Scales of head and carapace olive green. Skin pale yellowish green. Head with two pairs of prefrontals between the eyes. Carapace nearly circular and without patterning. Five costals on the side of the carapace, the first touching the nuchal.

May be confused with: Olive Ridley is similar but with six to nine elongated costals. Atlantic Ridley is slightly larger and grayer-colored than Olive Ridley, but such distinctions in the field are subject to viewing conditions and interpretation. Hawksbill is darker and has hawk-like head and strong back patterning. Loggerhead and Green are much larger with different shell patterns.

Range/distribution: Endangered. Principal range is the Gulf of Mexico. It is the most common species in the northern Gulf waters off Mississippi, Alabama, and Padre Island, Texas, where it may possibly breed. Also regular in the Gulf Stream and along the eastern seaboard north to Cape Cod.

135. OLIVE RIDLEY TURTLE (*Lepidochelys olivacea*)
Plate 39.

Identification: L. 22−27 in (56−68 cm); Wt. 80−100 lb (36−45 kg). Smallest sea turtle. Very similar to Atlantic Ridley but more olive-colored. Head with two pairs of prefrontals between the eyes. Carapace with six to nine elongated costal scutes, the first touching the nuchal.

May be confused with: Atlantic Ridley is grayer with five costals that are broader and hexagonal in shape. Hawksbill is much darker and different in color, with a patterned carapace and only four to five costals. Loggerhead and Green are much larger and darker.

Range/distribution: Most abundant sea turtle worldwide but rather rare in the northern Atlantic. Has been reported from the Florida Keys and Caribbean to western Africa.

Family DERMOCHELYIDAE (Leatherback Turtle): The single species in the family is the world's largest living turtle. Carapace appears solid and leathery, hence the name.

136. LEATHERBACK TURTLE (*Dermochelys coriacea*)
Plate 39.
Identification: L. 53−74 in (135−189 cm); Wt. 650−2,000+ lb (295−910 kg). Head mottled dark gray and white without obvious scales. Carapace solid, elongated, and covered with a smooth skin. Color is blackish blue to slate gray, generally marked with white to pinkish irregular blotches. The back has seven prominent ridges that run the full length of the shell.
May be confused with: Only Loggerhead and Green approach Leatherback in size. All other sea turtles have scutes on their carapaces and are olive to yellowish or reddish brown.
Range/distribution: The most widely distributed but also the most highly pelagic sea turtle. Breeds in Tropical waters, but known to occur as far north as Subarctic Canada, Iceland, and Norway and would be the most likely species to be found in cold, deep water.

RANGE ABUNDANCE CHARTS

Traditional field guides rely on range maps to give readers some idea of where a given species may be found. Owing to size constraints, such maps often cram thousands of square miles into mere square inches. With a geographic region the size of the Atlantic Ocean, one cannot glean much information by a map which illustrates 80 percent to 100 percent of the entire region as a possible range. Since this guide is primarily intended to serve those who venture forth on day-long trips (rather than extended research expeditions), it is reasonable to assume that the areas that may be explored are limited by three factors: (1) the availability of boats from specific departure locations, (2) the maximum distance one can travel offshore and return in a day, and (3) the presence of some feature that concentrates marine wildlife.

The following is a series of eighteen individual species lists, each referring to a popular or important observation locale. In most cases, reaching these locales requires two or more hours of travel by boat from the shore. The estimates of abundance are based on the theoretical (but often impractical) assumption that the preferred habitat is visited for a significant portion of the trip. Thus, a species expected in large numbers in deep water might be missed entirely if the boat remains in shallow water.

Interpreting the charts requires some understanding of what the abundance bars mean. First, they represent averages based on the best available information. Many species fluctuate in their abundance and different observers may interpret numbers in different ways. Also, our knowledge of the actual distribution of many species is limited and in some cases current knowledge may prove very different from what the future will reveal.

Four abundance codes are given as varying thickness of bars. Code 4 (thickest bar) is defined as "should see moderate to large numbers daily." The term "large numbers" means that multiple individuals should be seen repeatedly throughout the day in the proper habitat. The term "moderate numbers" signifies the regular or frequent observation of single individuals in the proper habitat. Code 3 is defined as "should see small to moderate numbers on most days." The term "small numbers" means that single individuals will be seen infrequently throughout the day in the proper habitat and that occasionally the species will be missed. It also implies that on rare occasion, the species may be seen in larger numbers. Code 2 is defined as "small numbers seen on some days." These species will often but not always be missed, and when seen, only one to a few individuals per day will likely be involved. Code 1 (thinnest line) is defined as "occurs but seldom if ever seen." This code is a bit different from the others in that it emphasizes the theoretical presence of a species rather than a probability of actually seeing it. Such a category was necessary because some species, even in their centers of distribution, are never seen by casual observers.

The following 18 land-based and 6 island-based locations (Map 1) represent some of the most important and frequently visited places to observe pelagic marine wildlife. From the North American continent in particular, these offshore destinations are associated with important submarine topographic features (Map 2). The range charts offer a broad overview of the relative abundance of all species regularly occurring at that location. However, not all species occur at all points along the way from shore to the destination. Therefore, on any given trip, observers might encounter some species in their predicted abundances only for a short period of time. In particular, nearshore species such as Northern Gannet, Parasitic Jaeger, Harbor Seal, and sea turtles would be more likely en route to and from the destination.

████ Should see in moderate to large numbers daily

███ Should see small numbers most days;
occasionally moderate numbers; occasionally missed

▬▬ May see small numbers on some days but often missed

—— Occurs but is seldom seen

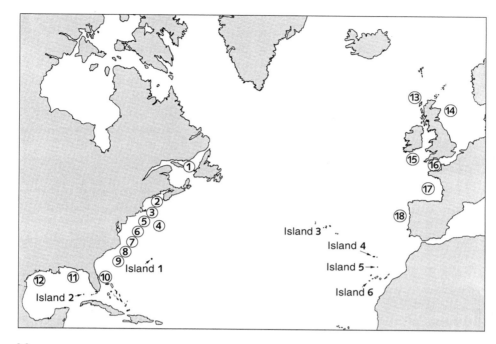

Map 1

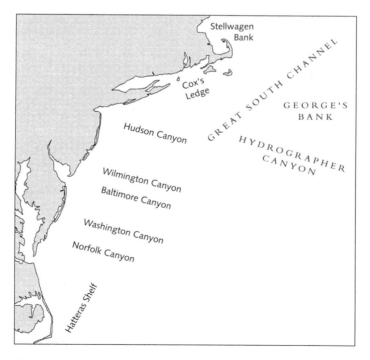

Map 2

Location 1: Gulf of St. Lawrence. These are the waters between New Brunswick, Quebec, and Newfoundland, and they include much of the St. Lawrence River. The accounts shown estimate a regional average from nearshore to deep offshore waters. Breeding species, particularly the alcids, will be far more abundant in close proximity to their breeding colonies than elsewhere. Several commercial ferryboats operate in the gulf from Nova Scotia, Newfoundland, and Labrador. In addition, organized tours operate from Big Bras d'Or, Cape Breton Island, Brier Island, and Halifax. Most of these are limited to the summer months. As one moves from the open gulf waters into the St. Lawrence River, the number of seabirds drops rapidly, but many of the whales become more common. In particular, Blue Whales and Belugas are far more common in the river than the gulf.

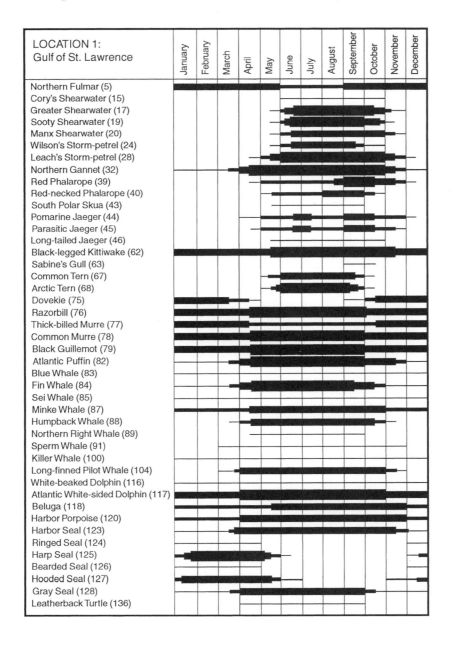

Location 2: Bay of Fundy, Gulf of Maine. Geographically the Bay of Fundy is the northernmost extension of the Gulf of Maine. The accounts estimate a compilation of the species seen both in the open gulf waters and nearshore in the vicinity of the breeding colonies. Several commercial ferryboats operate, most notably between Maine and Nova Scotia. There are also organized tours into nearshore waters to visit the puffin colonies on Machias Seal Island. These summer trips depart from Jonesport, Maine.

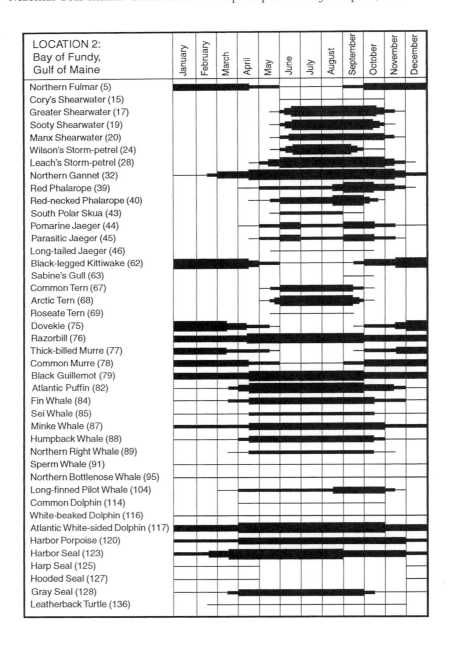

LOCATION 2: Bay of Fundy, Gulf of Maine	January	February	March	April	May	June	July	August	September	October	November	December
Northern Fulmar (5)												
Cory's Shearwater (15)												
Greater Shearwater (17)												
Sooty Shearwater (19)												
Manx Shearwater (20)												
Wilson's Storm-petrel (24)												
Leach's Storm-petrel (28)												
Northern Gannet (32)												
Red Phalarope (39)												
Red-necked Phalarope (40)												
South Polar Skua (43)												
Pomarine Jaeger (44)												
Parasitic Jaeger (45)												
Long-tailed Jaeger (46)												
Black-legged Kittiwake (62)												
Sabine's Gull (63)												
Common Tern (67)												
Arctic Tern (68)												
Roseate Tern (69)												
Dovekie (75)												
Razorbill (76)												
Thick-billed Murre (77)												
Common Murre (78)												
Black Guillemot (79)												
Atlantic Puffin (82)												
Fin Whale (84)												
Sei Whale (85)												
Minke Whale (87)												
Humpback Whale (88)												
Northern Right Whale (89)												
Sperm Whale (91)												
Northern Bottlenose Whale (95)												
Long-finned Pilot Whale (104)												
Common Dolphin (114)												
White-beaked Dolphin (116)												
Atlantic White-sided Dolphin (117)												
Harbor Porpoise (120)												
Harbor Seal (123)												
Harp Seal (125)												
Hooded Seal (127)												
Gray Seal (128)												
Leatherback Turtle (136)												

Location 3: Stellwagen Bank. This rich feeding area, especially for Fin and Humpback Whales, lies only a few miles north of Cape Cod Bay and the "hook" of Cape Cod. From April through October, numerous half-day whale-watching trips operate from Provincetown, Massachusetts, and elsewhere. Other, more extensive trips depart from Newburyport and Plymouth.

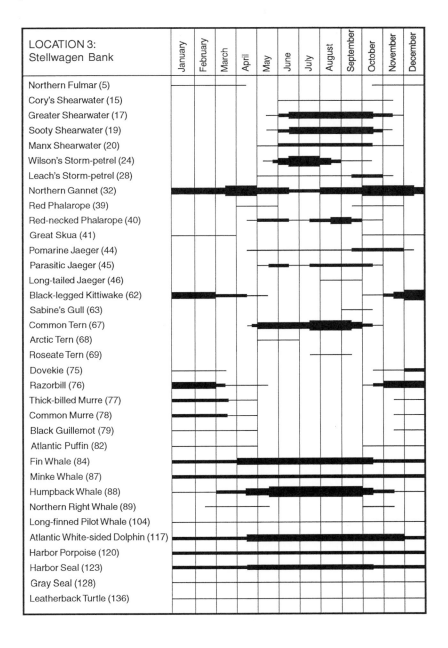

LOCATION 3: Stellwagen Bank	January	February	March	April	May	June	July	August	September	October	November	December
Northern Fulmar (5)												
Cory's Shearwater (15)												
Greater Shearwater (17)												
Sooty Shearwater (19)												
Manx Shearwater (20)												
Wilson's Storm-petrel (24)												
Leach's Storm-petrel (28)												
Northern Gannet (32)												
Red Phalarope (39)												
Red-necked Phalarope (40)												
Great Skua (41)												
Pomarine Jaeger (44)												
Parasitic Jaeger (45)												
Long-tailed Jaeger (46)												
Black-legged Kittiwake (62)												
Sabine's Gull (63)												
Common Tern (67)												
Arctic Tern (68)												
Roseate Tern (69)												
Dovekie (75)												
Razorbill (76)												
Thick-billed Murre (77)												
Common Murre (78)												
Black Guillemot (79)												
Atlantic Puffin (82)												
Fin Whale (84)												
Minke Whale (87)												
Humpback Whale (88)												
Northern Right Whale (89)												
Long-finned Pilot Whale (104)												
Atlantic White-sided Dolphin (117)												
Harbor Porpoise (120)												
Harbor Seal (123)												
Gray Seal (128)												
Leatherback Turtle (136)												

Location 4: Southern George's Bank, Hydrographer Canyon. Approximately 70 to 80 miles south-southeast of Cape Cod is the Great South Channel, separating Nantucket Shoals from George's Bank to the east and Hydrographer Canyon to the south. George's Bank is a vast area long famous for its rich fishing grounds and, in historic times, for whaling. Relatively shallow (only 20 to 30 fathoms), it is ecologically divisible into northern and southern halves. The latter has slightly warmer waters, particularly during summer, when spin-off eddies of the Gulf Stream reach the southern bank. Conversely, the northern half is more similar to the Gulf of Maine. To the south of George's Bank are a series of deep-water canyons. Of those, only Hydrographer Canyon, about 25 to 30 miles south of the Great South Channel, can be accessed on a day-long excursion. Collectively, an offshore excursion to southern George's Bank and Hydrographer Canyon could be

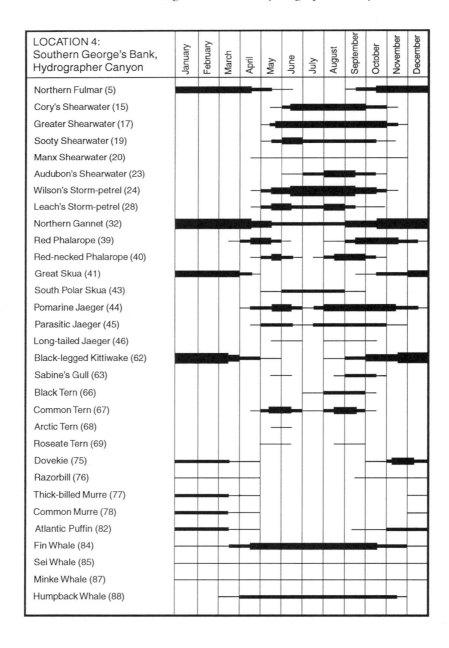

very rewarding but logistically somewhat difficult. The accounts shown estimate an average daily list for a 24-hour-long trip from the coast to and from these waters, assuming access by organized tour or private charter of a fishing boat from Point Judith, Rhode Island. Many of the species listed are more common in the nearshore waters transversed on the way out. Most notable are Parasitic Jaeger, most of the terns other than Arctic, and the alcids. Similarly, some of the larger whales, such as Humpback and Northern Right, are more likely in the nearshore waters. Of particular note is Wilson's Storm-petrel, which frequents nearshore waters early in the season and progressively moves offshore in summer.

LOCATION 4: (continued)	January	February	March	April	May	June	July	August	September	October	November	December
Northern Right Whale (89)												
Sperm Whale (91)												
Pygmy Sperm Whale (92)												
Dwarf Sperm Whale (93)												
Cuvier's Beaked Whale (94)												
Northern Bottlenose Whale (95)												
Sowerby's Beaked Whale (98)												
Blainville's Beaked Whale (99)												
Killer Whale (100)												
False Killer Whale (101)												
Long-finned Pilot Whale (104)												
Risso's Dolphin (106)												
Bottlenose Dolphin (108)												
Atlantic Spinner Dolphin (109)												
Atlantic Spotted Dolphin (112)												
Striped Dolphin (113)												
Common Dolphin (114)												
White-beaked Dolphin (116)												
Atlantic White-sided Dolphin (117)												
Harbor Porpoise (120)												
Loggerhead Turtle (131)												
Atlantic Ridley Turtle (134)												
Leatherback Turtle (136)												

Location 5: Cox's Ledge. This shallow-water (15–20 fathoms) location lies only 15 nautical miles south-southeast of Point Judith, Rhode Island, and may be accessed either from there or from Block Island, New York. The species present are those attracted by shallow offshore waters, and this location may be a better place to view species such as Sooty and Manx Shearwaters in summer and alcids, particularly Razorbill, in winter. Access is by organized tour or private charter, especially out of Point Judith, Rhode Island.

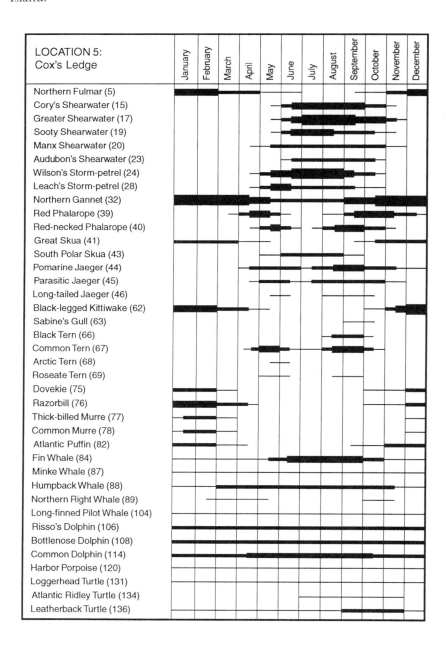

LOCATION 5: Cox's Ledge	January	February	March	April	May	June	July	August	September	October	November	December
Northern Fulmar (5)												
Cory's Shearwater (15)												
Greater Shearwater (17)												
Sooty Shearwater (19)												
Manx Shearwater (20)												
Audubon's Shearwater (23)												
Wilson's Storm-petrel (24)												
Leach's Storm-petrel (28)												
Northern Gannet (32)												
Red Phalarope (39)												
Red-necked Phalarope (40)												
Great Skua (41)												
South Polar Skua (43)												
Pomarine Jaeger (44)												
Parasitic Jaeger (45)												
Long-tailed Jaeger (46)												
Black-legged Kittiwake (62)												
Sabine's Gull (63)												
Black Tern (66)												
Common Tern (67)												
Arctic Tern (68)												
Roseate Tern (69)												
Dovekie (75)												
Razorbill (76)												
Thick-billed Murre (77)												
Common Murre (78)												
Atlantic Puffin (82)												
Fin Whale (84)												
Minke Whale (87)												
Humpback Whale (88)												
Northern Right Whale (89)												
Long-finned Pilot Whale (104)												
Risso's Dolphin (106)												
Bottlenose Dolphin (108)												
Common Dolphin (114)												
Harbor Porpoise (120)												
Loggerhead Turtle (131)												
Atlantic Ridley Turtle (134)												
Leatherback Turtle (136)												

Location 6: Hudson Canyon. This large canyon lies between 80 and 100 miles east of Barnegat Light, New Jersey. Accounts shown estimate a typical list of species expected on a day-long trip from coastal waters to and from the canyon. However, most day trips will not penetrate beyond the "upper" reaches of the canyon and thus will not be able to survey the deepest portions of this canyon. The best access is from Barnegat Light or Manasquan Inlet, New Jersey, requiring 15–24 hours at sea. Although sim-

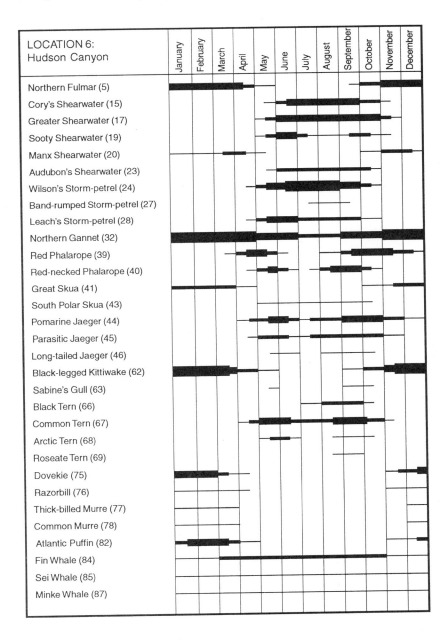

ilar to Hydrographer Canyon in species occurrence, it offers a better chance for viewing more of the warm-water species, such as Cory's and Audubon's Shearwaters. As with other deep-water locations, the shallow-water species (Sooty Shearwater, early-season Wilson's Storm-petrel, Parasitic Jaeger, and the winter alcids) are more likely to be seen en route than at the canyon itself.

LOCATION 6: (continued)	January	February	March	April	May	June	July	August	September	October	November	December
Humpback Whale (88)		———	———	———	———	———	———	———	———	———	———	
Northern Right Whale (89)				—							—	
Sperm Whale (91)	———	———	———	———	———	———	———	———	———	———	———	———
Pygmy Sperm Whale (92)					———	———	———	———	———			
Dwarf Sperm Whale (93)					———	———	———	———	———			
Cuvier's Beaked Whale (94)	———	———	———	———	———	———	———	———	———	———	———	———
Sowerby's Beaked Whale (98)	———	———	———	———	———	———	———	———	———	———	———	———
Blainville's Beaked Whale (99)	———	———	———	———	———	———	———	———	———	———	———	———
False Killer Whale (101)	———	———	———	———	———	———	———	———	———	———	———	———
Long-finned Pilot Whale (104)	▬▬▬	▬▬▬	▬▬▬	▬▬▬					▬▬▬	▬▬▬	▬▬▬	▬▬▬
Short-finned Pilot Whale (105)	———	———	———	———	———	———	———	———	———	———	———	———
Risso's Dolphin (106)				▬▬▬	▬▬▬	▬▬▬	▬▬▬	▬▬▬	▬▬▬	▬▬▬	▬▬▬	▬▬▬
Bottlenose Dolphin (108)	▬▬▬	▬▬▬	▬▬▬	▬▬▬	▬▬▬	▬▬▬	▬▬▬	▬▬▬	▬▬▬	▬▬▬	▬▬▬	▬▬▬
Atlantic Spinner Dolphin (109)					———	———	———	———	———	———	———	———
Atlantic Spotted Dolphin (112)	———	———	———	———	———	———	———	———	———	———	———	———
Striped Dolphin (113)	———	———	———	———	———	———	———	———	———	———	———	———
Common Dolphin (114)	▬▬▬	▬▬▬	▬▬▬	▬▬▬	▬▬▬	▬▬▬	▬▬▬	▬▬▬	▬▬▬	▬▬▬	▬▬▬	▬▬▬
Atlantic White-sided Dolphin (117)	———	———	———	———	———							
Harbor Porpoise (120)	———	———	———	———	———							—
Loggerhead Turtle (131)												
Atlantic Ridley Turtle (134)								———	———	———	———	———
Leatherback Turtle (136)												

Location 7: Wilmington Canyon, Baltimore Canyon. This pair of canyons lies farther south from Hudson Canyon and from 60 to 80 miles east of Delaware. Accounts shown estimate a daily list on a trip from coastal waters to the canyons and back. Access is by organized tour or charter from Ocean City, Maryland, and requires a 12-hour round trip. For the most part, the expected species are similar to those of Hudson Canyon, but with even greater influence of warm Gulf Stream water and the species associ-

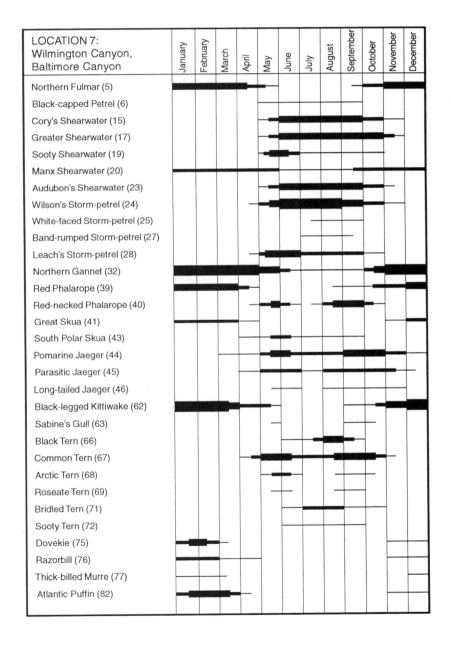

ated with it. Black-capped Petrel, Band-rumped Storm-petrel, and Sooty and Bridled Terns are possible when eddies of the Gulf Stream reach upward toward the north. Conversely, colder-water species such as Manx Shearwater and the rare White-faced Storm-petrel are more likely when the water is cold. Cetaceans seem to be less influenced by daily swings in ocean temperature.

LOCATION 7: (continued)	January	February	March	April	May	June	July	August	September	October	November	December
Fin Whale (84)			━	━	━	━	━	━	━	━		
Sei Whale (85)												
Minke Whale (87)												
Humpback Whale (88)												
Northern Right Whale (89)			─	─						─	─	
Sperm Whale (91)	━	━	━	━	━	━	━	━	━	━	━	━
Pygmy Sperm Whale (92)					─	─	─	─				
Dwarf Sperm Whale (93)					─	─	─					
Cuvier's Beaked Whale (94)												
Blainville's Beaked Whale (99)												
False Killer Whale (101)												
Long-finned Pilot Whale (104)												
Short-finned Pilot Whale (105)					━	━	━	━	━	━		
Risso's Dolphin (106)												
Bottlenose Dolphin (108)	▓	▓	▓	▓	▓	▓	▓	▓	▓	▓	▓	▓
Atlantic Spinner Dolphin (109)				─	─	─	─	─	─	─	─	─
Atlantic Spotted Dolphin (112)												
Striped Dolphin (113)												
Common Dolphin (114)	━	━	━	━	━	━	━				━	━
Atlantic White-sided Dolphin (117)	─	─	─	─	─	─	─	─	─	─	─	─
Harbor Porpoise (120)	─	─	─									
Loggerhead Turtle (131)					━	━	━	━	━			
Green Turtle (132)						─	─	─	─			
Atlantic Ridley Turtle (134)							─	─	─			
Leatherback Turtle (136)	─	─	─	─	─	─	─	─	─	─	─	─

Location 8: Washington Canyon, Norfolk Canyon. These two canyons, the southernmost canyons along the North American east coast, lie about 60 miles east of Maryland and Virginia respectively. Access is by organized tour or private charter from Virginia Beach (more commonly to Norfolk Canyon), requiring about 12 hours for a round trip. The expected

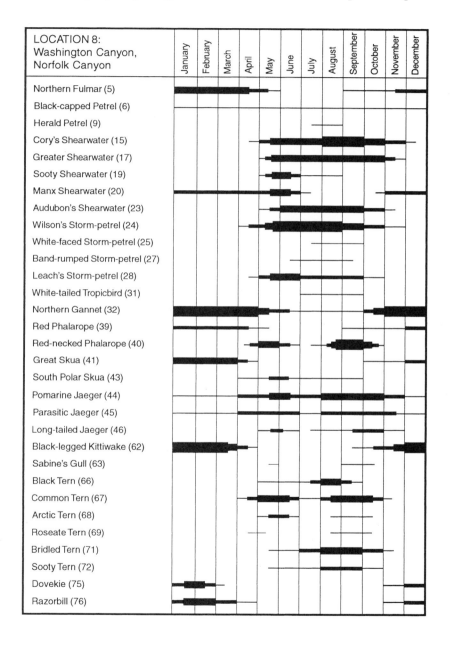

species should be similar to those of Wilmington and Baltimore Canyons, but access may be a bit easier. During winter, Razorbills and Humpback Whales occur in shallow water while Dovekie and Atlantic Puffin are found over the deep canyon waters.

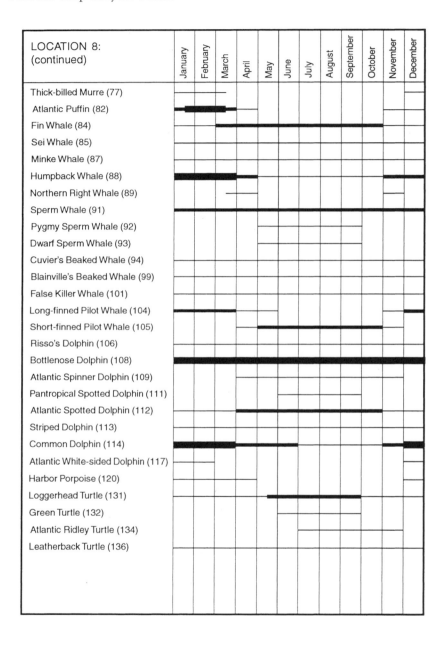

LOCATION 8: (continued)	January	February	March	April	May	June	July	August	September	October	November	December
Thick-billed Murre (77)												
Atlantic Puffin (82)												
Fin Whale (84)												
Sei Whale (85)												
Minke Whale (87)												
Humpback Whale (88)												
Northern Right Whale (89)												
Sperm Whale (91)												
Pygmy Sperm Whale (92)												
Dwarf Sperm Whale (93)												
Cuvier's Beaked Whale (94)												
Blainville's Beaked Whale (99)												
False Killer Whale (101)												
Long-finned Pilot Whale (104)												
Short-finned Pilot Whale (105)												
Risso's Dolphin (106)												
Bottlenose Dolphin (108)												
Atlantic Spinner Dolphin (109)												
Pantropical Spotted Dolphin (111)												
Atlantic Spotted Dolphin (112)												
Striped Dolphin (113)												
Common Dolphin (114)												
Atlantic White-sided Dolphin (117)												
Harbor Porpoise (120)												
Loggerhead Turtle (131)												
Green Turtle (132)												
Atlantic Ridley Turtle (134)												
Leatherback Turtle (136)												

Location 9: Hatteras Continental Shelf. East of North Carolina's Outer Banks, the continental shelf becomes straight and very steep. Here the Laborador Current meets the Gulf Stream, causing the latter to deflect to the northeast. From this intersection south for 100 miles is the greatest diversity of pelagic marine wildlife in the northern Atlantic. With the Gulf Stream only 10 to 20 miles offshore, access to rich shallow water habitats is relatively easy. However, the best diversity occurs 40 to 60 miles offshore, beyond the edge of the continental shelf. Access to the shallower water is by organized tour, private charter or "public" fishing boat (headboat) out of Manteo, Nagshead, or Hatteras. Access to the deeper water is by tour or private charter.

Near shore are the colder "green" non–Gulf Stream waters. Relatively

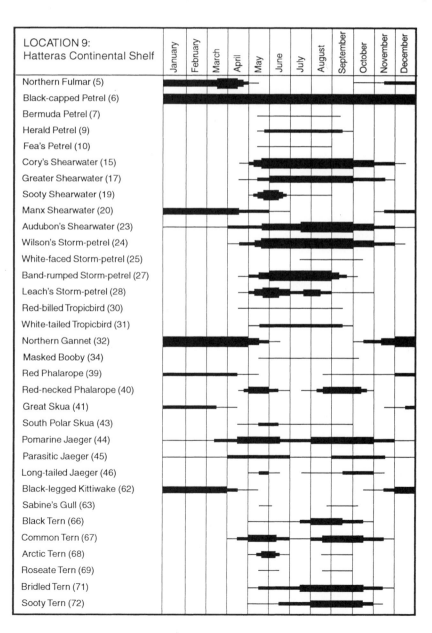

poor spring through fall except for spring bird migration, they have the best numbers and diversity of winter species. Where the green water meets the blue Gulf Stream, large numbers of shearwaters, phalaropes, and terns occur spring through fall, particularly when the transition is sharp and marked by a visible line of "weed" (*Sargassum*). Beyond is the deep Gulf Stream water that is home to *Pterodroma* petrels, storm-petrels, Sperm and beaked whales and oceanic dolphins. Water depth is important for finding target species. For example, Black-capped Petrels occur in water as little as 300 fathoms deep while Fea's and Herald petrels occur in 1000 fathoms. Wilson's Storm-petrels are common in shallow water while Band-rumped Storm-petrels are found in 800 fathoms or more. Sperm and Cuvier's Beaked whales are found in water 1,000 fathoms or deeper.

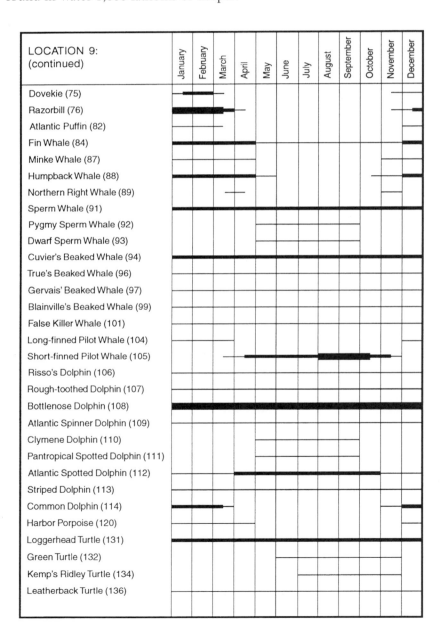

LOCATION 9: (continued)	January	February	March	April	May	June	July	August	September	October	November	December
Dovekie (75)												
Razorbill (76)												
Atlantic Puffin (82)												
Fin Whale (84)												
Minke Whale (87)												
Humpback Whale (88)												
Northern Right Whale (89)												
Sperm Whale (91)												
Pygmy Sperm Whale (92)												
Dwarf Sperm Whale (93)												
Cuvier's Beaked Whale (94)												
True's Beaked Whale (96)												
Gervais' Beaked Whale (97)												
Blainville's Beaked Whale (99)												
False Killer Whale (101)												
Long-finned Pilot Whale (104)												
Short-finned Pilot Whale (105)												
Risso's Dolphin (106)												
Rough-toothed Dolphin (107)												
Bottlenose Dolphin (108)												
Atlantic Spinner Dolphin (109)												
Clymene Dolphin (110)												
Pantropical Spotted Dolphin (111)												
Atlantic Spotted Dolphin (112)												
Striped Dolphin (113)												
Common Dolphin (114)												
Harbor Porpoise (120)												
Loggerhead Turtle (131)												
Green Turtle (132)												
Kemp's Ridley Turtle (134)												
Leatherback Turtle (136)												

Location 10: Central to South Florida, Atlantic. South of Hatteras the coastline angles westward and becomes increasingly farther from the Gulf Stream and the continental shelf. Thus, access to productive offshore habitats diminishes until one reaches central Florida. From Cape Canaveral through Miami, the Gulf Stream lies only a few miles offshore. In addition, this stretch of coast hosts numerous opportunities to get offshore aboard a fishing boat or one of the many cruise ships that sail between Florida and the Bahamas. The latter offers an excellent, comfortable way of surveying the deep offshore waters well beyond the reach of charter fishing boats. The only drawback to observing wildlife from a cruise ship is that the decks are very high above the water and observations will be at a distance.

LOCATION 10: Central to South Florida, Atlantic	January	February	March	April	May	June	July	August	September	October	November	December
Black-capped Petrel (6)				■	■							
Cory's Shearwater (15)						■	■	■	■			
Greater Shearwater (17)												
Sooty Shearwater (19)				■								
Manx Shearwater (20)												
Audubon's Shearwater (23)					■	■	■	■	■	■		
Wilson's Storm-petrel (24)					■	■	■					
Band-rumped Storm-petrel (27)												
Leach's Storm-petrel (28)												
White-tailed Tropicbird (31)												
Northern Gannet (32)	■	■	■								■	■
Masked Booby (34)								■				
Brown Booby (36)												
Magnificent Frigatebird (37)												
Red Phalarope (39)												
Red-necked Phalarope (40)												
Pomarine Jaeger (44)			■	■	■					■	■	
Parasitic Jaeger (45)			■	■	■							
Long-tailed Jaeger (46)									■			
Black-legged Kittiwake (62)	■	■	■									
Common Tern (67)	■	■	■									
Arctic Tern (68)												
Roseate Tern (69)				■	■	■	■	■	■			
Bridled Tern (71)				■	■	■	■	■	■			
Sooty Tern (72)						■	■	■	■			
Brown Noddy (73)												
Humpback Whale (88)												
Northern Right Whale (89)												
Risso's Dolphin (106)												
Rough-toothed Dolphin (107)												
Bottlenose Dolphin (108)	■	■	■	■	■	■	■	■	■	■	■	■
Atlantic Spinner Dolphin (109)												
Clymene Dolphin (110)												
Pantropical Spotted Dolphin (111)												
Atlantic Spotted Dolphin (112)												
Loggerhead Turtle (131)												
Green Turtle (132)												
Atlantic Ridley Turtle (134)												
Leatherback Turtle (136)												

Location 11: Northeastern Gulf of Mexico, Louisiana. Until recently, the Gulf of Mexico was considered poor for marine wildlife. However, the deep gulf waters beyond the edge of the continental shelf are quite rich, particularly for whales. The outflow of the Mississippi River effectively divides the gulf into eastern and western halves, which can be surprisingly different. About 50 miles south of Port Fourchon, Louisiana, lies the Mississippi Canyon. This area can be good for birds and fair for whales. It can be accessed with a 12-hour round trip by organized tour or private charter. Farther to the south and east lies the deep open waters of the gulf, which host an impressive diversity of cetaceans. Access would likely require at least 24 hours round trip. Presently, the only observational activities in these waters are by research vessels that put to sea for a month or more at a time.

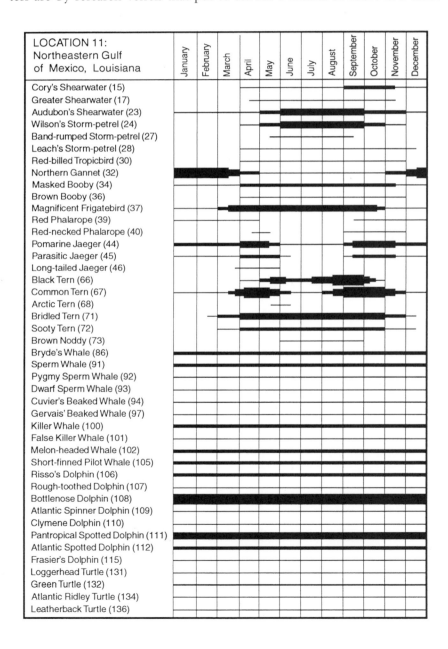

Location 12: Northwestern Gulf of Mexico, Texas. This area refers to the gulf waters west of the outflow of the Mississippi River. With somewhat less diversity than the eastern gulf, the deep offshore waters can be productive. However, the continental shelf lies 80 to 100 miles offshore and requires 30 to 46 hours at sea to access it. One of the biggest differences between eastern and western gulf waters is seen with the storm-petrels. In the eastern gulf, Wilson's is the only common species, but it is essentially nonexistent in the west. Conversely, Band-rumped is the common storm-petrel in the west, but not until the very deep offshore waters are reached. Currently, access is by organized tour or possibly private charter from Freeport, Texas.

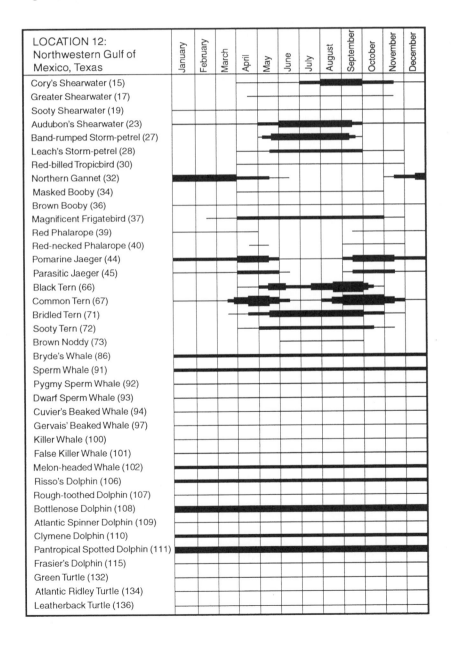

LOCATION 12: Northwestern Gulf of Mexico, Texas

Species	Jan	Feb	Mar	Apr	May	Jun	Jul	Aug	Sep	Oct	Nov	Dec
Cory's Shearwater (15)												
Greater Shearwater (17)												
Sooty Shearwater (19)												
Audubon's Shearwater (23)												
Band-rumped Storm-petrel (27)												
Leach's Storm-petrel (28)												
Red-billed Tropicbird (30)												
Northern Gannet (32)												
Masked Booby (34)												
Brown Booby (36)												
Magnificent Frigatebird (37)												
Red Phalarope (39)												
Red-necked Phalarope (40)												
Pomarine Jaeger (44)												
Parasitic Jaeger (45)												
Black Tern (66)												
Common Tern (67)												
Bridled Tern (71)												
Sooty Tern (72)												
Brown Noddy (73)												
Bryde's Whale (86)												
Sperm Whale (91)												
Pygmy Sperm Whale (92)												
Dwarf Sperm Whale (93)												
Cuvier's Beaked Whale (94)												
Gervais' Beaked Whale (97)												
Killer Whale (100)												
False Killer Whale (101)												
Melon-headed Whale (102)												
Risso's Dolphin (106)												
Rough-toothed Dolphin (107)												
Bottlenose Dolphin (108)												
Atlantic Spinner Dolphin (109)												
Clymene Dolphin (110)												
Pantropical Spotted Dolphin (111)												
Frasier's Dolphin (115)												
Green Turtle (132)												
Atlantic Ridley Turtle (134)												
Leatherback Turtle (136)												

Location 13: Outer Hebrides, Scotland. These islands off the northwestern coast of Scotland host some of the largest breeding seabird colonies in the United Kingdom. Although most marine wildlife observations are land-based, the accounts presented here include a theoretical mix of onshore and offshore observation such as would likely occur en route to St. Kilda, 45 miles west of Griminsh Point, North Uist, or the Flannan Isles, 17 miles northwest of Gallan Head, Lewis. However, these waters can be quite rough, and most observers would be quite content with the observations that can be made from shore.

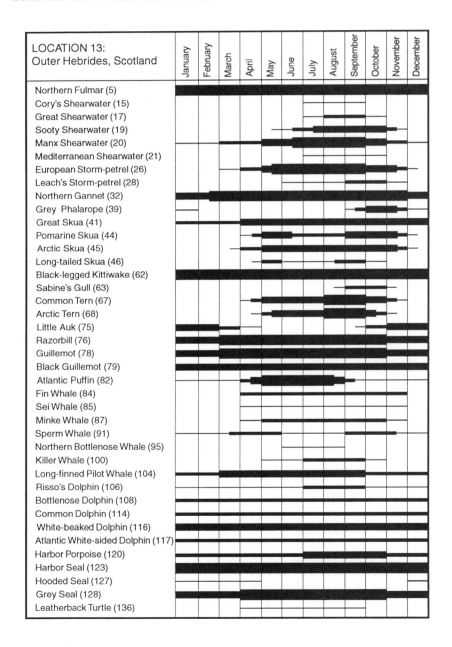

LOCATION 13: Outer Hebrides, Scotland	January	February	March	April	May	June	July	August	September	October	November	December
Northern Fulmar (5)												
Cory's Shearwater (15)												
Great Shearwater (17)												
Sooty Shearwater (19)												
Manx Shearwater (20)												
Mediterranean Shearwater (21)												
European Storm-petrel (26)												
Leach's Storm-petrel (28)												
Northern Gannet (32)												
Grey Phalarope (39)												
Great Skua (41)												
Pomarine Skua (44)												
Arctic Skua (45)												
Long-tailed Skua (46)												
Black-legged Kittiwake (62)												
Sabine's Gull (63)												
Common Tern (67)												
Arctic Tern (68)												
Little Auk (75)												
Razorbill (76)												
Guillemot (78)												
Black Guillemot (79)												
Atlantic Puffin (82)												
Fin Whale (84)												
Sei Whale (85)												
Minke Whale (87)												
Sperm Whale (91)												
Northern Bottlenose Whale (95)												
Killer Whale (100)												
Long-finned Pilot Whale (104)												
Risso's Dolphin (106)												
Bottlenose Dolphin (108)												
Common Dolphin (114)												
White-beaked Dolphin (116)												
Atlantic White-sided Dolphin (117)												
Harbor Porpoise (120)												
Harbor Seal (123)												
Hooded Seal (127)												
Grey Seal (128)												
Leatherback Turtle (136)												

Location 14: North Sea. This body of water is flanked by northeastern Great Britain to the west and Holland, Denmark, and Norway to the east. Although the vast majority of observations are land-based (sea watches) from England and Scotland, the accounts take into consideration offshore viewing, which usually produces larger numbers than from shore. However, land-based observations may be comparable to sea-based when wind and weather conditions conspire to blow birds close to the coast. Cetaceans would not likely be affected in a similar way. Shore-based observations can be made from any elevated vantage point overlooking the sea. Otherwise, access would be possible from private boat charter or commercial ferry service.

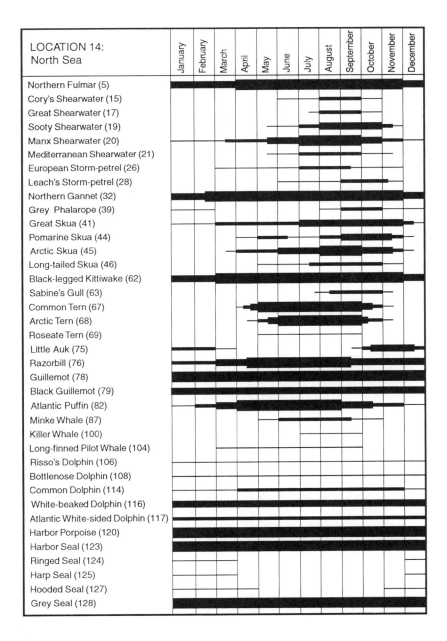

LOCATION 14: North Sea	January	February	March	April	May	June	July	August	September	October	November	December
Northern Fulmar (5)												
Cory's Shearwater (15)												
Great Shearwater (17)												
Sooty Shearwater (19)												
Manx Shearwater (20)												
Mediterranean Shearwater (21)												
European Storm-petrel (26)												
Leach's Storm-petrel (28)												
Northern Gannet (32)												
Grey Phalarope (39)												
Great Skua (41)												
Pomarine Skua (44)												
Arctic Skua (45)												
Long-tailed Skua (46)												
Black-legged Kittiwake (62)												
Sabine's Gull (63)												
Common Tern (67)												
Arctic Tern (68)												
Roseate Tern (69)												
Little Auk (75)												
Razorbill (76)												
Guillemot (78)												
Black Guillemot (79)												
Atlantic Puffin (82)												
Minke Whale (87)												
Killer Whale (100)												
Long-finned Pilot Whale (104)												
Risso's Dolphin (106)												
Bottlenose Dolphin (108)												
Common Dolphin (114)												
White-beaked Dolphin (116)												
Atlantic White-sided Dolphin (117)												
Harbor Porpoise (120)												
Harbor Seal (123)												
Ringed Seal (124)												
Harp Seal (125)												
Hooded Seal (127)												
Grey Seal (128)												

Location 15: Cape Clear, Ireland. Cape Clear and adjacent Cape Clear Island at the southernmost tip of Ireland provide one of the best shore-based observation points in the region. The accounts presented here pertain not only to this specific area but also to the open waters between southern Ireland and Cornwall at the southwesternmost tip of England. Shore-based observations are better during the migration seasons, particularly fall, than at other times. Offshore observations would likely be good at other times and offer better opportunity for viewing deep-water species such as Fea's petrel and the cetaceans. Offshore access by private charter would theoretically be possible from either Ireland or England.

LOCATION 15: Cape Clear, Ireland	January	February	March	April	May	June	July	August	September	October	November	December
Northern Fulmar (5)	■	■	■	■	■	■	■	■	■	■	■	■
Fea's Petrel (10)								—	—			
Cory's Shearwater (15)							—	■	■	—		
Great Shearwater (17)						—	—	■	■	—		
Sooty Shearwater (19)						—	—	■	■	—	—	
Manx Shearwater (20)	—		—	■	■	■	■	■	■	—		
Mediterranean Shearwater (21)	—							■	■	—		
Little Shearwater (22)							—	—	—			
Wilson's Storm-petrel (24)							—	—	—			
European Storm-petrel (26)					—	■	■	■	■	—		
Leach's Storm-petrel (28)								—	—			
Northern Gannet (32)	■	■	■	■	■	■	■	■	■	■	■	■
Grey Phalarope (39)									—	—		
Great Skua (41)					—	■	■	■	■	■	—	
Pomarine Skua (44)					—	■	—			—		
Parasitic Skua (45)					—	■	■	■	■	■	—	
Long-tailed Skua (46)					—	■	—			—		
Black-legged Kittiwake (62)	■	■	■	■	■	■	■	■	■	■	■	■
Sabine's Gull (63)								—	■	—		
Common Tern (67)					—	■	■	■	■	■	—	
Arctic Tern (68)					—	■	■	■	■	—		
Little Auk (75)	■	—									—	■
Razorbill (76)	■	■	■	■	■	■	■	■	■	■	■	■
Guillemot (78)	■	■	■	■	■	■	■	■	■	■	■	■
Black Guillemot (79)	—	—	—	—	—	—	—	—	—	—	—	—
Atlantic Puffin (82)				—	■	■	■	■	—			
Northern Bottlenose Whale (95)								—	—			
Risso's Dolphin (106)							■	■	—			
Bottlenose Dolphin (108)	—	—	—	—	—	—	—	—	—	—	—	—
Common Dolphin (114)	■	■	■	■	■	■	■	■	■	■	■	■
White-beaked Dolphin (116)	—	—	—	—	—	—	—	—	—	—	—	—
Atlantic White-sided Dolphin (117)	—	—	—	—	—	—	—	—	—	—	—	
Harbor Porpoise (120)	—	—	—	—	—	—	—	■	■	—	—	—
Harbor Seal (123)	—	—	—	—	—	—	—	—	—	—	—	—
Grey Seal (128)	■	■	■	■	■	■	■	■	■	■	■	■
Leatherback Turtle (136)							—	■	—			

Location 16: English Channel. This relatively narrow body of water between southeastern England and northwestern France hosts significantly fewer numbers of marine wildlife than the other regional points covered. However, offshore access is easier as there are multiple ferries that make the crossing daily.

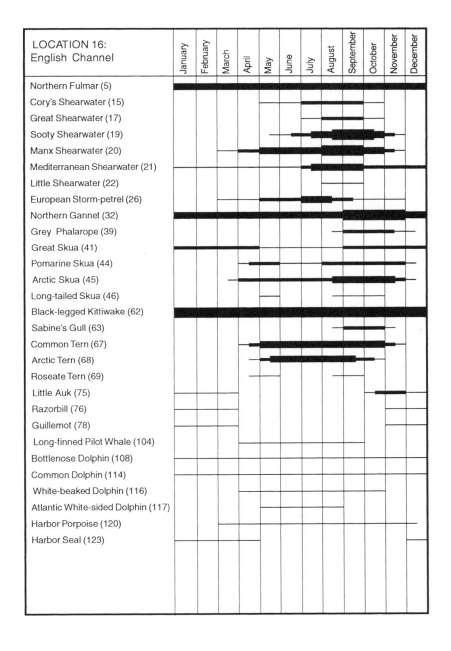

LOCATION 16: English Channel	January	February	March	April	May	June	July	August	September	October	November	December
Northern Fulmar (5)	███	███	███	███	███	███	███	███	███	███	███	███
Cory's Shearwater (15)							▬▬▬					
Great Shearwater (17)							───					
Sooty Shearwater (19)						─▬▬	▬▬	▬▬▬	───			
Manx Shearwater (20)				▬▬▬	▬▬	▬	▬▬	▬▬	▬▬▬	───		
Mediterranean Shearwater (21)							─▬▬	───				
Little Shearwater (22)							───					
European Storm-petrel (26)					───	▬▬	▬▬	─				
Northern Gannet (32)	███	███	███	███	███	███	███	███	███	███	███	███
Grey Phalarope (39)												
Great Skua (41)	───	───	───	───	───	───	───	───	───	───	───	───
Pomarine Skua (44)				───					───			
Arctic Skua (45)				─▬▬	▬	─	─	▬▬	▬▬▬	───		
Long-tailed Skua (46)					─			─				
Black-legged Kittiwake (62)	███	███	███	███	███	███	███	███	███	███	███	███
Sabine's Gull (63)								─	▬▬	───		
Common Tern (67)				─▬▬	▬	─	─	─▬▬	───			
Arctic Tern (68)					─▬	─	─	───				
Roseate Tern (69)					───			───				
Little Auk (75)	───										▬▬	─
Razorbill (76)	───											
Guillemot (78)	───											
Long-finned Pilot Whale (104)				───								
Bottlenose Dolphin (108)	───											
Common Dolphin (114)	───											
White-beaked Dolphin (116)				───					───			
Atlantic White-sided Dolphin (117)					───			───				
Harbor Porpoise (120)		───										───
Harbor Seal (123)	───											

Location 17: Bay of Biscay. This vast body of water lies between southern England and northern Spain. Access is by commercial ferry between Portsmouth, England, and Santander, Spain. The ferry ride is 24 hours each way. Access into nearshore and proximal offshore waters may also be possible by private charter from any port along the northern shore of Spain. However, at present, the ferry may be one of the best pelagic opportunities in Britain or Europe.

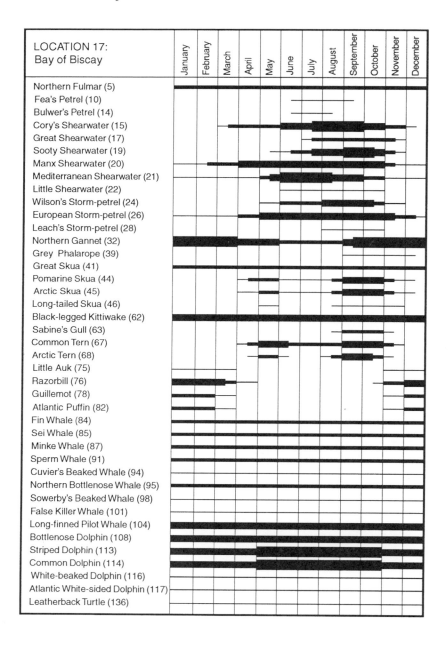

LOCATION 17: Bay of Biscay	January	February	March	April	May	June	July	August	September	October	November	December
Northern Fulmar (5)												
Fea's Petrel (10)												
Bulwer's Petrel (14)												
Cory's Shearwater (15)												
Great Shearwater (17)												
Sooty Shearwater (19)												
Manx Shearwater (20)												
Mediterranean Shearwater (21)												
Little Shearwater (22)												
Wilson's Storm-petrel (24)												
European Storm-petrel (26)												
Leach's Storm-petrel (28)												
Northern Gannet (32)												
Grey Phalarope (39)												
Great Skua (41)												
Pomarine Skua (44)												
Arctic Skua (45)												
Long-tailed Skua (46)												
Black-legged Kittiwake (62)												
Sabine's Gull (63)												
Common Tern (67)												
Arctic Tern (68)												
Little Auk (75)												
Razorbill (76)												
Guillemot (78)												
Atlantic Puffin (82)												
Fin Whale (84)												
Sei Whale (85)												
Minke Whale (87)												
Sperm Whale (91)												
Cuvier's Beaked Whale (94)												
Northern Bottlenose Whale (95)												
Sowerby's Beaked Whale (98)												
False Killer Whale (101)												
Long-finned Pilot Whale (104)												
Bottlenose Dolphin (108)												
Striped Dolphin (113)												
Common Dolphin (114)												
White-beaked Dolphin (116)												
Atlantic White-sided Dolphin (117)												
Leatherback Turtle (136)												

Location 18: Iberian Coast, Spain, Portugal. This area represents the western coast of Spain and Portugal collectively. Although not well surveyed, it may host some interesting surprises. Many of the species entries are speculative as the data are simply not available. Coastal waters may be surveyed by local ferry or shore-based observations, possibly best from August through October from Cape of Estaca de Bares, Spain. Offshore excursions may also be possible by private charter.

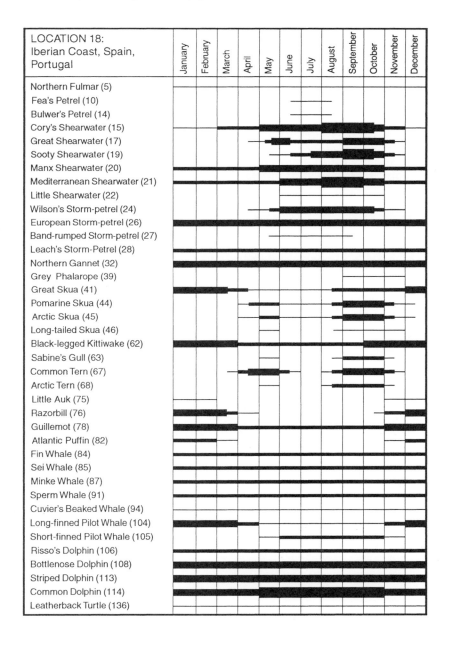

LOCATION 18: Iberian Coast, Spain, Portugal	January	February	March	April	May	June	July	August	September	October	November	December
Northern Fulmar (5)												
Fea's Petrel (10)												
Bulwer's Petrel (14)												
Cory's Shearwater (15)												
Great Shearwater (17)												
Sooty Shearwater (19)												
Manx Shearwater (20)												
Mediterranean Shearwater (21)												
Little Shearwater (22)												
Wilson's Storm-petrel (24)												
European Storm-petrel (26)												
Band-rumped Storm-petrel (27)												
Leach's Storm-Petrel (28)												
Northern Gannet (32)												
Grey Phalarope (39)												
Great Skua (41)												
Pomarine Skua (44)												
Arctic Skua (45)												
Long-tailed Skua (46)												
Black-legged Kittiwake (62)												
Sabine's Gull (63)												
Common Tern (67)												
Arctic Tern (68)												
Little Auk (75)												
Razorbill (76)												
Guillemot (78)												
Atlantic Puffin (82)												
Fin Whale (84)												
Sei Whale (85)												
Minke Whale (87)												
Sperm Whale (91)												
Cuvier's Beaked Whale (94)												
Long-finned Pilot Whale (104)												
Short-finned Pilot Whale (105)												
Risso's Dolphin (106)												
Bottlenose Dolphin (108)												
Striped Dolphin (113)												
Common Dolphin (114)												
Leatherback Turtle (136)												

Oceanic Islands

While the range charts are primarily devoted to offshore locales accessed from land-based departure points, there are several oceanic island groups in the northern Atlantic that host important breeding colonies of seabirds. The following accounts highlight these islands and the special-interest species in these areas.

Location Island 1: Dry Tortugas, Florida. This small group of islands about 70 miles west of Key West, Florida, hosts impressive breeding colonies of Magnificent Frigatebirds, Sooty Terns, and Brown Noddies. Within the Brown Noddy colonies are a few Black Noddies. There are also Brown and Masked Boobies and, on rare occasion, Red-footed. Access is by organized tour or private charter by boat or floatplane. Spring (mid-April through mid-May) is the peak season for professional tours, which often sail from Key West at night but return to Key West in the afternoon as an organized pelagic trip. Apart from Bridled Tern, a few shearwaters, Wilson's Storm-petrel, and an occasional jaeger, these trips often don't produce significant species lists.

Location Island 2: Bermuda. Lying about 650 miles east-southeast of Hatteras, North Carolina, Bermuda hosts the only known breeding ground for the endangered Bermuda Petrel. The current population of a little more than 50 breeding birds is limited to Nonsuch Island. Access to the island is restricted as part of a conservation effort. However, recent observations suggest that the breeding birds forage offshore in the waters to the northeast; a private charter might offer the chance of seeing one. Several other species occur, including White-tailed Tropicbird, which is locally abundant and even considered a pest to the petrel conservation project.

Location Island 3: Azores. This large group of oceanic islands about 900 miles west of Lisbon, Portugal, consists of four central islands plus outlying islands about 130 miles to the west-northwest and 120 miles to the east-southeast. A Portuguese territory, they host small breeding colonies of Cory's and Little Shearwaters and are home to the *atlantis* population of Yellow-legged Gull. The surrounding waters are also important feeding grounds for a number of nonbreeding species, particularly during summer.

Location Island 4: Madeira and the Desertas. This group of islands belonging to Portugal lies a little over 200 miles east of Morocco. They host breeding populations of Fea's Petrel, the critically endangered Zino's Petrel, and one of the few remaining populations of Mediterranean Monk Seal. Zino's Petrel breeds in the highlands of Madeira and is so rare that access to the breeding cliffs is prohibited. The more numerous Fea's Petrel breeds on Bugio Island, and Monk Seals breed on Grand Deserta Island, collectively about 12–15 miles southeast of Madeira. Access to these island is restricted, but one may easily charter a boat to explore adjacent waters. The offshore waters may also be accessed aboard a cruise ship or the ferry between Funchal and Porto Santo to the northeast. Other local species of interest include Bulwer's Petrel, Little Shearwater, and Band-rumped Storm-petrel.

Location Island 5: Salvage Islands. This small island group lies about 170 miles south of Madeira and about 185 miles north of the Canary Islands. Uninhabited, the islands host the largest breeding colony of Cory's Shearwater in the Atlantic, along with sizable colonies of Bulwer's Petrel, Little Shearwater, and Band-rumped and White-faced Storm-petrels. Fea's Petrel may possibly breed here. Direct access, possible only by organized tour or extended boat charter, is difficult. However, commercial shipping traffic between Funchal, Madeira, and Las Palmas, Grand Canary Island, passes directly by the Salvages.

Location Island 6: Canary Islands. This large group consists of seven main islands lying as little as 60 miles offshore from the African coast but stretching as much as 250 miles from east to west. They host breeding colonies of Bulwer's Petrel as well as Cory's and Little Shearwaters. Although the numbers of breeding birds are fewer than on the Salvages, access to the Canaries is much easier, and offshore forays may offer a good chance of seeing the species that don't breed locally. Offshore forays might be possible from Las Palmas by ferryboat or private charter. The Canaries are also far enough south that Cape Verde Shearwater may be a possibility.

REFERENCES

Ainley, D. G., L. B. Spear, and R. C. Wood. 1985. Sexual color and size variation in the South Polar Skua. *Condor* 87:427–428.

Allen, A. A. 1934. A new bird for North America. *University of the State of New York Bulletin to the Schools* 20:134–135.

Andrew, D. G. 1994. Spring passage of skuas in Outer Hebrides. *Scottish Birds* 17:172.

Baker, A. N. 1983. *Whales and Dolphins of New Zealand and Australia.* Wellington: Victoria University Press.

Baker, M. L. 1987. *Whales, Dolphins, and Porpoises of the World.* Garden City, N.Y.: Doubleday.

Balch, L. G. 1981. Identifying skuas in the ABA area. *Birding* 8:190–201.

Behler, J. L., and F. W. King. 1979. *National Audubon Society Field Guide to North American Reptiles and Amphibians.* New York: Alfred A. Knopf.

Bond, B. 1982. *The Handbook of Sailing.* New York: Alfred A. Knopf.

Bourne, W. R. P. 1983. The Soft-plumaged Petrel, the Gon-gon, and the Freira, *Pterodroma mollis, P. feae,* and *P. madeira. Bull. Brit. Ornithol. Club* 103:52–58.

———. 1986. Late summer seabird distribution off the west coast of Europe. *Irish Birds* 3:175–198.

———. 1990. The first dark-rumped petrel. *Birding World* 3:249.

Brady, A. 1988. Possible presence of an Antarctic Skua in New Jersey waters. *Cassinia* 62:7–11.

Brimley, H. H. 1943. A second specimen of True's Beaked Whale *Mesoplodon mirus,* from North Carolina. *J. Mamm.* 24:199–203.

Broom, A. 1987. Identification of juvenile Pomarine Skua. *British Birds* 80:426.

Burt, W. H., and R. P. Grossenheider. 1964. *A Field Guide to the Mammals.* Boston: Houghton Mifflin.

Caldwell, D. K., and M. C. Caldwell. 1973. Marine mammals of the eastern Gulf of Mexico. In *A Summary of Knowledge of the Eastern Gulf of Mexico,* edited by J. I. Jones, R. E. Ring, M. O. Rinkel, and R. E. Smith, pp. III-I-1 to III-I-10. Gainesville: State University System of Florida.

Committee of Sea Turtle Conservation. 1990. *Decline of the Sea Turtles.* Washington, D.C.: National Academy Press.

Conant, R., and J. T. Collins. 1991. *A Field Guide to Reptiles and Amphibians.* Boston: Houghton Mifflin.

Corbet, G. B., and S. Harris, eds. 1991. *The Handbook of British Mammals.* Oxford: Blackwell Scientific Publishers.

Cramp, S., and K. E. L. Simmons, eds. 1977. *Handbook of the Birds of Europe, the Middle East, and North Africa.* Vol. 1, *Ostrich to Ducks.* Oxford: Oxford University Press.

———. 1983. *Handbook of the Birds of Europe, the Middle East, and North Africa.* Vol. 3, *Waders to Gulls.* Oxford: Oxford University Press.

———. 1985. *Handbook of the Birds of Europe, the Middle East, and North Africa.* Vol. 4, *Terns to Woodpeckers.* Oxford: Oxford University Press.

Cubitt, M. 1991. The mystery petrels of Tyneside. *Birding World* 4:295–297.

Danielsen, F., H. Skov, J. Durinck, and D. Bloch. 1990. Marine distribution of seabirds in the Northeast Atlantic between Iceland and Scotland, June–September 1987 and 1988. *Dansk Orn. Tidsskr.* 84:45–63.

Davenport, D. L. 1975. The spring migration of the Pomarine Skua on British and Irish coasts. *British Birds* 68:456–462.

———. 1981. The spring migration of the Pomarine and Long-tailed Skuas at the south and western coasts of Britain and Ireland. *Irish Birds* 2:73–79.

———. 1992. The spring migration of Long-tailed and Pomarine Skuas in Britain and Ireland. *Birding World* 5:92–95.

Duncan, C. D., and R. W. Harvard. 1980. Pelagic birds of the northern Gulf of Mexico. *American Birds* 34:122–132.

Enticott, J., and D. Tripling. 1997. *Seabirds of the World.* Mechanicsburg, Pa.: Stackpole Books.

Evans, P. G. H. 1984a. The seabirds of Greenland: Their status and conservation. In *Status and Conservation of the World's Seabirds,* by J. P. Croxall, P. M. Ellis, P. G. H. Evans, and R. W. Schreiber, pp. 49–84. Cambridge, England: International Council for Bird Preservation.

———. 1984b. Status and conservation of seabirds in Northwest Europe. In *Status and Conservation of the World's Seabirds,* by J. P. Croxall, P. M. Ellis, P. G. H. Evans, and R. W. Schreiber, pp. 293–322. Cambridge, England: International Council for Bird Preservation.

Fussell, J. O. 1994. *A Birder's Guide to Coastal North Carolina.* Chapel Hill: University of North Carolina Press.

Grant, P. J. 1986. *Gulls: A Guide to Identification.* 2d ed. San Diego: Academic Press.

Griffin, R. B. 1999. Sperm Whale distributions and community ecology associated with a warm core ring off Georges Bank. *Marine Mammal Science* 15:33–51.

Gross, M. G. 1971. *Oceanography.* Columbus, Ohio: Charles E. Merrill Publishing.

Hamilton, J. E. 1934. The Sub-Antarctic forms of the Great Skua (*Catharacta skua skua*). *Discovery Reports* 9:161–174.

Harrison, C. 1982. *An Atlas of the Birds of the Western Palearctic.* Princeton, N.J.: Princeton University Press.

Harrison, P. 1983. *Seabirds: An Identification Guide.* Kent, England: Croom Helm.
———. 1987. *A Field Guide to Seabirds of the World.* Lexington, Mass.: Stephen Greene Press.

Hass, T. 1995. An additional record of Bulwer's Petrel *Bulweria bulweria* off the southeastern United States of America. *Marine Ornithol.* 23:161–162.

Houston, J. 1990. Status of True's Beaked Whale, *Mesoplodon mirus,* in Canada. *Can. Field Natur.* 104:135–137.

Howell, S. N. G. 1994. A new look at an old problem. *Birding* 26:400–414.

Hoyt, E. 1984. *The Whale-watcher's Handbook.* Garden City, N.Y.: Madison Press Books.

Imber, M. J. 1985. Origins, phylogeny, and taxonomy of the gadfly petrels *Pterodroma* spp. *Ibis* 127:197–229.

Jefferson, T. A. 1996. Estimates of abundance of cetaceans in offshore waters of the northwestern Gulf of Mexico, 1992–1993. *Southwestern Naturalist* 41:279–287.

Jefferson, T. A., and A. J. Schiro. 1997. Distribution of cetaceans in the offshore Gulf of Mexico. *Mamm. Review* 27:27–50.

Jepson, P. R., and B. Zonfrillo. 1986. Bird notes from Madeira, summer 1996. *Bocagiana* 117:1–10.

Joiris, C. 1972. Observations ornithologiques réalisées dans le sud-est de la Mer du Nord entre Juin 1971 et Janvier 1972. *Aves* 9:85–137.
———. 1978. Seabirds recorded in the northern North Sea in July: The ecological implications of their distribution. *Gerfaut* 68:419–440.
———. 1983a. Seabirds recorded in the Fladenground area, northern North Sea, in April, May, and June 1976. *JONSDAP '76 Contribution,* no. 1 (North Sea Dynamics): 675–686.
———. 1983b. Winter distribution of seabirds in the North Sea: an oceanological interpretation. *Gerfaut* 73:107–123.
———. 1992a. Summer distribution and ecological role of seabirds and marine mammals in the Norwegian and Greenland Seas (June 1988). *J. Marine Systems* 3:73–89.
———. 1992b. Summer distribution and ecological role of seabirds and marine mammals in the Norwegian and Greenland Seas (July 1988). *Royal Academy Overseas Science* 1992:113–133.
———. 1996. At-sea distribution of seabirds and marine mammals around Svalbard, summer 1991. *Polar Biol.* 16:423–429.

Joiris, C. R., J. Tahon, L. Holsbeek, and M. Vacauwenberghe. 1996. Seabirds and marine mammals in the eastern Barents Sea: Late summer at-sea distribution and calculated food intake. *Polar Biol.* 16:245–256.

Katona, S. K., V. Rough, and D. T. Richardson, 1993. *A Field Guide to Whales, Porpoises, and Seals from Cape Cod to Newfoundland.* Washington, D.C.: Smithsonian Institution Press.

Leatherwood, S., D. K. Caldwell, and H. E. Winn. 1976. *Whales, Dolphins, and Porpoises of the Western North Atlantic.* NOAA Technical Report NMFS CIRC 396.

Leatherwood, S., and R. R. Reeves. 1983. *The Sierra Club Handbook of Whales and Dolphins.* San Francisco: Sierra Club Books.

Leatherwood, S., R. R. Reeves, W. F. Perrin, and W. E. Evans. 1988. *Whales, Dolphins, and Porpoises of the Eastern North Pacific and Adjacent Arctic Waters.* New York: Dover.

Lutz, P. L., and J. A. Musick, eds. 1997. *The Biology of Sea Turtles.* Boca Raton, Fla.: CRC Press.

Malling Olsen, K. 1989. Field identification of the smaller skuas. *British Birds* 82: 143–176.

Malling Olsen, K., and H. Larsson. 1995. *Terns of Europe and North America.* London: Christopher Helm.

————. 1997. *Skuas and Jaegers: A Guide to the Skuas and Jaegers of the World.* New Haven, Conn.: Yale University Press.

Martin, A. R., S. K. Katona, D. Matilla, D. Hembree, and T. D. Waters. 1984. Migration of humpback whales between the Caribbean and Iceland. *J. Mammology* 65:330–333.

Mead, J. G. 1975. *Distribution of cetaceans along the Atlantic and Gulf Coasts of the United States.* Washington, D.C.: Smithsonian Institution.

Minasian, S. M., K. C. Balcomb, and L. Foster. 1984. *The World's Whales: The Complete Illustrated Guide.* Washington, D.C.: Smithsonian Books.

Nelson, J. B. 1978. *The Sulidae: Gannets and Boobies.* Oxford: Oxford University Press.

Norris, K. S., ed. 1966. *Whales, Porpoises, and Dolphins.* Los Angeles: University of California Press.

Olsen, K. M., and L. Jonsson. 1989. Field identification of the smaller skuas. *British Birds* 82:143–176.

Parmelee, D. F. 1988. The hybrid skua: A southern ocean enigma. *Wilson Bulletin* 199:345–356.

Perrin, W. F., E. D. Mitchell, J. G. Mead, D. K. Caldwell, P. J. H. van Bree, and W. H. Dawbin. 1987. Revision of the Spotted Dolphins *Stenella* spp. *Marine Mammal Sci.* 3:99–170.

Peterson, J. 1991. Avian wanderings and bruised egos: The documentation of rare birds in Texas. *Birding* 23:352–355.

Pietz, P. J. 1987. Feeding and nesting ecology of sympatric South Polar and Brown Skuas. *Auk* 104:617–624.

Powers, K. D. 1983. Pelagic distribution of marine birds of the northeastern United States. NOAA Techn. Memo. NMFSF/NEC 27. Woods Hole, Mass.

Prater, A. J., J. H. Marchant, and J. Vuorien. 1977. *Guide to the Identification and Ageing of Holoarctic Waders.* Field Guide 17. Herts, U.K.: British Trust for Ornithology.

Pritchard, P., and R. Marquez. 1973. Kemp's Ridley Turtle or Atlantic Ridley: *Lepidochelys kempi.* IUCN Monograph no. 2: Marine Turtle Series.

Reeves, R. R., B. S. Stewart, and S. Leatherwood. 1992. *The Sierra Club Handbook of Seals and Sirenians*. San Francisco: Sierra Club Books.

Ridgeway, S. H., and R. J. Harrison, eds. 1981a. *Handbook of Marine Mammals*. Vol. 1, *The Walrus, Sea Lions, Fur Seals, and Sea Otter*. London: Academic Press.

———. 1981b. *Handbook of Marine Mammals*. Vol. 2, *Seals*. London: Academic Press.

———. 1985. *Handbook of Marine Mammals*. Vol. 3, *The Sirenians and Baleen Whales*. London: Academic Press.

———. 1989. *Handbook of Marine Mammals*. Vol. 4, *River Dolphins and the Larger Toothed Whales*. London: Academic Press.

———. 1994. *Handbook of Marine Mammals*. Vol. 5, *The First Book of Dolphins*. London: Academic Press.

———. 1999. *Handbook of Marine Mammals*. Vol. 6, *The Second Book of Dolphins and the Porpoises*. London: Academic Press.

Roberson, D. 1996. Identifying Manx Shearwaters in the northeastern Pacific. *Birding* 28:18–33.

Ross, G. J. B. 1984. The smaller cetaceans of the southeast coast of southern Africa. *Annual Cape Province Mus.* (Nat. Hist.) 15:173–411.

Scott, S. L., ed. 1987. *Field Guide to the Birds of North America*. Washington, D.C.: National Geographic Society.

Sibley, C. G., and B. L. Monroe. 1990. *Distribution and Taxonomy of Birds of the World*. New Haven, Conn.: Yale University Press.

Swingle, W. M., S. G. Barco, and T. D. Pitchford. 1993. Appearance of juvenile humpback whales feeding in the nearshore waters of Virginia. *Marine Mammal Sci.* 9:309–315.

Tove, M. 1995. Live sighting of Mesoplodon C.F. *M. mirus* True's Beaked Whale. *Marine Mammal Sci.* 1:80–85.

Tove, M. H. 1993. Field Separation of Ring-billed, Mew, Common, and Kamchatka Gulls. *Birding* 25:386–401.

———. 1997a. Fea's Petrel in North America. Part 1, Taxonomy, distribution, and identification. *Birding* 29:207–214.

———. 1997b. Fea's Petrel in North America. Part 2, Documentation. *Birding* 29:309–315.

Warham, J. 1990. *The Petrels: Their ecology and breeding systems*. London: Academic Press.

Whitaker, J. O., Jr. 1980. *The Audubon Society Field Guide to North American Mammals*. New York: Alfred A. Knopf.

Whitehead, H., S. Gowans, A. Faucher, and S. W. McCarrey. 1997. Population analysis of Northern Bottlenose Whales in the Gulley, Nova Scotia. *Marine Mammal Sci.* 13:173–185.

Williams, L. E. 1965. Jaegers in the Gulf of Mexico. *Auk* 82:18–25.

Wingate, D. B., T. Hass, E. S. Brinkley, and J. B. Patteson. 1998. Identification of Bermuda Petrel. *Birding* 30:18–36.

Winn, H. 1982. A characterization of marine mammals and turtles in the mid- and North-Atlantic areas of the U.S. outer continental shelf, final report.

Cetacean and Turtles Assessment Program (CETAP) Contract No. AA551-CT8, U.S. Department of Interior, Bureau of Land Management, Washington, D.C.

Zino, P. A., and F. Zino. 1986. Contribution to the study of the petrels of the genus *Pterodroma* in the archipelago of Madeira. *Bol. Mus. Mun. Funchal.* 38:141–165.

Zottoli, R. 1973. *Introduction to Marine Environments*. St. Louis, Mo.: C. V. Mosby.

SPECIES INDEX

Species numbers are **boldface.** Page numbers for plates are roman. Page numbers for species accounts are *italic.*

SPECIES CHECKLIST

Species Name   *Date/Location Seen*

Albatrosses

- ☐ Black-browed   _____

- ☐ Wandering   _____

- ☐ Yellow-nosed   _____

Auks

- ☐ Ancient Murrelet   _____

- ☐ Atlantic Puffin   _____

- ☐ Black Guillemot   _____

- ☐ Common Murre
  or Guillemot   _____

- ☐ Dovekie or Little Auk   _____

- ☐ Long-billed Murrelet   _____

- ☐ Razorbill   _____

- ☐ Thick-billed Murre
  or Brunnich's Guillemot   _____

Species Name	Date/Location Seen
Boobies	
☐ Blue-footed	_____
☐ Brown	_____
☐ Masked	_____
☐ Red-footed	_____
Dolphins	
☐ Atlantic Spinner	_____
☐ Atlantic Spotted	_____
☐ Atlantic White-sided	_____
☐ Coastal Bottlenose	_____
☐ Common	_____
☐ Clymene	_____
☐ Frasier's	_____
☐ Offshore Bottlenose	_____
☐ Pantropical Spotted	_____
☐ Risso's	_____
☐ Rough-toothed	_____
☐ Striped	_____
☐ White-beaked	_____
Frigatebirds	
☐ Lesser	_____
☐ Magnificent	_____

Species Name

Date / Location Seen

Fulmars

☐ Northern _____

Gannets

☐ Northern _____

Gulls

☐ Black-headed _____

☐ Black-legged Kittiwake _____

☐ Bonaparte's _____

☐ Common _____

☐ Franklin's _____

☐ Glaucous _____

☐ Great or Greater Black-backed _____

☐ Herring _____

☐ Iceland _____

☐ Ivory _____

☐ Laughing _____

☐ Lesser Black-backed _____

☐ Little _____

☐ Mediterranean _____

☐ Ring-billed _____

☐ Ross' _____

☐ Sabine's _____

Species Name	Date/Location Seen
☐ Thayer's	_____
☐ Yellow-legged	_____

Jaegers

☐ Long-tailed or Long-tailed Skua	_____
☐ Parasitic or Arctic Skua	_____
☐ Pomarine or Pomarine Skua	_____

Manatees

☐ West Indian	_____

Noddies

☐ Black	_____
☐ Brown	_____

Petrels

☐ Bermuda	_____
☐ Black-capped	_____
☐ Bulwer's	_____
☐ Fea's	_____
☐ Herald	_____
☐ Mottled	_____
☐ Southern Giant	_____
☐ Stejneger's	_____
☐ White-chinned	_____
☐ Zino's	_____

Species Name

Date/Location Seen

Phalaropes

☐ Red or Grey

_____

☐ Red-necked

_____

Porpoises

☐ Harbor

_____

Seals

☐ Bearded

_____

☐ Gray or Grey

_____

☐ Harbor

_____

☐ Harp

_____

☐ Hooded

_____

☐ Mediterranean Monk

_____

☐ Ringed

_____

☐ Walrus

_____

Sea Lions

☐ California

_____

Shearwaters

☐ Audubon's

_____

☐ Buller's

_____

☐ Cape Verde

_____

☐ Cory's

_____

☐ Greater or Great

_____

Species Name   *Date/Location Seen*

☐ Little   _____

☐ Manx   _____

☐ Mediterranean   _____

☐ Sooty   _____

Skuas

☐ Brown   _____

☐ Great   _____

☐ South Polar   _____

Storm-petrels

☐ Band-rumped   _____

☐ European   _____

☐ Leach's   _____

☐ Swinhoe's   _____

☐ White-faced   _____

☐ Wilson's   _____

Terns

☐ Arctic   _____

☐ Black   _____

☐ Bridled   _____

☐ Common   _____

☐ Roseate   _____

☐ Sooty   _____

Species Name	*Date / Location Seen*

Tropicbirds

☐ Red-billed _____

☐ White-tailed _____

Turtles

☐ Atlantic Ridley _____

☐ Green _____

☐ Hawksbill _____

☐ Leatherback _____

☐ Loggerhead _____

☐ Olive Ridley _____

Whales

☐ Beluga _____

☐ Blainville's Beaked _____

☐ Blue _____

☐ Bowhead _____

☐ Bryde's _____

☐ Cuvier's Beaked _____

☐ Dwarf Sperm _____

☐ False Killer _____

☐ Fin _____

☐ Gervais' Beaked _____

☐ Humpback _____

Species Name

Date / Location Seen

☐ Killer _____

☐ Long-finned Pilot _____

☐ Melon-headed _____

☐ Minke _____

☐ Narwhal _____

☐ Northern Bottlenose _____

☐ Northern Right _____

☐ Pygmy Killer _____

☐ Pygmy Sperm _____

☐ Sei _____

☐ Short-finned Pilot _____

☐ Sowerby's Beaked _____

☐ Sperm _____

☐ True's Beaked _____